VENETIAN PALAZZI

PALÄSTE IN VENEDIG

PALAIS VÉNITIENS

Photographs by Gianluigi Trivellato
Text by Giuseppe Mazzariol · Attilia Dorigato

VENETIAN PALAZZI

PALÄSTE IN VENEDIG

PALAIS VÉNITIENS

EVERGREEN

EVERGREEN is an imprint of Benedikt Taschen Verlag GmbH

© for this edition: 1998 Benedikt Taschen Verlag GmbH
Hohenzollernring 53, D–50672 Köln
© 1998 Biblos srl, Cittadella, Padova (Italy)
General editor: Lanfranco Lionello
Text: Giuseppe Mazzariol, Attilia Dorigato
Photographs: Gianluigi Trivellato
Art director: Luciano Svegliado
Cover design: Catinka Keul, Cologne

Printed in Italy
ISBN 3–8228–7050–1 (English edition)
ISBN 3–8228–7112–5 (German edition)
ISBN 3–8228–7091–9 (French edition)

Contents
Inhalt
Sommaire

INTRODUCTION · EINLEITUNG

Whether it stands on the edge of the Grand Canal which winds through the city, or whether it faces onto a quiet secondary canal or a square, the Venetian palace has always been the object of unreserved admiration ever since the beginning of Venice's long history.

It is not only the richly structured façades of the palaces, in the formal refinement and the elegance of every single element, that have always aroused a sense of fascination in the visitor who can identify signs of the prestige and wealth of their owners. The interiors are also furnished and decorated with an incomparable magnificence that emphasizes the social standing and political influence of those who lived in them.

The luxury and opulence that marked the lifestyle within the palace walls is amply described, at the end of the 16th century, by Francesco Sansovino in his *Venetia città nobilissima:* "As for the incredible ornaments, furnishings and riches in the houses, whether they are large or small, it is impossible to imagine, let alone fully describe them in writing. And it is reasonable for this to be so, considering that by now 1159 years have passed since its

Seit den Anfängen Venedigs ist der Palazzo veneziano Objekt grenzenloser Bewunderung gewesen. Ganz gleich ob er am Ufer des Canal Grande liegt, der die Stadt in großen, geschwungenen Bögen durchfließt, ob er an einem der zahlreichen Nebenkanäle dieser Hauptader oder auf einem kleinen Platz steht – unvergeßlich prägt sich der mondäne Charakter dieser Paläste dem Betrachter ein.

Schon das Äußere der Palazzi fasziniert. An den reichgestalteten Fassaden mit all ihrem erlesenen Zierat lassen sich Macht, Status und Reichtum ihrer Besitzer ablesen. Aber auch die herrlichen Innenräume, die unvergleichlich prächtig ausgestattet wurden, lassen das Herz höher schlagen.

Luxus und Überfluß kennzeichneten das Leben in den Palazzi. Francesco Sansovino beschrieb die Ausstattung dieser besonderen »vier Wände« ausführlich Ende des 16. Jahrhunderts in seinem Werk *Venetia città nobilissima:* »Was die opulente Dekoration, die vornehme Möblierung und die unglaublichen Reichtümer der Häuser angeht – seien es nun kleine oder große Gebäude –, ist es unmöglich, sie sich vorzustellen oder gar zu beschreiben.

Qu'il se dresse aux bords du Grand Canal dont le cours sinueux traverse la ville ou qu'il donne sur un canal secondaire ou sur une place, le palais vénitien a toujours été l'objet d'une admiration inconditionnelle depuis l'origine de l'histoire millénaire de Venise.

Non seulement la structure architecturale du palais, dans sa recherche formelle et dans le raffinement de chaque élément particulier, a toujours suscité de l'étonnement chez le visiteur, qui y a repéré les signes du prestige et de la richesse des propriétaires de la demeure, mais les intérieurs, meublés et décorés avec un faste quasi incomparable, constituaient une mise au point ultérieure des conditions sociales et du poids politique de ceux qui les habitaient.

Le luxe et l'opulence qui caractérisent la vie à l'intérieur du palais est exhaustivement décrite, à la fin du XVIème siècle, par Francesco Sansovino dans son *Venetia città nobilissima :* « Quant aux ornements, aux bibelots et aux richesses incroyables de la maison, aussi bien des nantis que des petits bourgeois et des pauvres, il est impossible de les imaginer et même de les décrire de façon à les rendre pleinement.

foundation, without it ever being touched by a plundering or enemy hand, and continuing all the while in trading, by means of which it has always brought home the possessions of many a city ruined, dispersed and ill-treated by the barbarians for centuries, by those who wished to preserve them, so it must necessarily be extremely opulent and rich. What is more, the noble homes, which have thrived for hundreds of years thanks to the magistrates' success in the seafaring trades, have always increased their belongings to the brimful of happiness.

And however in the past they have been given to thrift, they were always splendidly liberal in the embellishment of their homes.

In countless buildings the wooden floors in the bedrooms and in other rooms are decorated with gold and other colours and the rooms are adorned with paintings and excellent illusionist devices. Almost all have the rooms lined with noble tapestries, silken fabrics, gilt stamped leathers, backing panels and other things according to the taste of the period. And the bedrooms are mainly decked with headboards and chests decorated with gold, and with paintings the frames of which are equally loaded with gold. There is no end to the amount of silver cutlery and porcelain dinner services, pewter, copper and bronze worked with azimine. In the main rooms there are racks of arms, with shields and banners of their ancestors who were in regiments on land or at sea. I have seen an auction of the goods and chattels of a nobleman condemned for a sinister incident and they would have still been excessive for any Duke of Italy."

The distribution of the space inside the Venetian palace underwent no substantial changes in the course of the centuries, and the tripartite layout of the main façade clearly illustrates its arrangement. The ground floor had a vast central room, or entrance hall that traversed the building, flanked on either side by rooms intended for the storage of merchandise ever since the time when the palace was used as a home-cum-warehouse for a society concerned mainly with trading.

From the great entrance hall, at the ends of which there were two main palace doors – one from the street and one from the water's edge – there was also the staircase for access to the first and second floors, which were the actual residential areas of

Da seit den Anfängen Venedigs nunmehr 1159 Jahre verstrichen sind, ohne daß es jemals von feindlicher Hand geplündert oder erobert worden ist, und da es sich von alters her dem Handel widmet, durch den seit jeher Reichtümer vieler zerstörter und jahrhundertelang von Barbaren heimgesuchter Städte nach Venedig gelangten, ist es geradezu zwangsläufig, daß die Bewohner der Lagunenstadt in Überfluß und Reichtum leben. Außerdem stehen die Adelshäuser seit Jahrhunderten in höchster Blüte. Sie verzeichnen für die Magistratsherren große Erfolge auf hoher See und haben ihre Häuser stets mit Reichtum gefüllt.

Obgleich sie immer schon in Sparsamkeit lebten, war die Ausstattung ihrer herrlichen Wohnsitze dennoch großartig. In unzähligen Bauten sind die Holzfußböden der Schlafgemächer und anderen Räume vergoldet oder zumindestens farbig gefaßt. Die Zimmer sind mit Gemälden und anderen Preziosen ausgestattet. Fast alle Gebäude haben Wohnräume, deren Wände edle Seidenteppiche oder Lederbespannungen mit Golddruck bedecken und in denen sich je nach dem jeweiligen Zeitgeschmack Spaliere und andere Dinge befinden. Die Schlafgemächer sind größtenteils mit Betten und goldenen Truhen ausgestattet, mit Malereien in Rahmen, in denen Gold dominiert. Unzählig sind die Kredenzen aus Silber und das fein gearbeitete Gerät aus Porzellan, Zinn, Kupfer oder Bronze. In den Hauptsälen befinden sich Waffen, Wappen und Banner der Vorfahren, die auf See oder zu Land kämpften. Auf einer Versteigerung habe ich den Hausrat eines zu Gefängnisstrafe verurteilten Adligen gesehen. Dieses Mobiliar wäre selbst für einen ›Herzog Italiens‹ zu verschwenderisch gewesen.«

Über Jahrhunderte blieb die venezianische Palastarchitektur bei aller Unterschiedlichkeit der aufeinander folgenden Stilperioden gewissen Grundprinzipien treu. Diese wurden lediglich variiert, aber nicht grundsätzlich verändert. Im Erdgeschoß durchmißt ein Korridor die gesamte Tiefe des Gebäudes. An diesen Hausflur schließen sich rechts und links Räume an, die der hauptsächlich vom Handel lebenden venezianischen Gesellschaft einst als Lagerstätten für Waren dienten.

Der venezianische Palast hat zwei Eingänge: einen vom Wasser her und einen auf der anderen Seite vom Land. Beide führen in den Hausflur, von wo man über

Et c'est logique, parce que 1159 ans s'étant désormais écoulés depuis le commencement de la vie de palais, sans qu'elle ait jamais été touchée par une main prédatrice et ennemie, et pratiquant le commerce pour lequel elle a toujours acheminé à la maison les richesses de nombreuses villes ruinées, dispersées et maltraitées par les barbares durant plusieurs siècles, il faut qu'elle soit très opulente et riche. A ceci s'ajoute que, pendant des siècles, les maisons nobles ont été rendues florissantes par les magistrats et leurs activités en mer couronnées de succès.

Et bien que les ancêtres aient vécu avec parcimonie, ils n'en étaient pas moins prodigues quand ils décoraient leurs maisons. On ne compte plus les édifices dont les plafonds des chambres et des autres pièces, ouvragés à l'or et en couleurs, décorés de peintures et d'ornements précieux. Presque tous les intérieurs sont revêtus de tapisseries de prix, de tissus de soie, de cuirs marqués à l'or, et d'autres choses selon les goûts de l'époque. Les chambres sont le plus souvent agrémentées de châlits, de coffres dorés et de peintures dont les cadres sont également rehaussés d'or. Les crédences d'argent et les autres bibelots de porcelaines, d'étain et de cuivre ou les bronzes travaillés à ‹ l'azimine › sont innombrables. Dans les salles principales, des râteliers d'armes présentent les écussons et les étendards des ancêtres qui combattirent sur la terre ou en mer. J'ai vu vendre aux enchères les biens d'un aristocrate condamné pour une sinistre affaire, biens qui auraient été trop dispendieux pour un duc d'Italie. »

La distribution intérieure des pièces du palais vénitien ne subit pas de modifications essentielles au cours des siècles, et nous retrouvons partout le même schéma tripartite de la façade extérieure qui la détermine. Au rez-de-chaussée, un large corridor se développant en profondeur est jouxté de salles destinées au stockage des marchandises depuis le temps où le palais servait d'entrepôt, dans une société vouée surtout au commerce. A partir du corridor aux extrémités duquel s'ouvrent les deux entrées du palais, l'une sur la terre, l'autre sur l'eau, on accède à l'escalier conduisant aux premier et second étages, dits *piani nobili,* qui constituent la zone résidentielle de la demeure. Le plan de ces étages correspond à celui du rez-de-chaussée ; ils pos-

the stately home. These upper floors were based on the same structure as the ground floor, i.e. with a vast central hall, called the *portego,* which received light from the great mullioned windows at each end and which gave access to the other rooms in the palace ranged along each side.

It was on the upper floors that the owners dedicated particular attention to both the decorations and the furnishings, as these reflected the social standing, power and prestige of the palace's inhabitants.

Naturally, in the course of the centuries, various kinds of renovation changed both the outside and the inside of the palaces and, as regards the interiors in particular, what survives today mainly reflects the most recent restorations, i.e. those of the 18th century – the last years of the Venetian Republic.

This was when the beamed ceilings of the 16th and 17th centuries recalled by Sansovino were replaced by the frescoed or painted ceilings created by the most famous of Venetian artists. These were often contained in elaborate frames of stucco work, done by the teams of stucco workers from the Ticino area who were much in demand and highly active in the city of Venice from the end of the 17th and throughout the 18th century.

The stucco work and paintings were extended to the walls, where they supplanted the previous upholstery of stamped leather, the famous *cuori d'oro,* which were no longer in fashion in the 18th century, so that unfortunately very few examples have survived to the present day.

Moreover, the rooms were enriched with elaborate fireplaces which became ornamental as well as useful, with complicated stucco decorations over the cowl. Rooms were also adorned with huge mirrors surrounded by precious carved and gilt frames or refined silks; the lighting was supplied by the sophisticated and colourful branching chandeliers, or *chioche,* produced in Murano.

Of course the stucco work, the frescoes and the paintings had a precise significance in relation to significant occurrences in the life of the family, such as marriages, elections to important political positions or accession to the nobility, often celebrated and handed down to posterity by means of mythological-allegorical compositions which naturally hardly concealed the family's vainglorious intentions.

eine Treppe in das erste und zweite Obergeschoß gelangt. Die beiden oberen Stockwerke, die sogenannten *piani nobili,* sind der Wohnbereich des Hauses. Ihre Raumaufteilung entspricht dem Erdgeschoß. So befindet sich über dem Hausflur ein großer zentraler Saal, der *portego* genannt und durch die großen Fassadenfenster erhellt wird. Von ihm gelangt man in die anderen Räumlichkeiten des Geschosses.

Da die *piani nobili* als Repräsentationsbereiche gesellschaftliche Stellung, Macht und Ansehen der jeweiligen Bewohner widerspiegelten, ist deren Ausstattung besonders bemerkenswert.

Heute findet man im Inneren der Paläste zumeist die Ausstattung aus dem 18. Jahrhundert vor, dem letzten Säkulum der Serenissima, der Republik Venedig.

Das von Sansovino erwähnte sichtbare Gebälk des 16. und 17. Jahrhunderts wurde im 18. Jahrhundert mit Deckengemälden der hervorragendsten venezianischen Künstler übermalt. Diese Fresken wurden oft mit erlesenen Stuckrahmen eingefaßt, für die die besten Stukkateure aus dem Tessin nach Venedig gerufen wurden. Seit Ende des 17. Jahrhunderts und das ganze 18. Jahrhundert hindurch arbeiteten sie in umfangreichen Maße in der Lagunenstadt.

Zu jener Zeit begannen Stukkaturen und Malereien auch die Wände zu überziehen. Sie ersetzten die älteren Wandverkleidungen aus Leder mit Golddrucken, die berühmten *cuori d'oro,* die im 18. Jahrhundert als unzeitgemäß empfunden wurden und von denen bis heute leider nur noch wenige Beispiele erhalten sind.

Die Zimmer wurden darüber hinaus mit fein gearbeiteten Kaminen ausgestattet. Neben ihrer eigentlichen Funktion als Wärmequelle waren sie wegen der komplexen Stuckdekorationen am Rauchfang wichtige Zierelemente. Desweiteren schmückten große Wandspiegel mit kostbar vergoldeten und geschnitzten Rahmen oder Wandbespannungen aus Seide die Räume. Wertvolle, farbige Kronleuchter aus Murano-Glas, oft mit feingearbeiteten Blütenornamenten versehen, sorgten für die Beleuchtung.

Natürlich zeigen die Arbeiten in Stuck und Farbe nicht irgendwelche Begebenheiten, sondern beziehen sich auf wichtige Ereignisse im Leben der jeweiligen Familie. Dargestellt sind zum Beispiel Hochzeitsfeierlichkeiten, die Übernahme wichtiger

sèdent en effet un vaste salon central, ou *portego,* éclairé par de vastes fenêtres polylobées et par lequel on accède aux autres pièces de la demeure.

Une attention particulière, aussi bien sur le plan de la décoration que de l'ameublement, est accordée aux étages « nobles » voués à la représentation, car ils reflètent le pouvoir et le prestige de celui qui y habite.

L'extérieur et les espaces intérieurs de la demeure ont évidemment fait l'objet de nombreuses restructurations au cours des siècles. Ce que nous admirons aujourd'hui est essentiellement le produit des interventions finales, c'est-à-dire celles auxquelles on a procédé au XVIIIème siècle, qui marque la fin de la Sérénissime.

Les poutrages des XVIème et XVIIème siècles, évoqués par Sansovino, ont été remplacés par des plafonds recouverts de fresques ou ornés de peintures des plus célèbres artistes vénitiens, souvent intégrés dans des cadres en stuc élaborés, pour lesquels on fit appel aux « quipes » de stucateurs d'origine tessinoise qui, depuis la fin du XVIIème, et pendant toute la durée du XVIIIème siècle, sont très recherchés à Venise.

Stucs et tableaux couvrent également les murs, remplaçant les tapisseries en cuirs marqués à l'or fin, les fameux « cœurs d'or » démodés au XVIIIème siècle, et dont malheureusement peu d'exemplaires nous sont parvenus.

De plus, les pièces s'enrichissent de cheminées élaborées qui, au-delà de leur fonction assument aussi un rôle ornemental avec les complexes décorations en stuc qui en recouvrent le manteau ; et elles s'ornent de grandes glaces aux précieux cadres dorés et gravés, ou de tentures de soie raffinées, tandis que l'éclairage est confié à des lustres colorés, présentant souvent une superbe décoration florale, fabriqués à Murano.

Les stucs, fresques et tableaux se réfèrent, c'est évident, aux événements fondamentaux de la vie de la famille tels que mariages, charges politiques très importantes ou admission au patriciat, qui sont souvent transmis à la postérité par l'intermédiaire de compositions à caractère mythologico-allégorique destinées à glorifier la famille.

En plus du mobilier réalisé par les habiles artisans vénitiens, célèbres surtout au XVIIIème siècle pour leurs fameux

The furnishings were either created by the able Venetian artisans who were famous, especially during the 18th century, for their lacquered furniture, or brought from exotic places far away to the East. Moreover, some Venetian stately homes also collected paintings, coins, medals and ceramics, creating some of the most amazing collections of the period and arousing the admiration of all visitors to the city. With the fall of the Republic and the consequent financial collapse, most of these riches were scattered or sold and now form the basis of many a collection in museums both in Italy and abroad.

The Venetian noble family's prestige and cultural role in the city was also emphasised by the great collections of books and manuscripts which, like the collections of art works, were given a specific place in the arrangement of the palace, in rooms especially equipped and decorated and at times even open to the public.

Finally, even the floors of these stately homes, which were lined with the famous Venetian *terrazzo,* had their own role to play. Here again, Sansovino's words offer a detailed illustration: "They use for the bedrooms, and for the other rooms in general, floors not of bricks but of a certain substance called *terrazzo,* which lasts for a very long time and is very charming to look at and clean. It is made with mortar and well-crushed tiles or bricks incorporated together. A portion of crushed Istrian marble chips is added and this highly dense mixture is spread on the floor of closely-laid planks nailed down so that the floor cannot twist and will stand the weight. Then they beat and stamp on the floor with special tools for a few days. When everything is smooth and equally hard, another layer of the same material is placed on top incorporating either vermillion or a red colouring. Then, after it has rested for a few days, it is spread with linseed oil so that the terrazzo becomes so shiny that a man can see his reflection in it. And even though this mixture is considered unhealthy because it is so cold, there is no flooring as beautiful, as elegant and as long-lasting as this…"

A further reason for admiration that only the Venetian palaces can offer lay, according to Sansovino, in the windows which "...are closed not with sheets of waxed fabric or paper, but with fine white glass, enclosed in wooden frames and held with iron and with lead, not only in the

politischer Ämter oder die Aufnahme in den Adelsstand – also entscheidende weil einschneidende Begebenheiten, die der Nachwelt überliefert werden sollten. Oft sind die Kompositionen in mythologisch-allegorische Darstellungen eingebettet, um den Clan zu zelebrieren.

Das Mobiliar stammte entweder aus den Werkstätten der venezianischen Kunsthandwerker, die besonders im 18. Jahrhundert für die Herstellung der berühmten Lackmöbel bekannt waren, oder aus den exotischen Ländern des Orients. In einigen Palazzi wurden zudem großartige zeitgenössische Kunstsammlungen angelegt: Gemälde, Münzen, Medaillen und Keramikgegenstände riefen bei den Betrachtern Bewunderung und Staunen hervor. Ein Großteil dieser Kunstsammlungen ging beim Untergang der Republik und dem daraus resultierenden finanziellen Zusammenbruch vieler Familien entweder verloren oder wurde verkauft. Heute sind diese Objekte Hauptattraktion zahlreicher italienischer und ausländischer Museen.

Zum Ruhm der Familie, und um deren kulturelle Rolle innerhalb der Stadt zu betonen, dienten auch die großen Bibliotheken, in denen zahlreiche Handschriften aufbewahrt wurden. Wie die anderen Preziosen fanden auch die Handschriften, die manchmal für die Öffentlichkeit zugänglich waren, in eigens dafür eingerichteten und dekorierten Räumen ihren Platz.

Schließlich weisen auch die Fußböden der venezianischen Paläste ganz spezifische Merkmale auf. Und es sind noch einmal die Worte Sansovinos, die sie am besten beschreiben: »In der Regel werden in den Schlafzimmern und Sälen keine Böden aus Ziegelsteinen verlegt, sondern aus einem besonderen Material, das *terrazzo* heißt. Es ist sehr widerstandsfähig und dabei doch anmutig. Es wird aus einer Mischung aus Kalkmörtel und zerstoßenen Ziegeln und Backsteinen sowie einem Anteil pulverisierten istrischen Marmors hergestellt. Dieses recht feste Gemisch wird auf dem Holzboden verteilt, dessen Bretter dicht verlegt wurden, damit sich das Holz nicht verzieht und dem Gewicht des Belags standhält. Dann bearbeitet man den Belag einige Tage lang mit speziellen Werkzeugen. Nachdem der Boden geglättet und gleichmäßig durchgehärtet ist, bedeckt man ihn mit einer zweiten Schicht des besagten Materials, die mit Zinnober oder roter Farbe angereichert ist. Dann streicht

meubles laqués, et des pièces originaires des lointaines contrées exotiques, certains palais abritaient des tableaux, monnaies, médailles et céramiques, formant les plus éclatantes collections de l'époque, qui provoquaient l'admiration de tous les visiteurs. A la chute de la République, avec la faillite financière qui en découla, la plus grande partie des collections fut dispersée ou vendue et elle constitue aujourd'hui le noyau des collections de nombreux musées, non seulement italiens, mais aussi étrangers.

Les livres et manuscrits qui, comme les autres objets précieux, étaient abrités dans des pièces expressément équipées et décorées, parfois ouvertes au public, contribuaient également à la gloire de la famille et à souligner le rôle culturel de celle-ci en milieu urbain.

Même les sols des demeures de la ville, les célèbres terrasses à la vénitienne, ont leur caractère spécifique. Ce sont encore les mots de Sansovino qui les illustrent : « Pour les chambres et les salles, les sols ne sont en général pas en brique, mais en *terrazzo,* une matière polie et très belle à voir tout en étant résistante. Cette substance est faite d'un mélange de calcaire, de tuiles et de briques écrasées. On y ajoute une part d'éclats de pierre d'Istrie pulvérisée, et on étend cette mixture plutôt dure sur le sol de planches bien fixé avec des clous, afin qu'il ne se déforme pas et résiste au poids de l'enduit. Ensuite, avec des outils conçus exprès, on bat et on tasse le sol pendant quelques jours. Quand il est lisse et durci, on y dépose une seconde couche de la dite matière, dans laquelle on incorpore soit du vermillon soit de la couleur rouge. Après avoir laissé reposer le sol pendant quelques jours, on l'astique à l'huile de lin, qui donne à la terrasse un tel brillant que l'on peut s'y mirer. Et bien que ce sol soit réputé nuisible à la santé parce qu'il est froid, on ne voit rien de plus beau ni de plus délicat et durable… »

Un autre sujet d'étonnement que seules présentent les demeures vénitiennes selon Sansovino : les fenêtres qui « …se ferment, non pas avec de la toile cirée ou du papier, mais avec des vitres très blanches et très fines, enfermées dans des cadres de bois et serties de fer et de plomb, pas seulement dans les palais et les bâtisses mais dans tous les lieux, aussi misérables qu'ils soient, au grand étonnement des étrangers. Rien qu'à cela on

palaces and large buildings but everywhere, however base the house might be, to the great astonishment of strangers to the city, as this fact in itself is proof enough of the infinite wealth that comes out of the glass kilns of Murano".

The fall of the Republic, with the consequent political upheaval and the collapse of the nobility, led to the scattering of the great wealth that had been preserved for centuries in the Venetian palaces, which were systematically plundered of what successive generations had brought together. But the treasures that were contained within their walls were so vast that not everything could be removed; thus what little has remained until the present day fortunately still bears ample witness to the magnificence and the glorious past of the city of Venice.

man, nachdem der Boden einige Tage geruht hat, Leinsamenöl darauf. So erhält der *terrazzo* einen Glanz, in dem man sich spiegeln kann. Und wenn dieser Fußboden wegen seiner Kälte auch als ungesund angesehen wird, so gibt es dennoch nichts Schöneres, nichts Anmutigeres und nichts Dauerhafteres als diesen…«

Einzigartig und besonders bemerkenswert waren – Sansovino zufolge – auch die Fenster, die »…nicht mit Wachstuch oder Papier geschlossen werden, sondern mit weißen und feinen Glasscheiben, die in Holzrahmen eingefaßt sind und Eisen- und Bleihalterungen aufweisen. Zum Erstaunen der Fremden finden sich diese Fenster nicht nur an den Palästen und Wohnhäusern, sondern auch an allen noch so unwichtigen Gebäuden. Allein daran kann der unermeßliche Reichtum begriffen werden, der aus den Öfen von Murano stammt…«

Das Ende der Republik, die daraus resultierenden politischen Unruhen und der Untergang der venezianischen Aristokratie ließen die jahrhundertealten Kostbarkeiten der venezianischen Paläste in alle Herren Länder gelangen. Was viele Generationen gesammelt hatten, konnte aber nicht in aller Vollständigkeit fortgeschafft werden. Die bis heute erhalten gebliebenen Schätze in der Lagunenstadt künden noch immer von der Herrlichkeit und großartigen Vergangenheit Venedigs.

peut mesurer la richesse infinie qui jaillit des creusets de Murano. »

La chute de la République, les bouleversements politiques qui en résultèrent et la décadence du patriciat conduisirent à la dispersion des biens séculaires conservés dans les palais vénitiens, systématiquement dépouillés de tout ce que des générations avaient recueilli ; mais les trésors conservés entre leurs murs étaient si nombreux que ce qui par chance est arrivé jusqu'à nous illustre encore parfaitement la splendeur et le passé glorieux de la ville.

PALAZZO PISANI

A' S. Tomaſo Sopra il Canal Grande

i Palazzo Barbarigo

PALAZZO PISANI
A' S. Tomaſo Sopra il Canal Grande

82.

Luca Carleuarijs del. et inc.

Palazzo Pisani Moretta

On the left bank of the Grand Canal, shut off from the horizon by the imposing mass of the Rialto Bridge, Palazzo Pisani Moretta demonstrates its Gothic origins in the delicate tracery decorating the façade around the balcony on the first floor and the open gallery on the second floor.

In its present form, the palace dates from around the mid-15th century and is one of the most representative examples of Venetian flamboyant Gothic. There are features in the mullioned windows with inbent arches in the first row and acute arches with quatrefoils in the second that are shared with other architectural examples of the period, though in this case they are distributed with a calibrated elegance and remarkable pictorial effect.

The palace belonged to the branch of the Pisani family bearing the nickname of "Moretta", a dialect form deriving from the name of the head of the family, Almorò. Unlike the Pisani of Santo Stefano, the Pisani Moretta never held important positions in the political life of the city, but they dedicated themselves actively to trading, accumulating a considerable fortune which was converted over the years into landed property.

The purchase of the palace actually dates back to 1629, but it was only occupied in the first decade of the 18th century by Francesco Pisani, nicknamed Piero. He was concerned with accumulating a fortune of his own to hand down to his only remaining daughter, Chiara. A trust of 1567 had destined all the family's goods entirely to the first male heir, who had to bear the name Francesco (and Francesco Piero's son having died, the entire heritage would have gone to the Pisani of Santo Stefano).

Pisani therefore obliged himself and his daughter to suffer such strict economies that, when he died in 1737, Chiara inherited a considerable amount of landed property and cash.

A year later she became a widow and set up house in Venice for good, abandoning Verona where she had lived with her husband. As the guardian of her six children, she administered her husband's fortunes alone.

Am linken Ufer des Canal Grande, der am Horizont von der imposanten Rialto-Brücke begrenzt wird, befindet sich der Palazzo Pisani Moretta. Das reiche Maßwerk des Balkons und der Loggia im ersten und zweiten Obergeschoß verweist auf die gotischen Wurzeln.

Der Palast in seiner heutigen Form wurde Mitte des 15.Jahrhunderts von der weitverzweigten Familie Pisani errichtet und ist eines der repräsentativsten Beispiele der venezianischen Gotik. Dem Grundmuster des Kielbogens und des Vierpasses begegnet man bei zeitgleichen Palästen immer wieder. Hier sind sie allerdings mit ausgewogener Eleganz und einzigartiger malerischer Wirkung eingesetzt worden.

Im 17. Jahrhunder gelangte der Palast in den Besitz eines anderen Zweigs der Familie Pisani, der sich durch den Beinamen Moretta unterschied, einer mundartlichen Abwandlung von Almorò. Im Gegensatz zu den Pisani di Santo Stefano haben die Pisani Moretta nie wichtige Ämter im politischen Leben der Stadt bekleidet. Sie trieben vielmehr erfolgreich Handel und legten ihr ansehnliches Vermögen in Grundbesitz an.

Der Palast wurde zwar bereits im Jahre 1629 erworben, aber erst im ersten Jahrzehnt des 18. Jahrhunderts von Francesco Pisani, auch Piero genannt, bewohnt. Dieser sparte sich ein eigenes Vermögen zusammen, das er seiner einzigen Tochter Chiara hinterlassen konnte. Ein Fideikommiß aus dem Jahre 1567 bestimmte nämlich, daß alle Güter der Familie einzig und allein dem erstgeborenen Sohn vererbt werden konnten, der außerdem den Namen Francesco tragen mußte. Da Pieros Sohn Francesco verstorben war, wäre das gesamte Vermögen an die Pisani di Santo Stefano übergegangen.

Pisani erlegte sich selbst und seiner Tochter strenge Sparsamkeit auf, so daß Chiara, als er 1737 starb, ein ansehnliches Vermögen in Grundstücken und Bargeld erbte.

Nachdem sie ein Jahr später Witwe geworden war, kehrte Chiara aus Verona, wo sie mit ihrem Ehemann gelebt hatte, nach Venedig zurück. Als Vormund ihrer sechs minderjährigen Kinder wurde sie zur Alleinverwalterin des Vermögens ihres Ehemannes.

Sur la rive gauche du Grand Canal fermé à l'horizon par la masse imposante du Pont de Rialto, le Palazzo Pisani Moretta dénonce ses origines gothiques dans les entrelacs aériens qui décorent le balcon et la galerie aux premier et second étages.

Le palais, dont la forme actuelle remonte à la moitié du XVème siècle, est l'un des exemples les plus représentatifs du Gothique flamboyant vénitien ; dans les fenêtres polylobées et les arcs fléchis de la première rangée et aigus de la deuxième, avec des croix quadrilobes, apparaissent, en effet, des éléments communs aux autres édifices de l'époque, répartis ici avec une élégance mesurée et la recherche d'un effet pictural très particulier.

Le palais appartenait à une branche des Pisani se distinguant par son surnom Moretta, forme dialectale dérivée du nom de la souche, Almorò ; les Pisani Moretta, contrairement aux Pisani de Santo Stefano, n'occupèrent jamais de charges importantes dans la vie politique de la ville, mais ils se vouèrent activement au commerce, amassant une fortune considérable en partie convertie, au cours des années, en biens fonciers.

L'acquisition du palais remonte à 1629 mais il ne fut effectivement habité que durant la première décennie du XVIIIème siècle par Francesco Pisani, dit Piero. Celui-ci accumula une fortune personnelle qu'il laissa à la seule fille qui lui fût restée, Chiara ; un fidéicommis de 1567 destinait en effet tous les biens de la famille au fils aîné, qui devait en outre s'appeler Francesco. Le fils de Francesco Piero étant décédé, la totalité du patrimoine aurait été transmise aux Pisani de Santo Stefano.

Par conséquent, Pisani se soumit ainsi que sa fille à un régime de sévère économie à tel point qu'à sa mort, en 1737, Chiara entra en possession d'un patrimoine considérable en biens fonciers et en argent liquide.

Un an plus tard, demeurée veuve, elle s'établit définitivement à Venise, abandonnant Vérone où elle avait vécu avec son mari, et devint l'administratrice unique de la fortune, en tant que tutrice de six enfants mineurs.

In Venice, Chiara concerned herself not only with modernizing and restoring the palace that her father's avarice had allowed to fall into disrepair, but also with satisfying those distinctly feminine whims that a life of strict economies had left unsatisfied. In the years after her return to Venice, she bought a great deal of jewelry: pearls, emeralds, rubies and diamonds (one of which cost 1 500 ducats) which were set in various ways or intended as pendant earrings.

In the meantime, in 1739, Chiara ordered certain works which mainly involved the interior of the palace, but she also had a third floor built with a terrace facing onto the Grand Canal, linking the three floors with an impressive double flight of stairs of unusual size, instead of the original Gothic outdoor staircase.

The interior decorations were coordinated by Francesco Zanchi, an illusionist painter who was to work for more than thirty years for Palazzo Pisani. He was responsible for the elaborate frames around the frescoes which decorated the ceilings of the palace after 1745 and also, possibly, for some of the floors and the landings on the staircase.

During these years, Palazzo Pisani Moretta also provided work for Giuseppe Angeli, Giambattista Tiepolo, Giambattista Piazzetta and Gaspare Diziani, as well as for stucco-workers, upholsterers, and layers of the *terrazzo* (marble mosaic) flooring peculiar to Venice. Even the lighting was not neglected and great branching chandeliers, which have unfortunately since been lost, were created by the most famous Murano glass-worker of the time, Giuseppe Briati.

In 1752, Chiara's oldest son, Pietro Vettore, married Caterina Grimani, the daughter of a Procurator and niece of the doge. On the death of Pietro's mother in 1767, it was he who took her place as administrator of the family fortune and continued the work of embellishing their home. It was also Pietro Vettore who commissioned Jacopo Guarana to fresco the ceiling of the *portego* on the first floor, which was completely renovated (taking on the appearance it retains today) for the marriage of his younger brother Vettore in 1773.

Guarana (1720 – 1808) produced two great mythological-allegorical representations of *Light Conquering Darkness* and *Apollo with Aurora and the Hours,* surrounded by the *Seasons* and the *Four Elements;* he also decorated the walls over the doors with six pairs of putti and the signs of the zodiac.

In der Lagunenstadt widmete sich Chiara nicht nur der Modernisierung und Restaurierung des Palastes, der durch die Sparsamkeit ihres Vaters recht verfallen war, sondern erfüllte sich auch einige Wünsche, die durch ihr bisheriges Leben unerfüllt geblieben waren. In den ersten Jahren nach ihrer Rückkehr erwarb sie zum Beispiel zahlreiche Schmuckstücke wie Perlen, Smaragde, Rubine und Diamanten, von denen alleine einer 1500 Dukaten wert war und die auf verschiedenste Weise gefaßt oder für Ohrringe bestimmt waren.

Im Jahre 1739 begann die Restaurierung, die vor allem die Innenräume des Palastes betraf. Es wurde außerdem ein drittes Stockwerk mit einer die gesamte Breite des Gebäudes einnehmenden Terrasse zum Canal Grande errichtet. Anstelle der gotischen Außentreppe ließ Chiara einen imposanten zweiarmigen Innenaufgang in recht ungewöhnlichen Dimensionen erbauen, der die drei Stockwerke miteinander verbindet.

Die Innendekoration wurde Francesco Zanchi anvertraut. Der Quadraturmaler sollte über dreißig Jahre lang für den Palazzo Pisani arbeiten. Ihm sind die feingearbeiteten Rahmen der Deckenmalereien, die ab 1745 entstanden, und wohl auch die Entwürfe für einige Fußböden und für die Treppenpodeste der Prunktreppe zu verdanken.

In jenen Jahren wirkten im Palazzo Pisani Moretta auch Giuseppe Angeli, Giambattista Tiepolo, Giambattista Piazzetta und Gaspare Diziani sowie zahlreiche Stukkateure, Polsterer und Terrazzo-Verleger. Für die Beleuchtung sorgte der damals angesehenste Glasbläser Muranos: Giuseppe Briati. Er lieferte die großen Kronleuchter, die leider nicht mehr erhalten sind.

1752 vermählte sich der erstgeborene Sohn Chiaras, Pietro Vettore, mit Caterina Grimani, Tochter des Prokurators und Nichte des Dogen. Nach dem Tod der Mutter im Jahre 1767 wurde er zum Verwalter des Familienvermögens und fuhr mit der Verschönerung des Wohnsitzes fort. Er beauftragte Jacopo Guarana mit der Ausmalung der Decke des portego im Obergeschoß, das anläßlich der Hochzeit des jüngeren Bruders Vettore im Jahre 1773 renoviert wurde.

Jacopo Guarana (1720 – 1808) malte zwei große mythologisch-allegorische Darstellungen: *Das Licht besiegt die Finsternis* und *Apoll mit Aurora und den Stunden.* Sie werden von den *Jahreszeiten* und den *Vier Elementen* umrahmt. Die Sopraporten schmücken sechs Puttenpaare und die Tierkreiszeichen.

A Venise, Chiara se consacra non seulement à la remodernisation et à la restauration du palais, que l'avarice de son père avait laissé se dégrader, mais aussi à la satisfaction d'exigences délicieusement féminines qu'une vie menée chichement avait laissées inassouvies. En effet, de retour à Venise, elle achètera de nombreux joyaux : perles, émeraudes, rubis et diamants, dont un d'une valeur de 1 500 ducats, sertis différemment ou destinés à des pendants d'oreilles.

En 1739 débutent les travaux qui concernent surtout les intérieurs du palais, mais Chiara fait également construire un troisième étage, avec terrasse donnant sur le Grand Canal, et pour relier les trois étages, un imposant escalier à double rampe, aux dimensions extraordinaires, qui remplace l'escalier extérieur d'origine gothique.

L'aménagement des décorations intérieures est confié à Francesco Zanchi, peintre quadratoriste qui travaillera plus de trente ans pour le Palazzo Pisani, et à qui l'on doit les cadres élaborés des fresques qui orneront les plafonds de la demeure à partir de 1745, et peut-être également les dessins réalisés pour quelques dallages et les paliers du grand escalier.

Ces années-là, sont en effet engagés au Palazzo Pisani Moretta : Giuseppe Angeli, Giambattista Tiepolo, Giambattista Piazzetta, Gaspare Diziani en plus des nombreux stucateurs, tapissiers et carreleurs ; le plus célèbre verrier de Murano, Giuseppe Briati, veilla à l'éclairage, fournissant les lustres malheureusement disparus.

En 1752, le fils aîné de Chiara, Pietro Vettore, épouse Caterina Grimani, fille du Procurateur et nièce du doge; à la mort de sa mère, en 1767, il lui succédera dans l'administration du patrimoine familial et continuera à embellir la demeure. C'est justement Pietro Vettore qui commande à Jacopo Guarana les fresques du plafond du *portego* de l'étage noble totalement rénové, qui revêtit l'aspect sous lequel il nous apparaît aujourd'hui, à l'occasion du mariage de son frère cadet, célébré en 1773.

Guarana (1720 – 1808) y développa deux grandes représentations allégorico-mythologiques, *La Lumière vainc les ténèbres* et *Apollon avec Aurore et les Heures* entourées des *Saisons* et des *Quatre Eléments.* En outre il décora les dessus-de-porte de six paires d'angelots et des signes du zodiaque.

Les deux thèmes semblent faire allusion à la nouvelle existence que Vettore s'apprêtait à passer avec son épouse Cornelia Grimani, après la dissolution d'un précédent mariage,

The two subjects seem to allude to the new life that Vettore was about to begin with his wife Cornelia Grimani, after the dissolution of a previous marriage that had not been well-received by the family, but from which he had had a son, Pietro Vettore.

Pietro Castelli was entrusted with the white and gold stucco work surrounding the frescoes, the great looking-glasses and the zodiac putti over the doors. Moreover, with the cooperation of a French craftsman, Antonio Rigotie, the furniture on the first floor was replaced. (Today, the *portego* still contains some armchairs, four console tables and the glass lamp-holders with wooden stands attached to the walls which go so well with the stucco decoration.)

According to the typical layout of the Venetian palace, the *portego* gives access to the other rooms, which contain frescoes dating from Chiara's time. In 1744, she had made a series of payments to Giuseppe Angeli for the paintings inserted in the ceiling of what is now the yellow drawing-room, to the left of the *portego,* including *Allegories of the Continents, Fortitude and Fame,* in pinkish and silvery tones which give an immaterial effect to the bold perspective compositions.

The well-known fresco by Giambattista Tiepolo of *The Meeting of Mars and Venus,* with its illusionist framing by Francesco Zanchi, dates from 1743 (in the Tiepolo room). Giambattista Piazzetta's great painting of the *Death of Dario* was produced around 1746 and is now preserved in the Museum of 18th-century Venetian Art in Ca' Rezzonico, as a result of a bequest made by Pisani Giusti del Giardino in 1926. Part of the artist's payment for this work was in the form of goods coming from the family's properties in Bagnolo and Montagnana.

Gaspare Diziani (1689 – 1767) also worked for Chiara Pisani, frescoing the ceilings of both the first and the second floors of the palace with mythological-allegorical subjects, with notable results from the point of view of composition and colour.

The natural complement to the paintings and frescoes is provided by the stucco work which, true to 18th-century custom, was used to decorate almost all the rooms in Palazzo Pisani. There are some particularly interesting stucco decorations on musical themes, with musical instruments and sheets of written music, made in 1769 by Giuseppe Ferrari on the mezzanine floor, where Chiara's younger son Vettore lived. There are others, done by the same artist a few years

Die beiden Hauptdarstellungen spielen wohl auf das neue Leben an, das Vettore mit seiner Frau Cornelia Grimani beginnen wollte, nachdem seine vorherige Ehe, aus der sein Sohn Pietro Vettore stammte, aufgelöst worden war.

Pietro Castelli wurde mit den weißen und vergoldeten Stuckarbeiten betraut, die die Fresken, die großen Wandspiegel und die Putten der Sopraporten rahmen. In Zusammenarbeit mit einem französischen Kunsthandwerker, Antonio Rigotie, wurde die Möblierung des Obergeschosses verändert, von der im *portego* die Sessel, die vier Konsoltische und die Wandglasleuchter mit Holzhalter erhalten sind. Letztere harmonieren perfekt mit den Stuckverzierungen.

Gemäß der typischen Raumfolge im venezianischen Palast öffnen sich zum *portego* hin die anderen Säle, deren Fresken Chiara in Auftrag gab. Im Jahre 1744 wies sie mehrere Zahlungen an Giuseppe Angeli an, um ihn für die Deckenmalereien des links vom *portego* befindlichen Gelben Salons zu entlohnen. Er malte die *Allegorien der Kontinente, der Stärke und des Ruhms* in rosa- und silberfarbenen Tönen, die kühne Kompositionen mit perspektivischen Verkürzungen zeigen.

Das berühmte Fresko *Zusammentreffen von Mars und Venus* von Giambattista Tiepolo stammt aus dem Jahre 1743. Francesco Zanchi versah diese Deckenmalerei (im Tiepolo-Saal) mit einem gemalten Rahmen. Um 1746 entstand das großartige Gemälde *Der Tod des Darius* Giambattista Piazzettas. Es wird heute im Museo del Settecento Veneziano in der Ca' Rezzonico aufbewahrt, dem es Pisani Giusti del Giardino 1926 vermachte. Für dieses Werk wurde der Maler teilweise auch in Naturalien bezahlt, die aus den Grundbesitzen der Familie in Bagnolo und in Montagnana stammten.

Im Dienste Chiara Pisanis stand auch Gaspare Diziani (1689 – 1767). Er schuf die Deckenmalereien des ersten und zweiten Obergeschosses. Die Fresken mythologisch-allegorischen Charakters bestechen durch ihre überaus geglückten Kompositionen und Farbgebungen.

Gemälde und Fresken ergänzen die Stukkaturen, die, wie im 18. Jahrhundert üblich, fast alle Säle des Palazzo Pisani schmückten. Besondere Aufmerksamkeit verdienen die Stuckdekorationen mit Motiven aus der Musik. Sie wurden 1769 von Giuseppe Ferrari in dem vom jüngeren Sohn Chiaras, Vettore, bewohnten Halbgeschoß ausgeführt. Es sind Musikinstrumente und

peu apprécié en famille, dont était né un fils, Pietro Vettore.

L'exécution des stucs blancs et or qui encadrent les fresques, les grands miroirs et les putti des dessus-de-porte fut confiée à Pietro Castelli. De plus, avec la collaboration d'un artisan d'art d'origine française, Antonio Rigotie, on veilla également à modifier l'ameublement de l'étage noble, dont il reste aujourd'hui, dans le *portego,* les fauteuils et les quatre consoles et, appliqués aux murs, les lampadaires en verre avec support en bois qui s'harmonisent à merveille avec les décors en stuc.

Selon le plan caractéristique du palais vénitien, le *portego* s'ouvre sur les autres salles abritant les fresques de l'époque de Chiara qui, en 1744, effectuait une série de paiements à Giuseppe Angeli pour les peintures intégrées au plafond de l'actuel Salon jaune, à gauche du portego, avec les *Allégories des continents, la Force et la Célébrité,* aux tons rosés et argentés qui prêtent un air aérien aux audacieuses compositions en perspective.

La célèbre fresque de Giambattista Tiepolo, *La Rencontre entre Mars et Vénus* (salle Tiepolo) remonte à 1743. Elle fut dotée d'un cadre peint par Francesco Zanchi. Giambattista Piazzetta réalisa vers 1746 *La Mort de Darius,* conservée aujourd'hui dans le Museo del Settecento Veneziano de la Ca' Rezzonico, suite au legs Pisani Giusti del Giardino de 1926. Le peintre reçut une partie du paiement en nature sous forme de produits des domaines de la propriété familiale de Bagnolo et de Montagnana.

Gaspare Diziani (1689 – 1767), lui aussi au service de Chiara Pisani, exécuta les fresques des plafonds du premier et du deuxième étage. Les peintures aux thèmes de caractère mythologico-allégorique sont extrêmement séduisantes sur le plan de la composition et de la couleur.

Les stucs qui, selon l'usage du XVIIIème siècle, ornent presque toutes les salles du Palazzo Pisani sont le complément naturel des tableaux et des fresques ; particulièrement intéressants : les stucs à thème musical réalisés en 1769 par Giuseppe Ferrari dans l'entresol habité par le fils cadet de Chiara, Vettore, avec instruments musicaux et papier à musique, et les autres stucs exécutés quelques années plus tard, avec lesquels le même artiste agrémenta l'actuelle salle à manger de l'étage noble : entre un riche appareil à caractère géométrique et floral s'intègrent les personnages d'Endymion et Séléné, semblables aux personnages du mythe d'Apollon que

later, decorating what is now the dining hall on the first floor: a rich arrangement of geometric and floral patterns encloses the figures of Endymion and Selene, which resemble those surrounding the myth of Apollo which Ferrari had created for Palazzo Pisani at Santo Stefano.

As mentioned previously, Chiara Pisani's restoration work on the palace was continued by her first son Pietro Vettore. Apart from the work of Guarana on the frescoes in the *portego* on the first floor, which was then called the "salone", it was Pietro Vettore who also commissioned Antonio Canova (1757 – 1822)to create the marble group of *Daedalus and Icarus,* one of the sculptor's juvenile masterpieces, rich in chiaroscuro vibrations, completed between 1778 and 1779. The sculpture was originally placed in the main entrance hall of the palace, between the doors on the water's edge; now it is in the Correr Museum, having been donated to the city of Venice by the three daughters of Vettor Daniele (Beatrice, Cornelia and Laura) in 1874.

Among the pictorial treasures that once belonged to the Pisani Moretta, there is an unforgettable masterpiece by Paolo Veronese (1528 – 1588): *Dario's Family before Alexander,* which the artist painted in a villa belonging to the family near Montagnana, from where the painting was subsequently transferred to the palace at San Polo. In 1857 it was sold by Vettor Daniele to the National Gallery in London for the sum of £ 13 650 sterling.

This fact caused a considerable uproar in the city, partly because of the value of the work and also because of the social standing of the family that had permitted the sale. The chroniclers of the time reported some of the comments made in Venice: "There is a great deal of noise and much satire, both spoken and written in the press, against the millionaire Pisani who sold the painting, instead of keeping it for the fame of his family… and donating it to the Municipality on his deathbed. He apologised by saying that, having no male heirs but three married daughters, there would have been quarreling on his death over the ownership of this indivisible painting, which would consequently have had to be sold, but for which certainly no-one would have paid 15 thousand gold napoleons, as the English consul had done (and from this point of view he was certainly right)…"

The palace remained constantly in the possession of the Pisani family until 1962, when it was left by legacy to the Sammartini, who have seen to its accurate restoration.

Notenblätter dargestellt. Etwas später schmückte derselbe Künstler den heutigen Speisesaal im ersten Obergeschoß aus: Reiche geometrische und florale Stuckdekorationen umfangen Endymion und Selene, die Ferraris Figuren zum Apoll-Mythos für den Palazzo Pisani in Santo Stefano ähneln.

Wie bereits erwähnt, führte der älteste Sohn Chiara Pisanis, Pietro Vettore, die Renovierungen seiner Mutter fort. Er ließ den *portego* im ersten Obergeschoß, der damals »Salon« genannt wurde, von Guarana ausmalen und gab bei Antonio Canova (1757 – 1822) die Marmorgruppe *Dädalus und Ikarus* in Auftrag. Canovas Jugendwerk, das starke Helldunkelkontraste prägen, entstand zwischen 1778 und 1779. Ursprünglich befand es sich im Hausflur des Palastes, zwischen den beiden Portalen zum Wasser. Heute wird es im Museo Correr aufbewahrt. Die drei Töchter Vettor Danieles, Beatrice, Cornelia und Laura, hatten die Marmorgruppe im Jahre 1874 der Stadt Venedig geschenkt.

Zu den Gemälden, die einst zum Besitz der Pisani Moretta zählten, gehört auch eines der Meisterwerke Paolo Veroneses (1528 – 1588): *Die Familie des Darius.* Der Künstler malte es in einer Villa der Familie Pisani in der Gegend von Montagnana, von wo das Bild später in den Palast von San Polo gelangte. Vettor Daniele verkaufte es schließlich im Jahre 1857 für 13 650 Pfund Sterling an die National Gallery in London.

Dieser Verkauf sorgte für großes Aufsehen in der Stadt. Zum einen wegen der Kostbarkeit des Werkes und zum anderen wegen der hohen Stellung der Familie, die es eigentlich nicht nötig hatte, solch ein wertvolles Bild zu veräußern. Ein Kommentator aus jenen Tagen schrieb dazu folgendes: »Viel Lärm und viel Satire in Wort und Schrift, in den Zeitungen, um den Millionär Pisani, der das Gemälde verkaufte, anstatt es zum Ruhm seiner Familie zu bewahren… und es bei seinem Tode der Stadt zu vermachen. Er entschuldigte sich mit der Ausrede, daß er, da er keine männlichen Erben, sondern nur drei verheiratete Töchter habe, Erbstreitigkeiten vorgebeugt habe, denn dieses unteilbare Gemälde hätte folglich verkauft werden müssen, wobei jedoch sicherlich niemand, wie der englische Konsul, 15 000 Napoleondore bezahlt hätte (womit er gewiß recht hat)…«

Bis 1962 war der Palast im Besitz der Pisani. Danach wurde er Sitz der Sammartini, die ihn restaurieren ließen.

Ferrari avait créés pour le Palazzo Pisani à Santo Stefano.

Comme il a déjà été mentionné, le fils aîné de Chiara Pisani, Pietro Vettore, poursuivit les travaux de restauration engagés par sa mère : outre les interventions de Guarana avec les fresques du portego de l'étage noble, le « salon » de l'époque, on lui doit la commande à Antonio Canova (1757 – 1822)du groupe de marbre *Dédale et Icare* – cette œuvre précoce du sculpteur, riche en vibrations de clairs-obscurs, fut exécutée entre 1778 et 1779 ; placée à l'origine dans le corridor du palais, entre les deux portes donnant sur l'eau, elle se trouve aujourd'hui au Museo Correr, les trois filles de Vettor Daniele, Beatrice, Cornelia et Laura l'ayant offerte en 1874 à la ville de Venise.

Parmi les trésors picturaux ayant appartenu aux Pisani Moretta, il faut mentionner l'un des chefs-d'œuvre de Véronèse (1528 – 1588), *La Famille de Darius devant Alexandre,* que l'artiste peignit dans une villa des Pisani près de Montagnana, d'où le tableau fut transféré, par la suite, au palais de San Polo, avant d'être finalement vendu par Vettor Daniele en 1857 à la National Gallery de Londres pour 13 650 livres sterling.

L'événement fit grand bruit en ville, aussi bien à cause de la valeur de l'œuvre que du prestige de la famille qui n'aurait pas dû consentir à la vente, à tel point que les chroniques de l'époque recueillent les commentaires que l'on fit à ce propos à Venise : « Le très grand tapage et de nombreuses satires orales et écrites imprimées dans les journaux au sujet du millionnaire Pisani qui a vendu le tableau plutôt que de le conserver en l'honneur de sa famille… et de le donner à sa mort à la Ville. Il s'est excusé en disant que n'ayant pas d'héritiers masculins mais trois filles mariées, il avait voulu anticiper les querelles d'héritage, et que ce tableau étant indivisible, il aurait donc dû être vendu, mais que certainement personne n'aurait payé 15 000 napoléons d'or, comme le fit le consul anglais (et en ceci il a certainement raison)… »

Avec les hauts et les bas à caractère patrimonial qui concernent surtout les dernières années du XVIIIème siècle et les premières années du XIXème, le palais a toujours été en possession des Pisani jusqu'en 1962, où il devint par legs testamentaire la propriété des Sammartini qui, après une restauration soignée, lui ont rendu la splendeur qu'il avait du temps de Chiara.

Palazzo Pisani Moretta

17 The great shell with horns of plenty which stands over the main entrance door onto the courtyard dates from the time of Chiara Pisani.

18/19 The majestic staircase with its double flight of steps. This was built by order of Chiara Pisani to replace the Gothic outdoor staircase which once linked the palace floors (which had become three with the extra floor and terrace she had added). The landings were probably designed by Pietro Zanchi, an illusionist painter who worked in the Palazzo Pisani for over thirty years.

20/21 The *portego* on the first floor. This was totally renovated in 1773 for the marriage of Vettore Pisani to Cornelia Grimani. The ceiling was then decorated with frescoes by Jacopo Guarana and white and gold stucco work by Pietro Castelli. The four armchairs, the four console tables and the glass chandeliers remain from the original furniture of the period which was designed by the French craftsman Antonio Rigotie. The Venetian *terrazzo* floor was the work of Bastian Crovato.

22 Jacopo Guarana and Pietro Castelli created the zodiac images over the doors of the first floor; the painting is the work of Guarana and the stucco decoration was done by Castelli. There are six doors with panels, each of which illustrates two zodiac signs.

23 Jacopo Guarana and Pietro Castelli: detail of the door which leads into the Yellow Room, topped by the panel decorated with zodiac signs.

24 Giambattista Tiepolo, *The Meeting of Mars and Venus*. This fresco was made in 1743 and was framed by the illusionist painter Francesco Zanchi; it decorates the ceiling of what is commonly called the "Tiepolo Room". The family accounts indicate that the painter received 2 200 lire for this work in 1745; this somewhat low figure is probably the balance, paid on completion of the work for which the artist had already received part payment in advance.

25 Giuseppe Angeli, *Allegory of the Continents: Europa*. This painting decorates the ceiling of the Yellow Room to the left of the *portego*. In 1744, when the paintings had already been completed, the family accounts mention that the artist was paid 165.4 lire.

26 Jacopo Guarana: detail of the fresco on the ceiling of the *portego*, where the decoration was renovated in 1773. The fresco is based on an allegorical-mythological theme and represents *Light Conquering Darkness* and *Apollo with Aurora and the Hours* surrounded by the *Seasons* and the *Four Elements*.

27 Gaspare Diziani, *Allegory of Faith*. This fresco was done around 1750 to decorate a passageway between two rooms. It dates from the time when Chiara Pisani had begun the palace's reconstruction and new decoration.

17 Die große Muschel mit Füllhörnern über dem Eingangstor zum Innenhof stammt aus der Zeit Chiara Pisanis.

18/19 Zweiarmige Prunktreppe in majestätischen Dimensionen. Chiara Pisani ließ sie anstelle der externen gotischen Treppe erbauen, die nur zwei Stockwerke miteinander verband. Da der Palazzo um ein weiteres Geschoß mit Terrasse aufgestockt wurde, gelangte man über die neue Treppe in drei Geschosse. Die Treppenpodeste entwarf vermutlich Pietro Zanchi, ein Quadraturmaler, der mehr als dreißig Jahre im Palazzo Pisani arbeitete.

20/21 Der *portego* im ersten Obergeschoß wurde anläßlich der Vermählung von Vettore Pisani mit Cornelia Grimani im Jahre 1773 komplett renoviert. Die Deckenmalereien führte Jacopo Guarana aus, die weißen und vergoldeten Stukkaturen Pietro Castelli. Das Mobiliar, von dem heute noch vier Polsterstühle, vier Konsoltische und die Wandleuchter aus Glas erhalten sind, entwarf der französische Kunsthandwerker Antonio Rigotie. Der *terrazzo alla veneziana* wurde von Bastian Crovato verlegt.

22 Die Gestaltung der sechs Sopraporten mit jeweils zwei Tierkreiszeichen im *portego* des ersten Obergeschosses nahmen Jacopo Guarana (Malereien) und Pietro Castelli (Stukkaturen) vor.

23 Jacopo Guarana und Pietro Castelli, eine Sopraporte mit Tierkreiszeichen. Durch diese Tür gelangt man vom *portego* in den Gelben Saal.

24 Giambattista Tiepolo, *Zusammentreffen von Mars und Venus*. Das Fresko, 1743 ausgeführt und mit Quadraturmalereien Francesco Zanchis gerahmt, schmückt die Decke des sogenannten Tiepolo-Saals. Im Jahre 1745 erhielt der Künstler für dieses Gemälde laut den Auszahlungsbelegen des Hauses 2 200 Lire. Die geringe Höhe des Betrages läßt darauf schließen, daß es sich bei dieser Summe um eine letzte Rate bei Vollendung der Arbeit gehandelt haben muß.

25 Giuseppe Angeli, *Allegorie der Kontinente: Europa*. Diese Deckenmalerei schmückt den Gelben Saal, links vom *portego* gelegen. Im Jahre 1744, als die Malereien bereits fertiggestellt waren, ist in der Buchhaltung der Familie eine Auszahlung an den Künstler in Höhe von 165,4 Lire eingetragen.

26 Jacopo Guarana, Detail der Deckenmalerei des *portego*, dessen Ausstattung 1773 renoviert wurde. Die Ausschmückung der Decke beinhaltet die mythologisch-allegorischen Themen *Das Licht besiegt die Finsternis* und *Apoll mit Aurora und den Stunden*, die von den *Jahreszeiten* und den *Vier Elementen* umgeben werden.

17 Grande coquille flanquée de deux cornes d'abondance qui surmonte la porte cochère donnant accès à la cour. Elle date de l'époque de Chiara Pisani.

18/19 Escalier à double rampe aux dimensions majestueuses. Chiara Pisani le fit construire pour remplacer l'escalier extérieur gothique qui ne reliait que deux étages du Palais, devenus trois à la suite de travaux de surélévation avec terrasse commandés par la noble dame. Les paliers auraient été exécutés selon les plans de Pietro Zanchi, peintre quadratoriste qui travailla plus de trente ans pour le Palais Pisani.

20/21 *Portego* du premier étage. Il fut complètement rénové en 1773 à l'occasion des noces de Vettore Pisani avec Cornelia Grimani. Le plafond fut alors orné de fresques de Jacopo Guarana et de stucs blancs et or de Pietro Castelli. L'ameublement dont il reste aujourd'hui quatre fauteuils, quatre consoles et les lustres de cristal fut imaginé par l'artisan d'art français Antoine Rigotie. Le *terrazzo alla veneziana* fut réalisé par Bastian Crovato.

22 Jacopo Guarana et Pietro Castelli, décoration du dessus-de-porte du *portego* de l'étage noble avec détail du zodiaque, dans laquelle Guarana a réalisé les peintures, et Castelli, les décorations en stuc qui servent de cadre. Il y a six décorations de dessus-de-porte et chacune d'elles illustre deux signes du zodiaque.

23 Jacopo Guarana et Pietro Castelli, une décoration zodiacale au-dessus de la porte qui mène du *portego* à la Salle jaune.

24 Giambattista Tiepolo, *La Rencontre entre Mars et Vénus*. La fresque réalisée en 1743 et entourée d'un cadre de Francesco Zanchi, orne le plafond de la Salle Tiepolo. Pour la réalisation de ce travail, il apparaît dans les registres de comptabilité de la maison que le peintre reçut 2 200 lires en 1745. Vu la somme peu élevée, on peut supposer qu'il s'agissait là du solde, et que l'artiste avait reçu un acompte sur le travail.

25 Giuseppe Angeli, *Allégorie des continents : l'Europe*. Cette peinture orne le plafond de la Salle jaune située à gauche du *portego*. En 1744, les peintures étaient alors terminées, il apparaît dans les registres de la maison un paiement de 165,4 lires au compte du peintre.

26 Jacopo Guarana, détail de la fresque du plafond du *portego* redécoré en 1773. La fresque à caractère allégorico-mythologique, représente *La Lumière vainc les ténèbres*, *Apollon avec Aurore et les Heures*, *Les Saisons* et *Les Quatre Éléments*.

27 Gaspare Diziani, *Allégorie de la Foi*. Fresque réalisée aux environs de 1750, elle décore un couloir reliant deux salles. Sa réalisation remonte à l'époque où Chiara Pisani avait commencé les travaux de restructuration et de décoration du palais.

28/29 The study on the first floor. The furniture is part of the palace's original 18th-century belongings. The great grey marble fireplace with the mirror is topped by the Pisani family's stucco coat-of-arms, possibly the work of Pietro Castelli.

31 The Sala delle Stampe. The grey marble fireplace with gilt bronze decorations is topped by a great mirror with ground-glass mythological and floral decorations, made in Murano around the mid-18th century.

32 The *portego* on the first floor: detail of the stucco decorations by Pietro Castelli and the glass chandelier with its wooden fixture.

32/33 Detail of a corner of the stucco frame on the ceiling of the Yellow Room, with branches of foliage, mythological figures, and the monogram of Pietro Vettore Pisani and Laura Zusto.

33 Jacopo Guarana and Pietro Castelli, chiaroscuro medallion representing one of the Four Elements, i.e. the Earth. There are four medallions in all; here again, the painting was done by Jacopo Guarana and the stucco frames are the work of Pietro Castelli.

27 Gaspare Diziani, *Allegorie des Glaubens.* Das Fresko, um das Jahr 1750 ausgeführt, ziert einen Verbindungsgang zwischen zwei Sälen. Es entstand im Rahmen der umfangreichen Palastrenovierung durch Chiara Pisani.

28/29 Studierzimmer im ersten Obergeschoß. Die Möbel gehören zur Ausstattung des 18. Jahrhunderts. Den großen Kamin aus grauem Marmor mit Spiegel bekrönt das Stuckwappen der Familie Pisani, das vielleicht Pietro Castelli schuf.

31 Saal der Drucke. Über dem Kamin aus grauem Marmor mit vergoldeten Bronzedekorationen hängt ein großer Spiegel mit mythologischen Figuren und Blumenverzierungen, die einem Rahmen gleich eingeritzt sind. Der Spiegel stammt aus Murano und entstand Mitte des 18. Jahrhunderts.

32 Im *portego* des Obergeschosses Stuckdekorationen Pietro Castellis und Wandleuchter aus Glas mit hölzerner Halterung.

32/33 Detail einer Ecke des Stuckrahmens an der Decke des Gelben Saals, mit Rankenverzierungen, mythologischen Figuren und Monogramm von Pietro Vettor Pisani und Laura Zusto.

33 Jacopo Guarana und Pietro Castelli, Medaillon in Helldunkeltechnik mit der Darstellung eines der vier Elemente, der Erde. Die Malereien der vier Medaillons stammen von Guarana, während die rahmenden Stuckdekorationen Pietro Castelli zuzuschreiben sind.

28/29 Bureau du premier étage. Le mobilier fait partie de l'aménagement du XVIIIème siècle. La grande cheminée en marbre gris avec miroir est surmontée d'un blason en stuc de la maison Pisani, et serait l'œuvre de Pietro Castelli.

31 Salle des gravures. Cheminée en marbre gris avec décorations en bronze doré, surmontée d'un grand miroir avec sujets mythologiques et décorations florales gravés. Le miroir fut réalisé à Murano au milieu du XVIIIème siècle.

32 *Portego* de l'étage noble, élément des décorations en stuc de Pietro Castelli avec lampadaire en verre doté d'un pied en bois.

32/33 Détail d'angle du cadre en stuc du plafond de la Salle jaune avec des volutes végétales, des personnages mythologiques et le monogramme de Pietro Vettore Pisani et Laura Zusto.

33 Jacopo Guarana et Pietro Castelli, médaillon à clair-obscur représentant un des Quatre Eléments, ici, la Terre. La partie peinte des quatre médaillons est due à Jacopo Guarana, et les stucs d'encadrement sont de Pietro Castelli.

PALAZZO BARBARO

a S. Stefano

PALAZZO BARBARO　＊　PALAIS BARBARO

a S. Stefano

à St Etienne

Venise Joseph Kier Editeur Place S. Marc 117.

Palazzo Barbaro

Not far from the Accademia bridge, the Gothic Palazzo Barbaro reflects its image onto the waters from the right bank of the Grand Canal. Its name is taken from the noble family, originally descended from a Roman Consul, which arrived in Venice from Eraclea, purchased the palace around 1460, and continued to live there for centuries.

As in the case of many other Venetian stately homes, the history of Palazzo Barbaro can be read on the inside and outside of the palace, from signs left over the years by successive generations of Barbaros. The completed changes, embellishments, and extensions illustrate the family's power and impressive position in the political, civic, artistic, and literary life of Venice.

After changing hands several times, the palace was purchased by Zaccaria Barbaro, a politician and subtle diplomat who held some of the highest positions in the city's government and administration. It has a Gothic façade with a door onto the water on the left-hand side and two rows of narrow, acutely-arched windows with balconies, which mark the two floors of its state apartments.

The palace has many Gothic elements, such as the capitals with foliage and cherubs and the brackets in the shape of rampant lions supporting the first-floor balcony. This balcony is one of the few 15th-century originals in Venice, which suggest the hand of the Bon stone-workers (who also created the Ca' d'Oro mullioned windows facing onto the water). Renaissance features were added to the façade towards the end of the 15th century, with the second door onto the water on the right-hand side and the medallions inserted between the central balconies and side windows.

At the turn of the 17th century, a new wing was added to the original Gothic building, according to a project by the architect Antonio Gaspari, for use as a ballroom. This was the time when the most extensive renovation work was done on the palace, replacing the balconies on the second floor (now the main floor) and extending them on both fronts.

In unmittelbarer Nähe zur Accademia-Brücke spiegelt sich auf der Wasseroberfläche des Canal Grande der Palazzo Barbaro. Der gotische Palast am rechten Ufer ist nach einer Patrizierfamilie benannt, die ursprünglich aus Herakleia stammte. Um 1460 erwarb sie den Palast, den sie mehrere Jahrhunderte lang bewohnte.

Wie auch bei vielen anderen venezianischen Palästen läßt sich die Geschichte des Palazzo Barbaro an den inneren und äüßeren Bauveränderungen ablesen. Die Um- und Ausbauten sowie die Innenausstattung verdeutlichen die Stellung der Familie innerhalb des politischen, zivilen und künstlerisch-literarischen Lebens in Venedig.

Nach verschiedenen Eigentümerwechseln gelangte der Palast schließlich in den Besitz von Zaccaria Barbaro, einem Politiker und feinsinnigen Diplomaten, der höchste Ämter in der Regierung und der städtischen Verwaltung bekleidete.

Die gotische Fassade des Palastes weist im Erdgeschoß links ein Portal zum Wasser auf. Zwei Reihen schlanker, spitzbogiger Fenster mit Balkonen rhythmisieren die beiden Obergeschosse. An der Fassade finden sich zahlreiche gotische Schmuckelemente, wie etwa Kapitelle mit Laubwerk und Cherubinen sowie als sich aufbäumende Löwen geformte Konsolen, die den Balkon des ersten Geschosses stützen. Dieser Balkon gehört zu den wenigen erhaltenen Originalen des 15. Jahrhunderts in Venedig und zeigt den Einfluß der Bildhauerwerkstatt Bon. Diese gestalteten auch die Fassade der berühmten Ca' d'Oro. Gegen Ende des 15. Jahrhunderts wurde die Fassade des Palazzo Barbaro im Stil der Renaissance verändert: ein zweites Portal zum Canal Grande wurde errichtet und zwischen den Balkonen und Seitenfenstern wurden Medaillons eingefügt.

Mit Beginn des 17. Jahrhunderts erhielt der gotische Bau einen neuen Flügel. Dieser Anbau, der den zukünftigen Ballsaal aufnehmen sollte, entstand nach einem Entwurf des Architekten Antonio Gaspari. Zu jener Zeit wurden die wichtigsten Renovierungsarbeiten durchgeführt, die auch die Erneuerung der Balkone des zweiten und nun zum

Situé sur la rive droite du Grand Canal, à peu de distance du Pont de l'Accademia, sur la rive droite, le Palazzo Barbaro se reflète dans les eaux ; l'édifice gothique porte le nom de la famille patricienne, d'antique descendance consulaire romaine et originaire d'Héraclée, qui l'acheta aux environs de 1460 et l'habita pendant des siècles.

Comme celle de la plupart des palais vénitiens, l'histoire du Palazzo Barbaro se manifeste, aussi bien à l'intérieur qu'à l'extérieur, par les traces de construction qu'ont laissées les générations successives de Barbaro, qui y apportèrent modifications, embellissements, agrandissements, faisant de lui l'emblème de leur pouvoir et du rôle déterminant de la famille dans la vie politique, civique, artistique et littéraire de Venise.

Acquis, après différents propriétaires, par Zaccaria Barbaro, homme politique et fin diplomate, qui occupa les plus hautes charges au gouvernement et dans l'administration de la ville, le palais présente une façade gothique dotée, sur la gauche, d'une porte donnant sur l'eau et de deux minces fenêtres ogivales, avec balcon, indiquant les deux étages nobles de l'édifice.

Aux éléments gothiques, tels que les chapiteaux avec feuillage et chérubins et les consoles en forme de lion rampant qui soutiennent le balcon du premier étage – un des rares originaux du XVème siècle à Venise, dans lesquels on reconnaît l'intervention des ouvriers des lapicides Bon, les mêmes à qui l'on doit la fenêtre polylobée de la façade donnant sur la Ca' d'Oro – s'en associèrent d'autres de caractère Renaissance, vers la fin du XVème siècle : la seconde entrée sur le Canal Grande, à droite, et les médaillons insérés entre les balcons centraux et les fenêtres latérales.

Au tournant du XVIIème siècle, une nouvelle aile fut ajoutée au corps gothique ; dessinée par l'architecte Antonio Gaspari, elle était destinée à accueillir la salle de bal. La restructuration la plus importante de la demeure – même les balcons du deuxième étage, devenu alors le principal, furent refaits et s'étendirent sur les deux façades – remonte à cette époque.

The fall of the Venetian Republic in 1797 saw the scattering of immense fortunes together with the systematic pillaging of rich collections of works of art, including frescoes and stucco work, that had been closely guarded in the Venetian palaces for centuries.

Palazzo Barbaro did not escape similar ruin: all that could be removed was taken from this stately home, which had seen the birth of three Patriarchs of Aquileia, and where Poliziano had received the gift of a Greek vase from the hands of Zaccaria Barbaro. Between those same walls, two other Barbaros, Daniele (Patriarch of Aquileia) and his brother Marc'Antonio (Procurator of St. Mark), decided half a century later to entrust Andrea Palladio with the construction of one of the most beautiful villas in the Venetian hinterland – Villa Barbaro at Maser, commissioning Paolo Veronese to do the fresco decorations. Another member of the family, Antonio, had celebrated the glory of his family name in the 17th century by commissioning the sculptured decoration of the façade of the Venetian church of Santa Maria del Giglio.

In the years after 1797, there seemed to remain nothing at all, not even the memory of the Humanist coterie, the subtle political and theological discussions, the learned interpretations of the works of Aristotle and Vitruvius, which had taken place in the tall and sunny rooms of the palace. But fortunately, in the Boston-born couple that purchased it in 1885, the palace found new owners who loved it and restored it to its original splendour.

The palace entrance from the street leads into a portico-lined courtyard from which a steep and wide staircase leads directly to the second floor, where the rest of the rooms lead off from the tall and spacious central hall, or *portego,* which faces with four balcony windows onto the Grand Canal.

Even though it is impossible to guess its original decoration, this room was hung in the late Baroque period with six equally large paintings ordered by Alvise Barbaro. Four were by Nicolò Bambini and two by Segala, mainly concerning Old Testament subjects and contained in rich frames of gilt stucco (*Judas and Thamar, The Finding of Moses, Lot and His Daughters,* and *Agar and Ishmael* by Bambini; the *Three Theological Virtues* and the *Judgement of Paris* by Segala).

The serious nature of the subject matter and the vast dimensions of the paintings are

Hauptgeschoß gewordenen Stockwerkes über beide Fassaden einschlossen.

Der Untergang der Republik Venedig im Jahre 1797 und die daraus resultierenden Unruhen trugen zu der systematischen Verstreuung der reichen Kunstsammlungen, der Fresken und Stuckarbeiten bei, die über Jahrhunderte hinweg in den venezianischen Palästen gehütet worden waren.

Auch der Palazzo Barbaro blieb von der Zerstörung nicht verschont: alle beweglichen Güter wurden aus dem Wohnsitz weggeschafft, in dem drei Patriarchen von Aquileia geboren worden waren und Poliziano von Zaccaria Barbaro eine griechische Vase zum Geschenk erhalten hatte. Zwischen diesen Mauern beschlossen Mitte des 16. Jahrhunderts zwei weitere Mitglieder der Familie Barbaro, der Patriarch von Aquileia, Daniele, und sein Bruder Marc'Antonio, Prokurator von San Marco, die Planung einer der schönsten Villen des venezianischen Festlands, die Villa Barbaro in Maser. Der Baumeister Andrea Palladio sollte diesen Wohnsitz errichten und der Maler Paolo Veronese ihn mit Fresken ausstatten. Ein anderes Familienmitglied, Antonio, hatte im 17. Jahrhundert die Skulpturen an der Fassade der venezianischen Kirche Santa Maria del Giglio in Auftrag gegeben.

In den Jahren nach 1797 scheint von den humanistischen Abendgesellschaften in den hohen, lichten Räumen des Palastes, den feinsinnigen politischen und theologischen Wortgefechten und den gelehrten Auslegungen der Werke eines Aristoteles oder eines Vitruv nicht einmal die Erinnerung geblieben zu sein. Zum Glück fand das Bauwerk 1885 in einem Ehepaar aus Boston neue Besitzer, die es liebevoll pflegten und so seinen ursprünglichen Glanz wiederherstellten.

Vom Palasteingang von der Landseite gelangt man in einen Innenhof mit Arkaden. Vom Hof aus führt eine steile, breite Treppe direkt zum zweiten Obergeschoß hinauf, wo sich der hohe und großzügige zentrale Saal, der *portego,* befindet. Seine vier Fenstertüren öffnen sich zum Balkon, von dem man auf den Canal Grande blickt.

Auch wenn es nicht möglich ist, die ursprüngliche Dekoration des *portego* zu rekonstruieren, so weiß man zumindest, daß er im Spätbarock auf Wunsch von Alvise Barbaro mit sechs gleichgroßen Gemälden ausgestattet wurde. Vier Gemälde stammten von Nicolò Bambini und zwei von Segala. Sie zeigten vorwiegend alttestamentliche Themen in üppigen vergoldeten Stuckrahmen (*Judas und Thamar; Die Auffindung*

La chute de la République de Venise, en 1797, entraîna la dispersion d'immenses patrimoines et le dépouillement systématique des très riches collections d'œuvres d'art, y compris les fresques et les stucs, gardés jalousement depuis des siècles dans les palais vénitiens.

Le Palais Barbaro ne fit pas exception : tout ce qui put être emporté quitta cette demeure qui avait vu naître trois patriarches d'Aquilée et où Zaccaria Barbaro avait offert un vase grec à Politien ; entre ces murs, d'autres Barbaro, Daniele, patriarche d'Aquilée, et son frère Marc'Antonio, procurateur de San Marco, décidèrent un demi-siècle plus tard, de confier le projet de construction de l'une des plus belles villas vénitiennes, Villa Barbaro à Maser, à Andrea Palladio, chargeant Paul Véronèse de la décorer de fresques ; et un autre membre de la famille, Antonio, glorifia la Maison au XVIIème siècle en commandant la décoration sculpturale de la façade de l'église vénitienne de Santa Maria del Giglio.

Durant les années qui suivirent 1797, il semble que même le souvenir des cénacles humanistes, des subtiles dissertations politiques et théologiques, des savantes interprétations des œuvres d'Aristote et de Vitruve qui s'étaient déroulées dans les hautes et lumineuses pièces du palais ait été effacé. Mais par chance un couple habitant Boston acquit l'édifice en 1885 ; les nouveaux propriétaires l'aimèrent, le restaurèrent et lui restituèrent sa splendeur passée.

L'entrée sur terre du palais introduit dans une cour à arcades à partir de laquelle un escalier raide et large conduit directement au second étage noble, où se trouve le vaste et haut salon central, ou *portego,* dont les quatre fenêtres s'ouvrent sur un balcon, d'où l'on voit le Grand Canal.

Même s'il est impossible d'en connaître la décoration d'origine, le *portego* fut recouvert à la fin de l'époque baroque, selon les vœux d'Alvise Barbaro, de six grandes œuvres de dimensions égales, dont quatre de Nicolò Bambini et deux de Segala, aux thèmes tirés principalement de l'Ancien Testament et enchâssées dans de riches cadres en stuc dorés (*Judas et Thamar ;* la *Découverte de Moïse ; Loth et ses filles* et *Agar et Ismaël* de Bambini ; et les *Trois Vertus théologales* et le *Jugement de Pâris* de Segala).

La gravité des sujets traités et les vastes dimensions des peintures s'adaptent bien aux proportions du *portego,* dont les caractéristiques spatiales restèrent intactes malgré le nouvel ameublement.

well-suited to the ample size of the *portego,* which the new owners have furnished with all due respect for its spatial features.

The Red Drawing-Room, where Robert Browning loved to read to the owners and their guests, leads into the great ballroom – what the documents of the period called the *cameron* and undeniably the most elaborately decorated in the palace.

Designed by Gaspari between 1694 and 1698, the ballroom appears completely lined with elaborate and highly refined stucco work, by the hand of Ticino workers. A circle and four ovals on the ceiling represent famous women of antiquity (Zenobia, Artemisia, Clelia Ersilia and Ipsocrateia), the work of Antonio Zanchi around 1695. The walls are hung with three large paintings by illustrious Venetian artists: *Coriolanus and the Women* by Antonio Balestra (1709), *The Rape of the Sabines* by Sebastiano Ricci, and *Mucius Scaevola at the Altar* by Giambattista Piazzetta.

The stucco decoration with floral motives, festoons and putti was done to replace the previous gilt leather wall linings around 1750 (when Almorò Barbaro was elected Procurator of St. Mark, after a life dedicated to the service of the State).

Almorò's prestigious new office was good enough reason for renovating his home and it is not surprising that the same date is attributed to the painting by Gianbattista Tiepolo which, according to recent interpretations, was to celebrate this particular event. The work is now at the Metropolitan Museum of New York (and a copy hangs in its place), but until 1874 it enhanced the ceiling of the great dining room with its splendid Venetian *terrazzo* floor decorated with ample floral scrolls inlaid with mother of pearl.

The condition of the ballroom when they bought the house is described in detail by the new owners: "We found a great deal to do in the large drawing-room… The fingers and the feet of many of the stucco putti were broken; children had apparently been allowed to throw some very hard little balls at them, because we found lots of them up on the frames! What is more, Mrs. Ker had covered the ceiling with tar, saying that she did not like having faces looking down on her! We had a huge scaffold built and we cleaned up the paintings, which were so confused that you could not say what they represented…"

The patient work of the most recent owners of the palace, and above all their love

Moses'; Loth und seine Töchter und *Agar und Ismael* von Bambini; *Die drei theologischen Tugenden* und *Das Urteil des Paris* von Segala). Der Ernst der Themen und die großzügigen Bildmaße paßten sich dem weiten *portego* an, so daß seine baulichen Charakteristika trotz der neuen Ausstattung perfekt erhalten blieben.

Durch den Roten Salon, in dem Robert Browning vorzugsweise seine »Lesungen« abhielt, gelangt man in den großen Ballsaal, der zu jener Zeit als *cameron* bezeichnet wurde und zweifellos der am prächtigsten ausgestattete Raum des Palastes ist.

Der von Gaspari zwischen 1694 und 1698 entworfene Ballsaal ist komplett mit überaus raffiniertem Stuck verziert. Es ist das Werk Tessiner Werkstätten. Zwischen den Stukkaturen der Decke sind ein rundes und vier ovale Bilder eingefügt, die berühmte Frauen der Antike (Zenobia, Artemis, Cloelia Ersilia und Hypsicrateia) zeigen. Die Deckenmalereien, die um 1695 fertiggestellt wurden, schuf Antonio Zanchi. An den Wänden befinden sich drei großformatige Gemälde berühmter venezianischer Maler: *Coriolanus und die Frauen* von Antonio Balestra (1709), *Der Raub der Sabinerinnen* von Sebastiano Ricci und *Mucius Scaevola am Altar* von Giambattista Piazzetta. Die Stuckdekorationen an den Wänden zeigen florale Motive, Girlanden und Putten und ersetzten um 1750 die vormals dort befindliche Wandbespannung aus vergoldetem Leder.

Zu jener Zeit war Almorò Barbaro nach einem Leben im Staatsdienst zum Prokurator von San Marco gewählt worden. Das ehrenvolle neue Amt Almoròs war der Anlaß für die Renovierung des Wohnsitzes. Bei Giambattista Tiepolo wurde ein Gemälde in Auftrag gegeben, das neueren Forschungen zufolge dieses Ereignis rühmen sollte. Das Bild, das sich heute im Metropolitan Museum in New York befindet und durch eine Kopie im Palazzo Barbaro ersetzt wurde, schmückte bis 1874 die Decke des Speisesaals.

Den Zustand des Ballsaals beim Ankauf des Hauses beschreibt die neue Besitzerin ausführlich: »Es gab viel zu tun im großen Salon… Die Finger und Füße vieler Stuckputten waren beschädigt. Anscheinend hatte man den Kindern erlaubt, sie mit harten Kugeln, die wir in großer Anzahl auf den Rahmen gefunden haben, zu bewerfen! Wir haben ein großes Gerüst aufstellen und die Deckenmalereien reinigen lassen, die derart unkenntlich geworden waren, daß man kaum feststellen konnte, was sie eigentlich darstellen sollten…«

En passant par le Salon rouge, où Henry James aimait lire ses œuvres aux maîtres de maison et à leurs hôtes, on accède à la grande Salle de bal, celle que les documents de l'époque appellent *cameron,* et qui est indiscutablement la pièce la plus fastueusement décorée du palais.

Conçue par Gaspari entre 1694 et 1698, la Salle de bal apparaît complètement revêtue de stucs élaborés et très raffinés, œuvre d'ouvriers tessinois, parmi lesquels s'insèrent, au plafond, un cercle et quatre ovales représentant des femmes célèbres de l'Antiquité (Zénobie, Artémise, Clélie Ersilie et Hypsicratée), peintes par Antonio Zanchi qui s'y appliqua aux alentours de 1695, et aux murs, trois grandes toiles d'illustres peintres vénitiens : *Coriolan et les femmes* de Antonio Balestra (1709), *L'Enlèvement des Sabines* de Sebastiano Ricci et *Mucius Scaevola à l'autel* de Giambattista Piazzetta.

La décoration en stucs à motifs floraux, festons et putti fut exécutée autour de 1750, pour remplacer les revêtements muraux en cuir doré, à l'occasion de l'élection de Almorò Barbaro à la fonction de Procurateur de San Marco, après une vie passée à servir l'Etat.

La prestigieuse charge d'Almorò fut l'occasion de restaurer la demeure, et ce n'est pas par hasard si on attribue la même date à la toile de Giambattista Tiepolo qui, selon de récentes interprétations, célébrerait cet événement. La peinture, qui se trouve aujourd'hui au Metropolitan Museum de New York et a été remplacée par une copie, décorait jusqu'en 1874 le plafond de la grande salle à manger, qui possède une splendide terrasse à la vénitienne décorée de grandes volutes florales ornées de nacre.

L'état de la Salle de bal au moment de l'achat de la maison est décrit dans le détail par la nouvelle propriétaire : « Nous trouvâmes beaucoup à faire dans le grand salon… Les doigts et les pieds de nombreux putti en stuc étaient cassés ; à ce qu'il semble, étant donné que nous en trouvâmes plusieurs sur le cadre, on avait permis aux enfants de tirer dessus des billes très dures ! Nous fîmes construire un grand échafaudage et nettoyâmes les tableaux, qui étaient en si piteux état que l'on ne réussissait pas à définir ce qu'ils pouvaient représenter… »

Le travail patient des derniers propriétaires, et surtout leur amour pour la maison, réussirent à recréer cette atmosphère enchantée que Henry James (1843 – 1916) sut exprimer avec tant de subtilité dans *Les Ailes de la colombe* qu'il écrivit en 1902 au Palazzo

for the house, succeeded in re-creating the enchanted atmosphere that Henry James (1843 – 1916) described so well through Milly Theale, his leading lady in *The Wings of the Dove*, which he wrote in 1902 at Palazzo Barbaro, sitting at a lacquered desk with Chinese decorations that is still preserved today: "…gratefully glad that the warmth of the Southern summer was still in the high florid rooms, palatial chambers where hard cool pavements took reflexions in their lifelong polish, and where the sun on the stirred seawater, flickering up through open windows, played over the painted 'subjects' in the splendid ceilings – medallions of purple and brown, of brave old melancholy colour, medals as of old reddened gold, embossed and beribboned, all toned with time and all flourished and scalloped and gilded about, set in their great moulded and figured concavity (a nest of white cherubs, friendly creatures of the air)…"

In this book the reference to the ballroom of Palazzo Barbaro is quite obvious, though it became Palazzo Leporelli in James' work. But the same magic pervades all the rooms where the 18th-century frescoes and stuccoes melt in delicate merging colours – especially in the library. Among stucco work and elegant bookshelves, this is where the American writer on a visit to Isabella Stewart Gardner (who had rented the house several times) was to sleep in a four-poster bed. Fascinated by the enchantment of the long, low hall looking out over the small square behind the palace, James later wrote to Mrs. Curtis: "If you have not raised your eyes from your resting place, in the pinkish dawn or during the afternoon siesta (after lunch), to admire the medallions and arabesques of the ceiling, permit me to say that you do not really know Palazzo Barbaro…"

The many guests to the palace included the painter John Singer Sargent (who is responsible for the painting of the owners in the ballroom) and Claude Monet (who drew inspiration from here for his languid evocations of Venice), together with personalities of the highest social rank (the Empress Victoria, wife of Frederick of Prussia, the Queen of Sweden, and the Princess of Denmark, whom the lady of the house judged as "interesting people", regretting that she had never kept a visitors' book).

Even the eccentric Isabella Stewart Gardner could not escape the seduction of the stately home, to the point of taking it as inspiration for the building of her own home in Boston, now the Fenway Court Museum.

Dem geduldigen und liebevollen Einsatz seiner letzten Käufer ist es zu verdanken, daß die bezaubernde Atmosphäre, die Henry James (1843 – 1916) in *Die Flügel der Taube* schildert, wiederhergestellt wurde. James schrieb seinen Roman 1902 im Palazzo Barbaro: »…sie war froh und dankbar, daß die Wärme des südlichen Sommers noch immer die hohen, überladenen Räume, die palastartigen Gemächer erfüllte, in denen harte, kühle Fußböden, von jeher gewachst und poliert, das Licht reflektierten, und wo die Sonnenstrahlen vom leicht bewegten Meer her zuckend durch offene Fenster drangen und spielerisch über die gemalten ›Sujets‹ an den herrlichen Decken huschten – purpurne und braune Medaillons in einer schönen, alten, melancholischen Farbe, Medaillen, die aussahen, als seien sie aus rotem Gold, bossiert und bändergeschmückt, alle vom Alter getönt und reich ornamentiert, mit muschelförmigen Rändern, über und über vergoldet und eingebettet in ihre große konkave und plastisch gearbeitete Wölbung voller Gestalten (einem Nest weißer Cherubs, freundlicher Geschöpfe der Luft)…«

Der Bezug auf den Ballsaal des Palazzo Barbaro, den James in seinem Roman »Palazzo Leporelli« nennt, ist nur allzu deutlich. Der gleiche Zauber haftet aber jedem Raum an, in dem sich Fresken und Stukkaturen des 18. Jahrhunderts in delikaten Farbübergängen befinden – vor allem in der Bibliothek. Dort ließ Isabella Stewart Gardner, die den Palazzo wiederholt mietete, den amerikanischen Schriftsteller zwischen Stuck und erlesenen Bücherregalen in einem Himmelbett schlafen. James schrieb voller Begeisterung über den langen, niedrigen, auf einen hinter dem Palast befindlichen kleinen Platz blickenden Saal, folgendes an die Hausherrin: »…Sollten Sie noch nie ihren Blick von Ihrem Ruhelager in die Höhe gerichtet haben, um beim Morgengrauen oder während der Mittagsruhe nach dem Mittagessen die Medaillons und Arabesken an der Decke zu bewundern, so erlauben Sie mir zu sagen, daß Sie den Palazzo Barbaro noch nicht kennen…«

Zu den zahlreichen Gästen des Palastes gehörten die Maler John Singer Sargent, der das Bild der Hausbesitzer im Ballsaal schuf, und Claude Monet, der hier Anregungen zu seinen venezianischen Bildthemen fand. Auch Persönlichkeiten höchsten gesellschaftlichen Ranges, wie Kaiserin Viktoria, verheiratet mit Friedrich von Preußen, die Königin von Schweden und die Prinzessin von Dänemark verkehrten in dieser Villa.

Barbaro sur un bureau laqué à chinoiseries qui existe encore : « …heureuse et reconnaissante que la chaleur de l'été méridional fût encore présente dans les pièces hautes et florissantes, salles de palais dans lesquelles les sols durs, frais, se reflétaient dans les polissages sans fin et où le soleil sur l'eau agitée, montant par éclairs et lueurs et entrant par les fenêtres grand ouvertes jouait sur les ‹ sujets › peints aux plafonds, de splendides médaillons violets et brunis, d'une ancienne et courageuse couleur mélancolique, médailles travaillées en repoussé et ornées de rubans, toutes patinées par le temps, en forme de coquillages dorés, cannelées et fleuries, dans les grandes concavités modelées et décorées de personnages (un nid de chérubins blancs, bienveillantes créatures de l'air)…»

La référence à la Salle de bal de Palazzo Barbaro, qui dans l'œuvre de James devient Palazzo Leporelli, est évidente ; mais la même magie pénètre chaque pièce où stucs et fresques du XVIIIème siècle se fondent en de délicates transitions de couleur ; et surtout dans la bibliothèque, où entre les stucs et les librairies raffinées, Isabella Stewart Gardner, qui loua à plusieurs reprises la maison, fit dormir dans un lit à baldaquin l'écrivain américain, lequel, fasciné par le charme de la salle longue et basse, dont la vue donne sur une petite place située derrière le palais, écrivait ainsi à la maîtresse de maison : « …si vous n'avez pas encore levé les yeux, depuis votre couche, à l'aube rosée ou pendant la sieste de l'après-midi (après le repas) pour admirer les médaillons et les arabesques du plafond, permettez-moi de vous dire que vous ne connaissez pas le Palazzo Barbaro… »

Parmi les nombreux hôtes du palais, on note John Singer Sargent, à qui l'on doit le tableau représentant les propriétaires de la maison dans la Salle de bal, et Claude Monet qui trouva ici l'inspiration pour ses languissantes évocations vénitiennes, ou bien des personnages de la meilleure société : l'impératrice Victoria, épouse de Frédéric de Prusse, la reine de Suède et la princesse du Danemark, que la maîtresse de maison considérait comme « des personnes intéressantes », regrettant de n'avoir jamais eu de livre d'hôtes.

Même l'excentrique Isabelle Stewart Gardner ne put se soustraire à la séduction de la demeure, à tel point qu'elle s'en inspira pour construire sa maison de Boston qui abrite aujourd'hui le Fenway Court Museum.

PALAZZO BARBARO

41 The bedroom overlooking the Grand Canal. The particularly noteworthy bed dates from the end of the 16th or early 17th century.

42/43 The ballroom on the second floor. Designed by the architect Antonio Gaspari between 1694 and 1698 and mentioned by documents of the period as the *cameron*. Around 1750, it was completely lined with highly elegant stucco work by Ticino workers. The ceiling contains four ovals and a circle, surrounded by stucco work, representing famous women of antiquity; these are the work of Antonio Zanchi and date from around 1695. The walls are hung with three huge paintings: *Coriolanus and the Women* by Antonio Balestra, *The Rape of the Sabines* by Sebastiano Ricci and *Mucius Scaevola at the Altar* by Giambattista Piazzetta.

44 The library, its ceiling decorated with a rich carpet of 18th-century stucco work with geometric and floral patterns surrounding paintings of the same period. The room is lined with the original 18th-century bookshelves.

45 18th-century fresco on a mythological theme, in a rich frame of stucco work with foliage scrolls. It decorates the ceiling of one of the bedrooms.

47 The Red Drawing-Room. This room faces onto the Grand Canal and links the *portego* with the ballroom. It was Robert Browning's favourite room, where he used to read aloud to entertain the owners of the house and their guests.

48 Girolamo Brusaferro, *Flora.* This painting was created in 1730 and is surrounded by a stucco frame. It is hung in one of the passageways.

49 The *portego* on the second floor with a balcony onto the Grand Canal. In the late Baroque period, Alvise Barbaro had this decorated with six equally huge paintings (four by Nicolo Bambini and two by Giovanni Segala), all on themes from the Old Testament except for Segala's *Judgement of Paris.*

50 Detail of one of the doors leading from the central hall, or *portego,* to the side rooms; there is a stucco panel over the door, supported by putti.

51 The entrance from the street with a portico-lined courtyard and an ample, steep open staircase leading to the second floor. It is one of the few outdoor Gothic staircases still in existence, as subsequent renovation of the Gothic palaces generally included the elimination of outdoor staircases and their replacement with new staircases indoors.

41 Schlafzimmer mit Ausblick auf den Canal Grande. Das wertvolle Bett stammt aus dem späten 16. oder frühen 17. Jahrhundert.

42/43 Den Ballsaal im zweiten Obergeschoß entwarf der Architekt Antonio Gaspari zwischen 1694 und 1698. Er wurde zu jener Zeit *cameron* (großer Raum) genannt und um 1750 vollständig mit äußerst raffinierten Stuckdekorationen ausgestattet, die das Werk tessinischer Handwerker sind. Antonio Zanchi führte um 1695 ein Rundbild und vier Ovale an der Decke aus. Die Deckenmalereien zeigen berühmte Frauen des Altertums. An den Wänden befinden sich drei berühmte Gemälde, *Coriolanus und die Frauen* von Antonio Balestra, *Der Raub der Sabinerinnen* von Sebastiano Ricci und *Mucius Scaevola am Altar* von Giambattista Piazzetta.

44 Die Decke der Bibliothek überziehen prächtige geometrische und florale Stuckarbeiten aus dem 18. Jahrhundert, die einige Gemälde aus demselben Jahrhundert einfassen. An den Wänden stehen Bücherregale, die ebenfalls aus dem 18. Jahrhundert stammen.

45 Das Fresko aus dem 18. Jahrhundert mit mythologischem Thema schmückt die Decke eines Schlafzimmers. Den prächtigen Stuckrahmen zieren florale Motive.

47 Der Rote Salon hat Ausblick auf den Canal Grande und verbindet den *portego* mit dem Ballsaal. Es war der bevorzugte Raum Robert Brownings, der hier mehrere »Lesungen« für die Hausherren und deren Gäste abhielt.

48 Girolamo Brusaferro, *Flora.* Das Gemälde aus dem Jahre 1730 mit Stuckrahmen schmückt einen Verbindungsraum.

49 *Portego* im zweiten Obergeschoß mit Balkon und Blick auf den Canal Grande. Im Spätbarock ließ Alvise Barbaro den zentralen Saal mit sechs gleichgroßen Gemälden dekorieren, von denen vier Nicolò Bambini und zwei Giovanni Segala schufen. Die Bildthemen sind vorwiegend aus dem Alten Testament gewählt, nur ein Werk Segalas stellt ein antikes Thema dar: *Das Urteil des Paris.*

50 Eine der Türen, durch die man vom zentralen Saal oder *portego* zu den seitlichen Räumen gelangt, mit von Putten gehaltener Stucksopraporte.

51 Vom Eingang von der Landseite gelangt man in einen Hof mit Bogengang und breiter, steiler Treppe, die zum zweiten Obergeschoß führt und eine der wenigen noch erhaltenen gotischen Außentreppen ist. Bei den späteren Restaurierungen gotischer Gebäude wurden die externen Zugangstreppen zu den Stockwerken abgerissen und durch interne Aufgänge ersetzt.

41 Chambre à coucher avec vue sur le Grand Canal. Le lit de grande valeur date de la fin du XVIème siècle ou du début du XVIIème.

42/43 Salle de bal du deuxième étage. Dessinée par l'architecte Antonio Gaspari, entre 1694 et 1698, et appelée *cameron* dans les documents de l'époque, elle fut complètement ornée de stucs très raffinés par des ouvriers du Tessin vers 1750. Sur le plafond, entre les stucs, quatre peintures représentent des femmes célèbres de l'Antiquité et ont été réalisées par Antonio Zanchi aux environs de 1695. Sur les murs on admire trois grandes toiles d'Antonio Balestra *(Coriolan et les femmes),* de Sebastiano Ricci *(L'Enlèvement des Sabines)* et de Giambattista Piazzetta *(Mucius Scaevola à l'autel).*

44 Bibliothèque au plafond garni d'un superbe revêtement de stuc du XVIIIème siècle à formes géométriques et florales encadrant des peintures de la même époque. Les bibliothèques qui recouvrent les murs font également partie de l'ameublement du XVIIIème siècle.

45 Fresque du XVIIIème siècle représentant des sujets mythologiques, avec un encadrement raffiné en stuc à volutes végétales. Elle orne le plafond d'une chambre à coucher.

47 Salon rouge. La pièce donne sur le Grand Canal et relie le *portego* avec la salle de bal. C'était la pièce préférée de Robert Browning qui y lisait ses œuvres aux maîtres de maison et à leurs hôtes.

48 Girolamo Brusaferro, *Flore.* La peinture réalisée vers 1730, est encadrée de stucs et agrémente une pièce de passage.

49 *Portego* du deuxième étage avec balcon donnant sur le Grand Canal. A la fin de l'ère baroque, Alvise Barbaro le fit décorer de six grandes peintures de taille égale, quatre de Nicolò Bambini et deux de Giovanni Segala, aux thèmes vétéro-testamentaires à l'exception du *Jugement de Pâris,* de Segala, d'inspiration mythologique.

50 Une des portes du salon central ou *portego,* qui s'ouvrent sur les pièces latérales. Le dessus-de-porte en stuc est soutenu par des putti.

51 Entrée côté terre avec cour à arcades et grand escalier raide conduisant au deuxième étage. Il s'agit d'un des rares escaliers gothiques encore conservés. De fait, au cours des restructurations successives des édifices gothiques, les escaliers d'accès aux étages, toujours extérieurs à l'origine, furent éliminés et remplacés par des escaliers intérieurs.

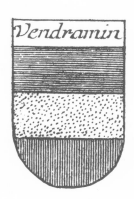

Vendramin

PALAZZO VENDRAMIN CALERGI

ora di S. A. R. la Duchessa di Berry

PALAZZO VENDRAMIN CALERGI   PALAIS VENDRAMIN CALERGI

ora di S. A. R. la Duchessa di Berry   maintenant de S. A. R. la Duchesse de Berry

Venise, Joseph Kier Editeur, Place S Marc 117

PALAZZO LOREDAN VENDRAMIN CALERGI

The palace represents the most significant architectural epoch of Renaissance Venice. It is mentioned by Sansovino, in his *Venetia città nobilissima* of 1581, as being "among the most important of all the palaces on the Grand Canal"; it is described as having "great body and great height… very noble with regard not only to the layout of the rooms inside but also to the façade covered with Greek marble, with great windows all colonnaded in the Corinthian style…"

The construction of the palace was ordered by Andrea Loredan, who entrusted the project to the architect Mauro Codussi of Bergamo.

Recent studies have demonstrated that it was built very quickly, between 1502 and 1509, when it would appear to have already been inhabited. There is no doubt that its size and formal refinement surpassed all contemporary constructions.

The Istrian marble façade, with its double row of mullioned windows crowned with an arch enclosing a circle and divided into three by the harmonious scansion of its mullions, is a reflection of the distribution of the rooms inside according to the typical scheme of the Venetian stately home. In fact there are side rooms in line with the first and last windows, whereas the great hall for state receptions and for access to all the others is indicated by the three central windows.

Codussi died in 1504 and did not see his work completed, but he must have left detailed plans, because it was finished with such a coherence of composition (probably by his son Domenico, who also succeeded him in the completion of other works).

The history of the palace proceeded in step with that of its owner and those who inhabited it after him. Andrea Loredan was a personality of great prestige who had held important political positions. In 1513, during the war of Cambrai, he had to accept the role of quartermaster-general for the army, which had closed ranks near Vicenza. Being without an heir and almost guessing his destiny, he made a will to the effect that, apart from the usufructuary rights of his wife, the building was to be assigned to the son of a cousin,

Der Palazzo Loredan Vendramin Calergi repräsentiert die venezianische Renaissance und wird von Sansovino in seinem Werk *Venetia città nobilissima* aus dem Jahre 1581 »als einer der wichtigsten Palazzi des Canal Grande« erwähnt. Sansovino beschreibt ihn als »sehr groß und hoch… sehr vornehm, da er neben der Raumanordnung im Innern eine mit griechischem Marmor verkleidete Fassade mit großen Fenstern besitzt, deren Mittelsäulen korinthische Kapitelle aufweisen…«

Der Palazzo entstand im Auftrag Andrea Loredans, der den Bau dem Architekten Mauro Codussi aus Bergamo anvertraute.

Neueren Studien zufolge ist der Palast innerhalb eines relativ kurzen Zeitraums entstanden, nämlich zwischen 1502 und 1509. Im Jahre 1509 war er bereits bewohnt. Sein riesiger Baukörper und seine raffinierte Ausstattung übertrafen zweifellos alle zeitgenössischen Gebäude.

Die dreigeteilte Fassade aus istrischem Marmor mit ihren zwei Reihen Zwillingsfenstern, die von zwei Rundbögen mit einem kleinen Okulus unter einem übergreifenden Bogen gebildet werden, spiegelt die Raumfolge wider, die dem venezianischen Wohnsitz eigen ist: Das erste und das letzte Fenster entsprechen seitlichen Zimmern, während der zentrale Repräsentationssaal, von dem aus alle anderen Räume des Stockwerkes erreicht werden, sich hinter den mittleren drei Fenstern verbirgt.

Codussi, der 1504 starb, konnte die Vollendung seines Werkes nicht mehr erleben. Er hinterließ aber so detaillierte Pläne, daß der Bau in letzter Konsequenz fertiggestellt werden konnte – wahrscheinlich von seinem Sohn Domenico, der auch andere Gebäude seines Vaters vollendete.

Die Geschichte des Palastes verläuft parallel zum Schicksal seines Auftraggebers und seiner späteren Bewohner. Andrea Loredan war eine sehr angesehene Persönlichkeit und bekleidete wichtige politische Ämter. Als er 1513 während der Liga von Cambrai zum Generalinspekteur des Heeres, das in der Nähe von Vicenza Stellung bezogen hatte, ernannt wurde, setzte er, seinen nahen Tod vielleicht erahnend, sein Testament auf. Da

Ce Palais est l'exemple architectural le plus significatif de la Renaissance vénitienne. Sansovino le signale dans son livre *Venetia città nobilissima* de 1581, comme l'un des plus importants palais du Grand Canal. Il est décrit comme « un édifice vaste et haut… très distingué car en plus des pièces intérieures, sa façade est couverte de marbres grecs et ses grandes fenêtres sont toutes ornées de colonnes corinthiennes… »

On doit la construction de ce bâtiment à la volonté d'Andrea Loredan qui confia le projet à l'architecte bergamasque, Mauro Codussi.

Des études récentes ont révélé que le palais fut édifié très rapidement, entre 1502 et 1509, époque à laquelle il est déjà habité. Les proportions du corps de bâtiment et le raffinement de l'aménagement dépassèrent indubitablement les autres constructions de l'époque.

La façade en pierre d'Istrie, avec deux rangées de fenêtres jumelées couronnées par un arc qui contient un cercle, et divisée harmonieusement en trois parties par des colonnes, traduit la distribution des espaces intérieurs caractéristique des demeures vénitiennes. De fait, les pièces latérales correspondent à la première et à la dernière fenêtre, alors que le salon de représentation qui s'ouvre sur les autres pièces se trouve derrière les trois fenêtres du milieu.

Codussi, qui mourut en 1504, ne vit pas son œuvre terminée mais il en laissa un plan détaillé selon lequel elle fut achevée avec la même cohérence dans la composition, vraisemblablement par son fils Domenico, qui lui succéda également dans l'achèvement d'autres travaux.

L'histoire du palais est liée à l'histoire de son concepteur et de ceux qui l'ont habité après lui. Andrea Loredan fut un personnage de grand prestige. Il avait obtenu des mandats politiques importants et en 1513, pendant la guerre de Cambrai, devant assumer la charge d'intendant général de l'armée, délégué aux environs de Vicence, il semble avoir eu l'intuition de sa mort prochaine. N'ayant pas d'héritier, il établit par testament que, exception faite de l'usufruit de sa femme,

also named Andrea, with the obligation to keep it in good order, preserving all the works of art it contained and handing it down to his heirs according to the rights of primogeniture.

Andrea Loredan died in battle in that same year near Creazzo. His heirs proved totally unworthy of the ideals of greatness and dignity of the Venetian nobility and in 1581 they obtained permission from the Council of Ten to sell off the palace to the Duke of Brunswick for fifty thousand ducats. More changes of hands took place, however, and two years later the palace was purchased by William III Gonzaga, Duke of Mantua, who sold it again shortly afterwards to a rich merchant named Calergi, originally from Crete, whose family had opposed the Venetian Republic's domination of the island for centuries and who, with the purchase of the palace, intended to establish his social position in the city on the same level as the Venetian nobility.

The merchant's daughter and sole heiress, Marina, was married in 1608 to a nobleman, Vincenzo Grimani, who belonged to a family of ancient and well-rooted cultural traditions (which had, among other things, created a real museum of antique sculptures, transferred by Vincenzo Scamozzi to the Sansovinian Library towards the end of the 16th century).

These were years of splendour for the palace, which received illustrious guests and was renovated inside and extended outside by Vincenzo Scamozzi with a new, so-called White Wing that faced onto the great garden along the bank of the Grand Canal.

Marina Grimani provided in her will for the integrity of the palace and for its preservation (for which she instituted a rich fund, establishing that the property was subject to primogeniture and that the heirs were to add the name Calergi to their own surname).

Despite the noble lady's precautions, however, the palace suffered considerable risks: in 1681, Marina's heirs – who had a reputation for violence – assassinated their indomitable enemy Francesco Querini Stampalia inside the palace. The scandal was so great that the Senate ordered the perpetual banishment of the guilty parties, the confiscation of their goods and the destruction of their home. Because of its magnificence, the palace was actually only confiscated and its White Wing was razed to the ground. The Grimani Calergi succeeded in regaining possession of their goods, nonetheless, thanks to the payment of considerable sums of money,

er keine direkten Erben hatte, sollte der Palast unter Vorbehalt der Nutznießung seitens seiner Ehefrau Andrea, dem Sohn eines Cousins ersten Grades zufallen, mit der Verpflichtung, das Bauwerk stets in gutem Zustand zu halten, alle Kunstwerke zu bewahren und den Palast unter Beachtung des Erstgeburtsrechts seinen Erben zu vermachen.

Andrea Loredan fiel noch im selben Jahr bei Creazzo. Seine Erben erwiesen sich aber keineswegs den Idealen von Größe und Anstand der venezianischen Aristokratie würdig: 1581 erhielten sie vom Zehnerrat die Erlaubnis, den Palast an den Herzog von Braunschweig zu verkaufen, der ihn für 50 000 Dukaten erwarb. Bereits zwei Jahre später ging das Gebäude in den Besitz von Guglielmo III. Gonzaga, dem Herzog von Mantua, über. Dieser wiederum verkaufte den Palazzo nach kurzer Zeit an einen reichen Händler namens Calergi, der aus Kreta stammte und dessen Familie jahrhundertelang die Herrschaft der Serenissima bekämpft hatte. Mit dem Kauf dieses Palastes wollte Calergi seine gesellschaftliche Stellung in der Stadt festigen und sich auf eine Stufe mit der venezianischen Aristokratie stellen.

Seine Tochter und Alleinerbin Marina hatte im Jahre 1608 den Adligen Vincenzo Grimani geheiratet. Grimani entstammte einer Familie, die sich antiker und tief verwurzelter kultureller Traditionen rühmte und unter anderem ein Museum antiker Skulpturen gegründet hatte. Diese Antikensammlung ordnete Vincenzo Scamozzi gegen Ende des Cinquecento in die Libreria Sansoviniana ein.

In jenen glanzvollen Jahren gingen in dem Palast illustre Gäste ein und aus. Die Säle wurden renoviert, und unter der Leitung von Vincenzo Scamozzi um den sogenannten Weißen Flügel zum großen Garten am Canal Grande hin erweitert.

In ihrem Testament traf Marina Grimani Vorkehrungen für den Erhalt des Palastes und richtete einen Fonds ein. Außerdem setzte sie fest, daß der Besitz dem Erstgeburtsrecht unterliegen sollte und die Erben ihrem Familiennamen den Namen Calergi anhängen müßten.

Trotz aller Vorsichtsmaßnahmen der Adligen stand der Palast ernsthaft in Gefahr: 1681 metzelten die Erben Marinas, die für ihre Gewalttätigkeit bekannt waren, ihren Feind Francesco Querini Stampalia im Palazzo nieder. Es gab einen so großen Skandal, daß der Senat beschloß, die Schuldigen lebenslänglich zu verbannen, ihr Vermögen zu konfiszieren und ihren Wohnsitz zu zerstören, der jedoch wegen seiner besonderen

l'édifice devait revenir au fils, portant le même nom que lui, d'un cousin germain, avec obligation de maintenir le palais en bon état, de conserver toutes les œuvres d'art qu'il renfermait et de le léguer à ses héritiers en respectant le droit d'aînesse.

Andrea Loredan mourut sur le champ de bataille cette année-là, près de Creazzo, mais ses héritiers ne se montrèrent pas dignes des idéaux de grandeur et de décorum de l'aristocrate vénitien, car en 1581, ils obtinrent l'accord du Conseil des Dix (Consiglio dei Dieci) pour vendre le palais au duc de Brunswick qui l'acheta pour 50 000 ducats. Les changements de propriété n'étaient pas pour autant terminés, puisque deux ans plus tard, l'édifice fut acheté par Guillaume III Gonzague, duc de Mantoue, qui, à son tour le revendit, peu après, à un riche commerçant originaire de Candie, Calergi, dont la famille avait pendant des siècles contrecarré la domination de la Sérénissime dans l'île. Ce palais lui permettrait d'affirmer sa position sociale dans la ville, en se mettant au même niveau que la noblesse vénitienne.

Sa fille et unique héritière, Marina, avait épousé en 1608 le noble Vincenzo Grimani, qui appartenait à une famille de traditions culturelles fort anciennes, et qui avait notamment réuni un véritable musée de sculptures antiques, installé par Vincenzo Scamozzi dans la Libreria Sansoviniana à la fin du XVIème siècle.

Ce furent alors des années de splendeur pour le palais qui reçut la visite de personnages illustres. Les espaces intérieurs furent rénovés, l'extérieur fut enrichi par la construction, dirigée par Vincenzo Scamozzi, d'une aile nouvelle appelée « aile blanche », donnant du côté des jardins sur le Grand Canal.

Dans son testament, Marina Grimani prit les dispositions pour garantir l'intégrité du palais, instituant un fonds important pour sa conservation, établissant notamment que la propriété serait léguée à l'aîné et que les héritiers devraient ajouter à leur nom celui de Calergi.

Malgré les précautions de la noble dame, l'édifice allait courir des risques sérieux. De fait, en 1681, les héritiers de Marina, bien connus pour leur tempérament violent, y massacrèrent Francesco Querini Stampalia pour lequel ils nourrissaient une haine irréductible. Le scandale fut terrible, et le Sénat décréta le bannissement perpétuel des coupables, la confiscation de leurs biens et la destruction de la demeure. En raison de sa beauté, elle fut seulement confisquée et

and they rebuilt the wing that had been demolished.

In 1739, there being no heirs, the property passed into the hands of Nicolò Vendramin, who added the name Calergi to his own, thus giving the palace the name it still carries today.

The Vendramins decorated the interior with works of art from their own ancestral collections, including two jasper columns brought to Venice by Caterina Cornaro, Queen of Cyprus, and donated to her sister Cornelia, who had married Paolo Vendramin.

It would seem that a good deal of the furnishings remained in place when Maria Carolina, Duchess of Berry, purchased the palace from the last of the Vendramins in 1844.

During the time when it was inhabited by the Duchess and her husband, Count Ettore Lucchesi-Palli, the palace was completely renovated by Giovan Battista Meduna and returned to a period of great pomp, was reopened for receptions and enriched with a number of paintings and even a theatre.

Economic difficulties deriving from the changing political conditions led to the subsequent sale of the collections by Paris auction in 1865, and the palace passed to the Count of Chambord, the Duchess' son, who divided it into apartments, one of which, on the mezzanine floor, was the home of Richard Wagner for some years (where he composed his *Parsifal*).

In 1926, Ca' Vendramin Calergi passed from the heirs of the Count of Chambord to Count Giovanni Volpi of Misurata, who used the second floor for his research into electricity, leaving the residence on the first floor unchanged. Finally, in 1946, the palace was ceded to the Municipality of Venice and is now the winter residence of the Municipal Casino.

Despite the complex and sometimes gloomy events it witnessed and the rapid succession of so many owners, with consequent renovations and the pillaging and dispersion of its artistic contents, the palace's imposing internal structure remains intact, partly preserving indications of its glorious past. The ample and luminous *portego* (or main entrance hall) on the ground floor, which opens scenographically into a "T" on the side of the façade, extending the full depth of the building, still preserves marks of the passage of the Duchess of Berry (in the great coat-of-arms in the shape of a shield with the arms of France).

Pracht nur beschlagnahmt wurde. Lediglich der Weiße Flügel wurde abgerissen. Den Grimani Calergi gelang es dank größerer Zahlungen allerdings, wieder in den Besitz ihrer Güter zu kommen und den Weißen Flügel wieder aufzubauen.

Da es im Jahre 1739 keine Nachkommen gab, ging der Palazzo in den Besitz von Nicolò Vendramin über, der seinem Familiennamen den Namen Calergi anhängte. So erhielt der Palast den Namen, den er auch heute noch trägt. Die Vendramin schmückten die Innenräume mit Kunstwerken ihrer Familiensammlungen aus.

Als Maria Carolina, Herzogin von Berry, im Jahre 1844 den Palast von den letzten Vendramin erwarb, war ein Großteil der Einrichtung noch erhalten. Sie ließ den Palazzo von Giovan Battista Meduna pompös umbauen und um eine ansehnliche Gemäldesammlung bereichern. Sogar ein Theater ließ sie erbauen. Im Palast fanden nun prunkvolle Empfänge statt.

Die veränderte politische Lage zwang die Herzogin von Berry jedoch dazu, die Kunstsammlung 1865 in Paris zu versteigern. Der Palast wurde Eigentum des Grafen von Chambord, dem Sohn der Herzogin, der ihn in Wohnungen aufteilte. In einer von ihnen, im Halbgeschoß, lebte einige Jahre Richard Wagner, der dort seinen *Parsifal* komponierte.

Von den Erben des Grafen von Chambord ging Ca' Vendramin Calergi im Jahre 1926 in den Besitz des Grafen Giovanni Volpi di Misurata über. 1946 schließlich wurde der Palast der Stadtverwaltung Venedigs überlassen. Heute ist er der Wintersitz des Städtischen Spielkasinos.

Trotz der zuweilen recht düsteren Vorfälle, des raschen Wechsels der zahlreichen Besitzer und der daraus resultierenden Umbauten und Veräußerungen der Kunstwerke blieben die imposanten Innenräume unversehrt. Zum Teil bewahrt der Palazzo noch heute Zeugnisse seiner glorreichen Vergangenheit.

So befindet sich etwa im großzügigen *portego* (Eingangshalle) im Erdgeschoß, der sich korrespondierend zur Fassade T-förmig verbreitert und sich über die gesamte Tiefe des Gebäudes erstreckt, das große Wappen, das die Herzogin von Berry anbringen ließ.

Durch ein solides Bogenportal gelangt man zur zweiarmigen Treppe, die zum ersten Obergeschoß führt. Dort wiederholt der zentrale Saal die Anlage der darunter befindlichen Eingangshalle. Vom Querflügel blickt man auf den Canal Grande und gelangt in die seitlichen Räume. Unter anderem befinden

privée de son « aile blanche » qui fut complètement rasée. Néanmoins, grâce à des dons substantiels, les Grimani Calergi réussirent à rentrer en possession de leurs biens et à reconstruire l'aile abattue.

En 1739, par manque d'héritiers, la propriété passa à Nicolò Vendramin qui ajouta à son nom celui de Calergi, donnant ainsi au Palazzo le nom qu'il porte encore aujourd'hui.

Les Vendramin enrichirent l'intérieur avec des œuvres d'art de leurs collections familiales dont deux colonnes en jaspe amenées à Venise par Catherine Cornaro, reine de Chypre, et offertes à sa sœur Cornelia, épouse de Paolo Vendramin.

Il semble qu'une bonne partie du mobilier soit restée en place quand Marie Caroline, duchesse de Berry, acheta en 1844 le palais aux derniers Vendramin.

Pendant la période où la Duchesse y vécut avec son mari, le comte Ettore Lucchesi-Palli, la demeure fut complètement restructurée par Giovan Battista Meduna et connut à nouveau une période de grand éclat, se rouvrant aux réceptions et s'enrichissant d'une galerie de tableaux et même d'un théâtre.

Les difficultés économiques dues à l'instabilité politique, entraînèrent la vente aux enchères de la collection à Paris, en 1865, et le palais passa au comte de Chambord, fils de la Duchesse, qui le divisa en appartements, l'un d'eux, à l'entresol, fut habité pendant quelques années par Richard Wagner qui y composa son *Parsifal.*

Des héritiers du comte de Chambord, le Ca' Vendramin Calergi passa en 1926, au comte Volpi di Misurata qui utilisa le deuxième étage comme laboratoire de recherches électriques, conservant, autant que possible, l'aspect du premier étage noble. Finalement, le palais fut cédé en 1946 à la ville de Venise et il est aujourd'hui le siège d'hiver du Casino Municipal.

Malgré les événements parfois vraiment sombres et la succession rapide de nombreux propriétaires ayant mené à des restructurations, au pillage et à la dispersion des objets d'art, le palais possède encore son imposante architecture intérieure et des témoignages de son glorieux passé.

Le grand et clair *portego,* ou hall d'entrée du rez-de-chaussée qui s'élargit en forme de « T » en accord avec la façade et s'étend sur toute la profondeur du bâtiment, conserve encore les signes du passage de la duchesse de Berry dans les grandes armoiries en forme de bouclier aux armes de France.

A sturdy arched portal gives access to the double flight of stairs rising to the first floor, where the *portego* repeats the layout of the underlying entrance, with the crosswise gallery which faces onto the Grand Canal and leads to the corner rooms. Among other things, this hall still contains paintings of battles and triumphs by Nicolò Bambini, a Venetian painter of the end of the 17th century, probably dating back to the time when the palace was inhabited by the Grimani. Over the doors there are mythical and allegorical figures and also three portraits, some of which are the work of Palma Giovane.

The rooms which face onto the Grand Canal, on either side of the *portego,* are of particular interest. One has leather-covered walls with Baroque gilt impressions, dating back to the time of the Calergi Grimani. It contains a monumental fireplace of pinkish marble, topped by a stucco cowl with allegorical figures of Justice between two enchained Moors, the work of the school of Alessandro Vittoria (the greatest Venetian sculptor of the 16th century). The other room displays the renovations ordered by the Duchess of Berry above all in the lacunar arch with its fluted columns and Corinthian capitals. The room must have been for the Duchess's collection of favourite paintings because spaces have clearly been left free in the decoration for the hanging of pictures.

The next room, called the Sala del Camino, is one of the most magnificent in the palace; it takes its name from the huge fireplace in Veronese marble with African marble columns, topped by an imposing and elaborate scroll-decorated cowl with a niche in the centre containing a winged figure, possibly Peace, with Fortitude and Astronomy on either side. This work can be attributed to the school of Vittoria and dated around the early years of the 17th century. The stucco decorations over the doors belong to the same period.

The White Wing which faces onto the garden was probably the last part to be restored and redecorated in the 18th century.

It has a ceiling frescoed towards the mid 18th-century by Giambattista Crosato with a *Nuptial Allegory* in which a young man with a plumed beret sits on a cloud with a girl dressed in white, in the centre of a ring of winged putti with flowers and mythological figures. The subject probably refers to the marriage of Nicolò Vendramin to Marina Grimani Calergi which had taken place about a century earlier.

sich dort noch heute Gemälde Nicolò Bambinis, die Kämpfe und Triumphe darstellen. Diese Werke des venezianischen Malers aus dem späten 17. Jahrhundert gehen vermutlich auf die Zeit zurück, als der Palast von den Grimani bewohnt wurde. Die Sopraporten schmücken mythische und allegorische Figuren und drei Porträts, von denen einige Palma il Giovane schuf.

Die Zimmer, die sich rechts und links an den *portego* anschließen und zum Canal Grande weisen, sind besonders edel ausgestattet. Die Wände eines Raumes sind mit gold bedrucktem Leder im Barockstil verkleidet. Diese Wandbespannung stammt aus der Zeit der Calergi Grimani. Über dem monumentalen Kamin aus rosa Marmor befindet sich ein Rauchfang aus Stuck, der die Allegorie der Gerechtigkeit zwischen zwei in Ketten gelegten Mohren zeigt. Diese Stuckarbeit stammt aus der Schule Alessandro Vittorias, des größten venezianischen Bildhauers des Cinquecento. In dem anderen Zimmer sind die von der Herzogin von Berry veranlaßten Neuausschmückungen klar erkennbar, etwa an dem Portikus mit Kassetteneinwölbung, den kannelierte Säulen mit korinthischen Kapitellen tragen. Hier muß sich die Gemäldesammlung der Herzogin befunden haben, denn die undekorierten Flächen sollten sicher Bilder aufnehmen.

Der angrenzende Raum ist einer der prunkvollsten des ganzen Palastes und verdankt seinen Namen (Kaminsaal) dem großen Kamin aus veronesischem Marmor mit Säulen aus afrikanischem Marmor. Er hat einen fein gearbeiteten Rauchfang mit Voluten. Die geflügelte Figur in der Mitte des Rauchfangs stellt vielleicht den Frieden dar, den Stärke und Astronomie flankieren. Dieses Werk kann der Schule Vittorias zugeschrieben werden und ist auf den Beginn des 17. Jahrhunderts datierbar. Aus dieser Epoche stammen auch die Stucksopraporten auf vergoldetem Hintergrund.

Der Weiße Flügel, von dem man auf den Garten blickt, ist vermutlich zuletzt im 18. Jahrhundert hergerichtet und neu ausgeschmückt worden. Dort befindet sich aus der Mitte des Settecento eine Deckenmalerei Giambattista Crosatos, die eine *Allegorie der Hochzeit* zeigt. Ein junger Mann mit Federhut sitzt zusammen mit einem weiß gekleideten Mädchen auf einer Wolke. Putten mit Blumen und mythologische Figuren sind um das Paar herumgruppiert. Die Darstellung bezieht sich vermutlich auf die Vermählung Nicolò Vendramins und Marina Grimani Calergis, die etwa ein Jahrhundert zuvor stattgefunden hat.

Un vaste portail arqué donne sur l'escalier à double rampe qui monte au premier étage noble où le *portego* reproduit la disposition de l'entrée inférieure avec le bras transversal qui, face au Grand Canal, conduit aux salles d'angle. Elles abritent encore des toiles de batailles et de victoires réalisées par Nicolò Bambini, peintre vénitien de la fin du XVIIème siècle, et qui remontent certainement à l'époque à laquelle les Grimani habitaient le palais. Les dessus-de-porte sont décorés de personnages mythico-allégoriques et de trois portraits, certains de la main de Palma il Giovane.

Les pièces s'ouvrant sur le *portego* et donnant sur le Grand Canal sont aménagées avec un luxe particulier. L'une est tapissée en cuir doré à l'or fin dans le style baroque ; elle remonte à l'époque des Calergi Grimani et possède une cheminée monumentale en marbre rose surmontée d'un manteau en stuc présentant une figure allégorique de la Justice entre deux maures enchaînés, œuvre de l'école d'Alessandro Vittoria, le plus grand sculpteur vénitien du XVIème siècle. L'autre pièce met en évidence les interventions voulues par la duchesse de Berry, par exemple dans l'arcade à caissons flanquée de colonnes cannelées avec des chapiteaux corinthiens. Cette pièce devait être la galerie de la Duchesse comme en témoignent les espaces laissés nus et destinés à recevoir des tableaux.

La pièce contiguë, une des plus somptueuses du palais, est appelée Salle de la cheminée, en raison de la grande cheminée en marbre de Vérone avec colonnes de marbre africain, surmontée d'un impressionnant manteau à volutes très élaboré sur lequel au centre, dans une niche, se trouve une figure ailée, peut-être la Paix, flanquée de la Force et de l'Astronomie. Cette œuvre, attribuable à l'école de Vittoria, remonte aux premières années du XVIIème siècle, époque de laquelle datent également les bas-reliefs garnissant les dessus-de-porte en stuc sur fond doré.

« L'aile blanche » qui donne sur le jardin a probablement été réaménagée et redécorée pour la dernière fois au XVIIIème siècle. On y trouve un plafond décoré de fresques vers le milieu du XVIIIème siècle par Giambattista Crosato et qui représente une *Allégorie Nuptiale :* un jeune homme coiffé d'un chapeau à plumes et une jeune fille vêtue de blanc sont assis sur un nuage entouré de putti aux ailes fleuries et de personnages mythologiques. La peinture se rapporte peut-être au mariage de Nicolò Vendramin et Marina Grimaldi Calergi qui avait eu lieu environ un siècle auparavant.

PALAZZO LOREDAN VENDRAMIN CALERGI

57 Gilt lacunar arch contained by fluted columns with Corinthian capitals. The archway, like the rest of the decorations in the room, dates from the time of the Duchess of Berry, who had arranged her favourite paintings here. The double door inlaid with precious wood and ivory is particularly noteworthy.

58/59 The Sala del Camino. The walls are lined with leather decorated with gilt impressions. There is an image of Minerva over the door, surrounded in stucco work, dating from the early 17th century. The cowl over the Veronese marble fireplace has a winged figure, possibly Peace, between Fortitude and Astronomy, a stucco work by the school of Alessandro Vittoria. The ceiling has painted beams with elegant brackets.

60 Inlaid door surrounded by painted stone columns with a lintel. The wall covering is made of green leather with gold and silver-coloured floral patterns. This kind of wall covering was very popular between the 15th and 17th centuries in Venice, where it was called *cuori (cuoi) d'oro.* The city was renowned for its leather-work during that period.

61 Giambattista Crosato, *Nuptial Allegory.* The fresco was made around the mid-18th century and decorates the ceiling of one of the rooms in the palace's White Wing. The image of the couple seated on a cloud, amidst winged putti and mythological figures, probably celebrates the marriage of Nicolò Vendramin and Marina Grimani Calergi, which had taken place a hundred years previously. The rich stucco frame decorated with foliage and scrolls is the work of the illusionist decorator Pietro Visconti.

62 Detail of the stucco cowl over the fireplace to which the Sala del Camino owes its name. The palace is rich in fireplaces that are similar but of smaller dimensions.

62 Detail of the monumental staircase which leads to the first floor from about halfway down the entrance hall. The beginning of the staircase is emphasised by a solid arched portal borne by pilasters with Corinthian capitals. Over the door opposite the staircase is the great shield with the arms of France, dating from when the Duchess of Berry purchased the palace and lived there for a few years in the mid-19th century.

63 Detail of one of the doors inlaid with Oriental-style motives in the Sala del Camino.

57 Portikus mit vergoldeter Kassetteneinwölbung, getragen von kannelierten Säulen mit korinthischen Kapitellen. Die gesamte Ausstattung dieses Saals veranlaßte die Herzogin von Berry, die hier auch ihre Lieblingsgemälde beherbergte. Die zweiflügelige Tür mit Edelholz- und Elfenbeinintarsien ist besonders bemerkenswert.

58/59 Kaminsaal. Die Wände schmückt gold bedrucktes Leder. Die Stucksopraporte mit der Darstellung der Minerva stammt aus dem frühen 17. Jahrhundert. Den Kamin aus veronesischem Marmor krönt der Rauchfang aus Stuck, in dessen Mitte sich eine geflügelte Figur befindet – vielleicht eine Allegorie des Friedens. Rechts und links sind Astronomie und Stärke dargestellt. Diese Stuckarbeiten stammen aus der Schule Alessandro Vittorias. Die Decke weist bemalte Balken und elegante Auskragungen auf.

60 Inkrustierte Türrahmung. Der Architrav wird von zwei bemalten Steinsäulen getragen. Die Wandbespannungen sind aus grünem Leder mit floralen Motiven in Gold- und Silbertönen. Diese »Tapeten« waren in Venedig zwischen dem 15. und dem 17. Jahrhundert sehr verbreitet und wurden *cuori (cuoi) d'oro* genannt. Zu jener Zeit war die Lagunenstadt berühmt für ihre Lederbearbeitung.

61 Giambattista Crosato, *Allegorie der Hochzeit.* Die Deckenmalerei, die einen Saal des Weißen Flügels schmückt, entstand gegen Mitte des 18. Jahrhunderts. Die Darstellung des auf einer Wolke sitzenden jungen Ehepaares zwischen Putten und mythologischen Figuren preist wahrscheinlich die Vermählung von Nicolò Vendramin und Marina Grimani Calergi, die etwa ein Jahrhundert zuvor stattfand. Der reich verzierte Stuckrahmen ist ein Werk Pietro Viscontis.

62 Detail des Kaminrauchfangs aus Stuck, der dem Kaminsaal seinen Namen gab. Der Palast ist reich an ähnlichen, jedoch kleineren Kaminen.

62 Detail der Prunktreppe, die von der Eingangshalle zum ersten Obergeschoß führt. Ein kräftiger Rundbogen, den Pilaster mit korinthischen Kapitellen tragen, betont den Beginn des monumentalen Treppenaufgangs. Der Treppe gegenüber über der Tür befindet sich das Wappen, das die Herzogin von Berry anbringen ließ, als sie gegen Mitte des 19. Jahrhunderts den Palast erwarb.

63 Detail einer Tür im Kaminsaal mit Intarsien, die orientalisch inspirierte Motive aufweisen.

57 Arche dorée soutenue par des colonnes cannelées avec chapiteaux corinthiens. Toute la décoration de la salle date de l'époque de la duchesse de Berry qui avait aussi installé ici les peintures auxquelles elle tenait particulièrement. La porte à deux battants aux incrustations de bois précieux et d'ivoire est particulièrement intéressante.

58/59 Salle de la cheminée. Les murs sont tendus de cuir à impressions dorées. La décoration en stuc des dessus-de-porte qui représente Minerve date du début du XVII siècle. Le manteau de la cheminée, en marbre de Vérone, présente un personnage ailé, en stuc – peut-être la Paix entourée de la Force et de l'Astronomie –, œuvre de l'école d'Alessandro Vittoria. Plafond à poutres peintes avec des décorations élégantes.

60 Porte marquetée encadrée de colonnes en pierre peinte soutenant un architrave. Les tentures murales sont en cuir vert orné de motifs floraux dorés et argentés. Ces « tapisseries » étaient très répandues entre le XVème et le XVIIème siècle à Venise où on les appelait « cœurs(cuirs) d'or ». A cette époque, la ville était renommée pour les travaux du cuir.

61 Giambattista Crosato, *Allégorie Nuptiale.* La fresque réalisée vers le milieu du XVIIIème siècle décore le plafond d'une salle de « l'aile blanche ». La représentation du jeune couple sur un nuage, entouré d'angelots et de figures mythologiques, rend probablement hommage au mariage de Nicolò Vendramin et Marina Grimani Calergi, célébré un siècle auparavant. Le magnifique encadrement en stuc décoré de végétaux et de volutes est l'œuvre du peintre quadratoriste Pietro Visconti.

62 Détail du manteau en stuc auquel la Salle de la cheminée doit son nom. Le palais possède beaucoup d'autres cheminées semblables mais plus petites.

62 Détail de l'escalier monumental qui mène de l'entrée au premier étage. Un arc en plein cintre soutenu par des pilastres à chapiteaux corinthiens souligne le début de l'escalier. Face à l'escalier, un grand écusson aux armes de France surplombe la porte. La duchesse de Berry l'y fit poser quand elle acheta le palais vers le milieu du XIXème siècle.

63 Détail d'une des portes de la Salle de la cheminée. Les incrustations s'inspirent de motifs orientaux.

PALAZZO LOREDAN

in Campo St Stefano

M. Moro dis.   Pt lit Kier

PALAZZO LOREDAN   ✦   PALAIS LOREDAN

in Campo St Stefano   Place St Etienne

Venise Joseph Kier Edit Place St Marc 72

PALAZZO LOREDAN

The palace occupies a vast oblong area between the two churches of San Vidal and Santo Stefano (which lends its name to the square onto which the building faces).

Like almost all Venetian palaces, its history is indissolubly linked with that of the family – the Loredans – who lived in it for nearly three centuries. According to legend, the family traced its origins back to Mucius Scaevola; but in historical terms they appeared on the Venetian scene in the first half of the 14th century, with the Procurators Marco and Paolo (the latter is remembered as one of those who elected the Doge Andrea Dandolo).

The family could boast that it had twice served the Republic of Venice at the highest possible level, with the Doges Leonardo (1501–1521) and Francesco (1752–1762). The Loredans had begun to make their fortune at the end of the 15th century, thanks to the goods accumulated with trading activities in Africa and the East by Leonardo himself, who became Procurator of St. Mark in 1492 and was elected doge in 1501, governing the State for twenty years.

This shrewd and determined politician succeeded in preserving and consolidating Venice's liberty in a crucial period of its history. As doge, he was admired and praised by the major contemporary historian Marin Sanudo and he left the Republic in thriving economic conditions. Moreover, through his artistic patronage he furthered the city's architectural and urbanistic revival.

In fact, it was during the years of his government that Venice saw alterations and new decorations for the Zen chapel in St. Mark's, the restoration of the Rialto market area, and the reconstruction of the Fondaco dei Tedeschi on the Grand Canal (for which he ordered the outer façade to be decorated by Giorgione). Official orders were also issued to Vittore Carpaccio and Giovanni Bellini for the cycles of portraits and paintings to decorate the Sala del Maggior Consiglio in the Palazzo Ducale (which, however, was destroyed by the devastating fire of 1577).

It was Bellini who portrayed the doge with his children in the *Portrait of Doge Leo-*

Der Palazzo Loredan befindet sich auf einem großen rechteckigen Platz zwischen den Kirchen San Vidal und Santo Stefano. Breit lagert er an der westlichen Längsseite des Campo Santo Stefano. Wie bei fast allen venezianischen Palästen ist auch seine Geschichte untrennbar mit der Historie der Familie verbunden, die ihn fast drei Jahrhunderte lang bewohnte. Die Loredan, die ihre Abstammung auf Mucius Scaevola zurückführten, waren in der ersten Hälfte des Trecento mit den Prokuratoren Marco und Paolo nach Venedig gekommen. Letzterer gehörte zu den Wählern des Dogen Andrea Dandolo.

Die Erfolge der Familie, die sich rühmen durfte, der Republik von Venedig mit den Dogen Leonardo (1501–1521) und Francesco (1752–1762) sogar zweimal an höchster Stelle gedient zu haben, begannen Ende des 15. Jahrhunderts. Leonardo hatte durch den Handel in Afrika und im östlichen Mittelmeer ein enormes Vermögen angehäuft. 1492 wurde er Prokurator von San Marco und 1501 zum Dogen gewählt. Leonardo lenkte das Schicksal Venedigs zwei Jahrzehnte lang.

Als umsichtiger und entschlossener Politiker gelang es ihm, in einer kritischen Zeit die Freiheit Venedigs zu bewahren und zu festigen. Bewundert und gefeiert von dem wichtigsten zeitgenössischen Historiker, Marin Sanudo, verließ der Doge die Serenissima in blühenden wirtschaftlichen Verhältnissen und zeichnete als Mäzen maßgeblich für die architektonische und städtebauliche Erneuerung Venedigs verantwortlich.

In seine Regierungszeit fallen der Umbau und die neue Ausschmückung der Zen-Kapelle in der Markuskirche, die Umstrukturierung des Marktbereiches an der Rialto-Brücke und der Wiederaufbau des Fondaco dei Tedeschi (Deutsches Handelshaus) am Canal Grande, dessen Fassade er von Giorgione dekorieren ließ. Außerdem vergab er offizielle Aufträge an Vittore Carpaccio und Giovanni Bellini, im Dogenpalast den Saal des Großen Rates auszuschmücken, der jedoch im Jahre 1577 bei einem Brand zerstört wurde.

Le Palazzo Loredan occupe un vaste terrain rectangulaire entre les églises de San Vidal et de Santo Stefano ; sa façade jouxte le Campo Santo Stefano sur sa longueur.

Comme pour presque tous les palais vénitiens, son histoire est indissolublement liée à celle de la famille qui l'habita pendant presque trois siècles, les Loredan. Ceux-ci faisaient remonter d'une manière mythique l'origine de leur lignée à Mucius Scaevola, mais ils n'apparaissent sur la scène vénitienne que dans la première moitié du XIVème siècle avec les Procurateurs Marco et Paolo, ce dernier étant l'un des électeurs du doge Andrea Dandolo.

Les bonnes fortunes de la maison, qui pouvait se glorifier d'avoir servi la République de Venise deux fois, et au plus haut niveau, avec les doges Leonardo (1501–1521) et Francesco (1752–1762), débutent à la fin du XVème siècle grâce aux énormes biens dus au commerce en Afrique et dans le Levant accumulés par Leonardo. Devenu Procurateur de San Marco en 1492, il fut élu doge en 1501 et tint pendant vingt ans les comptes de l'Etat.

Homme politique avisé et déterminé, il sut préserver et consolider le liberté de Venise durant une période cruciale de son histoire ; admiré et célébré par le plus grand historien de son temps, Marin Sanudo, le doge laissa la Sérénissime dans des conditions économiques très florissantes, pourvoyant de surcroît, avec une évidente inclination au mécénat, à la rénovation architecturale-urbanistique de Venise.

Les années de son gouvernement virent la transformation et la nouvelle décoration de la Chapelle Zena à San Marco, la restructuration du Fondaco dei Tedeschi (entrepôt des négociants allemands) sur le Grand Canal, dont la façade qu'il voulut décorée par Giorgione, mais également les commandes officielles à Vittorio Carpaccio et à Giovanni Bellini qui peignirent les cycles décorant la Salle du Grand Conseil du Palais ducal, détruits ensuite dans l'incendie qui la dévasta en 1577.

Bellini encore représenta le doge avec ses fils dans le *Portrait du Doge Leonardo Lore-*

nardo Loredan with Four Counsellors (now at the State Museum in Berlin), a work which was probably ordered privately by Leonardo himself, as it is recorded as hanging at Palazzo Loredan around the middle of the 17th century.

The purchase of the palace came after the death of the doge, however, who lived in another part of the city, in the parish of San Canciano. In 1536 his son bought most of the late 15th-century building in Campo Santo Stefano from the Mocenigo family.

Little remains today of the original 15th-century building, apart from the arches with late-Gothic capitals decorated with acanthus leaves in the inner courtyard. Here too is a well-curb decorated with festoons, garlands and lions' heads, the work of an anonymous Lombard sculptor.

A few years after its purchase, the building underwent a somewhat radical reconstruction, entrusted to the architect Antonio Abbondi (nicknamed "Scarpagnino"), who had already worked for Doge Leonardo Loredan on the eastern wing of the Palazzo Ducale and in the Rialto area.

Scarpagnino's most significant work on the palace in Campo Santo Stefano is the monumental staircase, of unusual size for Venetian buildings. The first, double flight of stairs has pillars at either end with sculpted baskets of flowers and fruit and the marble gratings in the balustrade each have different decorations and interlacing effects.

As for the façade onto the Campo, there is an evident harmonic discord between the mullioned windows at the centre and the other windows. The architect's project clearly took into account a plan for fresco decorations in which architectural trompe-l'œil elements, statues and illusionist perspective effects would create a balance which is difficult to imagine today.

The frescoes on the outside were entrusted to Giuseppe Porta (nicknamed "Salviati"), who was much admired by his contemporaries for the complexity of his compositions, on which he lavished all his remarkable inventive ability. He was required to celebrate the Loredan family by representing episodes – such as those of Lucrece, Clelia, Porsenna, and Mucius Scaevola – taken from Roman epic to emphasise domestic, civic, and military virtues that could also be found in the Loredan family.

The inside of the building seemed rather plain and unusual in comparison to the outside. Two large doors (from the *rio*, or small canal, and from the Campo) gave onto

Es war auch Bellini, der den Dogen mit seinen Söhnen in dem Gemälde *Der Doge Leonardo Loredan mit vier Räten* porträtierte, das heute zu den Sammlungen der Staatlichen Museen Preußischer Kulturbesitz in Berlin gehört. Vermutlich war dieses Bild ein privater Auftrag Leonardos, denn Mitte des 17. Jahrhunderts soll es sich im Palazzo Loredan befunden haben.

Der Erwerb des Palazzo Loredan erfolgte jedoch erst nach dem Tod des Dogen, dessen Wohnsitz im Stadtteil San Canciano gelegen war. Sein Sohn kaufte im Jahre 1536 der Familie Mocenigo einen Großteil des Gebäudes aus dem späten Quattrocento am Campo Santo Stefano ab.

Von dem ursprünglichen Bauwerk aus dem 15. Jahrhundert zeugen heute nur noch wenige Reste, wie die Bögen im Innenhof, die spätgotische Kapitelle mit Akanthusblättern zieren. Im Innenhof befindet sich auch eine mit Girlanden und Löwenköpfen versehene Brunneneinfassung, das Werk eines unbekannten lombardischen Bildhauers.

Bereits wenige Jahre nach dem Erwerb des Gebäudes wurde es umfassend umstrukturiert. Der Umbau wurde dem Architekten Antonio Abbondi, genannt lo Scarpagnino, anvertraut, den der Doge Leonardo Loredan vorher schon mit Arbeiten am Ostflügel des Dogenpalastes und im Gebiet um die Rialto-Brücke beauftragt hatte.

Der einschneidendste Eingriff Scarpagninos am Palazzo Loredan ist die monumentale Treppe mit für venezianische Gebäude ungewöhnlichen Dimensionen. An der ersten doppelten Rampe stehen an jedem Ende Pfeiler, die gemeißelte Blüten- und Früchtekörbe tragen. Die Marmorsäulen der Brüstung unterscheiden sich durch ihre verschiedenen Dekorelemente voneinander.

Die Fassadengliederung zum Platz hin wirkt recht unausgewogen: Neben dem mehrbögigen Fenster über dem Portal gibt es weite Wandflächen mit einfachen Fenstereinfassungen. Einst hatten Außenfresken die Fassade geschmückt, und mit ihren gemalten Architekturelementen, Statuen und Scheinperspektiven schufen sie jene Ausgeglichenheit, die man sich heute nur noch schwer vorstellen kann.

Die Außenfresken hatte Giuseppe Porta, genannt Salviati, ausgeführt, den seine Zeitgenossen vor allem wegen seiner äußerst komplexen Werke bewunderten. Dargestellt waren Episoden aus der römischen Epik, die das Geschlecht der Loredan preisen sollten. Die Mythen um Lucretia, Cloelia, Porsenna

dan avec quatre Conseillers, qui fait actuellement partie des collections des Staatlichen Museen Preußischer Kulturbesitz à Berlin. Cette œuvre fut très probablement réalisée sur commande privée de Leonardo, puisqu'elle se trouvait au milieu du XVIIème siècle dans le Palazzo Loredan.

L'achat du palais eut toutefois lieu après la mort du doge, dont la demeure était située dans la paroisse de San Canciano. En effet, c'est son fils qui acquit en 1536 une grande partie de l'édifice datant de la fin du XVème siècle et qui appartenait aux Mocenigo à Campo Santo Stefano.

De la construction du XVème siècle, il ne reste que quelques vestiges, les arcades à chapiteaux du gothique flamboyant avec feuilles d'acanthe dans la cour intérieure, où se trouve aussi une margelle de puits ornée de festons, guirlandes et protomés léonins, œuvre d'un sculpteur lombard anonyme.

Quelques années après l'achat, l'édifice fut soumis à une restructuration radicale, confiée à l'architecte Antonio Abbondi, dit Scarpagnino, qui avait déjà prêté son concours pour l'aile orientale du Palais ducal et pour la zone de Rialto, sur commission du doge Leonardo Loredan.

L'intervention la plus significative de Scarpagnino dans le palais de Santo Stefano est l'escalier monumental aux dimensions inhabituelles pour les édifices vénitiens, dont la première rampe double présente, au début et à la fin, des piliers qui soutiennent des corbeilles de fleurs et de fruits sculptées, tandis que les colonnes de marbre de la balustrade diffèrent l'une de l'autre par l'ornement et les entrelacs.

En ce qui concerne la façade sur la place, des déformations harmoniques entre la fenêtre polylobée centrale et les autres fenêtres s'avèrent évidentes, mais le projet de l'architecte tenait évidemment compte de la décoration picturale à fresque prévue qui – avec de fausses architectures, statues et cadres perspectifs – créait cet équilibre difficile à imaginer aujourd'hui.

L'exécution des fresques extérieures fut confiée à Giuseppe Porta, dit Salviati, très admiré de ses contemporains pour la complexité de ses compositions.

Il s'agissait en fait de célébrer la lignée des Loredan à travers la représentation d'épisodes, tels que ceux de Lucrèce, Clelia, Porsenna et Mucius Scaevola, tirés de l'épopée romaine qui mirent en lumière les vertus domestiques, civiques et militaires vérifiables également au sein de la famille Loredan.

a square entrance with a monumental stairway leading to the first floor, where three rooms led off from the main hall, which corresponded to the entrance-hall below.

The renovations made by architect and painter demonstrate the evident growth of the family fortune. Reputed to be one of the richest families in the city, the Loredans had acquired highly-profitable landed properties after the doge's death and also enjoyed a considerable income from the commendam on Vangadizza Abbey, which they continued to hand down until 1608. In 1598, with the purchase from the Mocenigo family of the adjacent part of the palace, the building took on its present layout, with the addition of the new north-eastern façade facing towards the church. This was designed by Giovanni Girolamo Grapiglia, who had already designed the architectural elements of the funeral monument commemorating Doge Leonardo, erected in the church of SS. Giovanni e Paolo.

Probably because of the state of extensive disrepair of Salviati's frescoes, Grapiglia preferred to cover the new façade with Istrian marble, decorating it with festoons, female busts and two Virtues. These were the work of the sculptors from Vincenzo Scamozzi's atelier, who were also responsible for the more or less contemporary Procuratie Nuove.

There is also documentary evidence regarding the decorations inside the palace's new wing: Filippo Zaniberti painted the ceiling with an allegorical fresco on the myth of Adonis which has since been lost. The interior now contains only the 18th-century decorations ordered by the second and last Loredan doge, Francesco.

In fact, it is not certain whether the late 16th-century ceiling with episodes from the Old Testament, pagan divinities, genii and virtues (a work done in collaboration by Aliense, Palma il Giovane and Sante Peranda) was originally carried out for the palace. In any case, its analogy with other 16th-century ceilings suggests that it could only have been intended for the mezzanine floor.

Renowned as the "father of the poor" for his generosity, Francesco Loredan had most of the palace redecorated, adapting the late 16th-century decorations in some of the rooms (which were further manhandled in the 19th century).

The frescoes on the ceiling of one of the inner halls belong to the time of the second Doge Loredan, around 1760. Here the painter Giuseppe Angeli represented *Apollo*

und Mucius Scaevola spielten auf die verschiedenen Tugenden der Familie Loredan an.

Die Innenräume des Gebäudes erschienen im Gegensatz zur Außengestaltung recht einfach: Durch zwei große Türen, die eine an der Kanalseite, die andere an der Platzfront gelegen, gelangte man in eine quadratische Eingangshalle, von der aus die monumentale Treppe zum ersten Stock führte. Im *piano nobile* befand sich der der darunter liegenden Eingangshalle entsprechende Hauptsaal, von dem wiederum drei weitere Zimmer zu erreichen waren.

Die Gebäudeveränderungen, die sowohl Architekt als auch Maler durchführten, bekunden das offensichtliche Anwachsen des Familienvermögens. Die Loredan galten als eine der reichsten Familien der Stadt. Nach dem Tod des Dogen hatten sie ertragreichen Landbesitz erworben. Zudem erhielten sie hohe Pfründe aus der Abtei Vangadizza, die die Loredan bis 1608 an ihre Nachkommen weitervererbten. Im Jahre 1598 kauften die Loredan der Familie Mocenigo den an den Palast angrenzenden Teil ab. Durch die neue nordöstliche, von Giovanni Girolamo Grapiglia entworfene Fassade zur Kirche erhielt das Gebäude sein heutiges Aussehen. Grapiglia hatte schon zuvor die Architekturelemente für das Grabmal des Dogen Leonardo entworfen, das in der Kirche Santi Giovanni e Paolo errichtet worden war.

Wahrscheinlich wegen des fortschreitenden Verfalls der Fresken Salviatis entschied Grapiglia, die neue Fassade mit istrischem Marmor zu versehen. Bildhauer aus der Werkstatt Vincenzo Scamozzis schufen die Fassadenschmuckelemente, wie Girlanden, weibliche Büsten oder die zwei Tugenden. Denselben Bildhauern sind die ungefähr gleichzeitig fertiggestellten Procuratie Nuove zu verdanken.

Anhand überlieferter Quellen kennt man die ehemalige Ausschmückung im Inneren des neuen Flügels: Filippo Zaniberti hatte dort ein allegorisches Deckenfresko mit dem Mythos des Adonis gemalt, das leider nicht erhalten ist. Heute zeigen die Säle die Dekorationen des 18. Jahrhunderts, die der zweite und letzte Doge der Familie Loredan, Francesco, in Auftrag gegeben hat.

Nicht sicher ist, ob die Deckenmalerei aus dem späten 16. Jahrhundert, die alttestamentliche Episoden, heidnische Götter, Genien und Tugenden zeigt und an der Aliense, Palma il Giovane und Sante Peranda arbeiteten, ursprünglich für den Palast ausgeführt wurde. Im Vergleich mit anderen

L'intérieur de l'édifice apparaissait en revanche plutôt simple et inhabituel : deux grandes portes d'entrée, depuis le canal et la place, introduisaient dans une salle carrée, à partir de laquelle l'escalier monumental conduisait à l'étage noble où se trouvait le *portego* s'ouvrant sur trois pièces, et correspondant à la salle située à l'étage inférieur.

Les interventions de l'architecte et du peintre témoignent de l'évidente croissance des biens de la famille, évoquée comme l'une des plus riches de la ville, et qui après la mort du doge avait acquis des propriétés terriennes à haut revenu et jouissait en plus de rentes considérables provenant de la commende sur l'abbaye de la Vangadizza que les Loredan se transmirent jusqu'en 1608. En 1598, avec l'achat par les Mocenigo de la partie voisine du palais, l'édifice prit la structure actuelle avec l'adjonction de la nouvelle façade au nord-est, du côté de l'église, imaginée par Giovanni Girolamo Grapiglia qui avait déjà projeté les éléments architecturaux du monument funéraire du doge Leonardo dressé dans l'église Santi Giovanni e Paolo.

Probablement en raison de l'état de dégradation avancé des fresques de Salviati, Grapaglia préféra réaliser la nouvelle façade en pierre d'Istrie qui fut ornée de festons, de protomés féminins et de deux Vertus, œuvre de sculpteurs de l'atelier de Vincenzo Scamozzi, auquel on doit les Procuratie Nuove achevées vers la même époque.

Les sources donnent également des indications sur la décoration intérieure de la nouvelle aile du palais : Filippo Zaniberti y avait peint, au plafond, une frise allégorique avec le mythe d'Adonis, aujourd'hui perdue ; les intérieurs conservent donc seulement les décorations du XVIIIème siècle, commandées par le second et dernier doge de la famille Loredan, Francesco.

Il n'est pas certain que le plafond fin XVIème siècle avec épisodes de l'Ancien Testament, divinités païennes, génies et vertus, œuvre à laquelle collaborèrent Aliense, Palma le Jeune et Sante Peranda, ait été exécuté à l'origine pour le palais, où de toute façon il devait être destiné, par analogie avec d'autres plafonds du XVIème siècle, à l'entresol.

Connu comme « père des pauvres » pour sa générosité, Francesco Loredan fit redécorer une grande partie du palais ; il modifia dans certaines pièces les décorations fin XVIème, qui furent ensuite retouchées au XIXème siècle.

La fresque du plafond d'un salon intérieur dans laquelle le peintre Giuseppe

with Aurora, Eternity and Time, using a bright and lively colouring reminiscent of Piazzetta's teaching. The stucco illusionist effects on the walls may possibly be attributed to Abbondio Stazio and represent the *Four Seasons.*

In a boudoir not far away, the same painter and the same stuccoworkers drew upon a more frivolous subject, representing *Leda and the Swan* on the ceiling and decorating the walls with rich, coloured jugs containing little rampant horses, within elaborate panels.

With Francesco Loredan, the fortunes of the family came to an end and the last descendant, Caterina Loredan in Pisani, sold the palace to a furniture-dealer, who passed it on, in 1805, to the Austrian government. With the arrival of the French in 1806, it became the home of the first Governor, and in subsequent years it was transformed into offices, until it was handed over to the Royal Venetian Institute of Sciences, Letters and the Arts in 1891, when the rooms were furnished as we see them today.

Deckenmalereien des 16. Jahrhunderts könnte dieses Fresko für das Halbgeschoß des Palastes bestimmt gewesen sein.

Francesco Loredan, der wegen seiner Großzügigkeit als »Vater der Armen« bekannt war, ließ einen Großteil des Palastes neu ausstatten. In manchen Räumen veränderte er die Dekorationen des späten Cinquecento, an die im 19. Jahrhundert erneut Hand angelegt wurde.

In der Zeit des zweiten Dogen Loredan, nämlich um 1760, entstand das Deckenfresko eines Salons, auf dem der Maler Giuseppe Angeli *Apoll mit Aurora, der Ewigkeit und der Zeit* in lebhaften und leuchtenden Farben darstellte. Dieses Werk nimmt die kompositorischen Lektionen Piazzettas auf. Die Stuckpaneelen an den Wänden zeigen die *Vier Jahreszeiten* und können Abbondio Stazio zugeschrieben werden.

In einem diesem Salon benachbarten Boudoir arbeiteten derselbe Maler und die gleichen Stukkateure ein frivoleres Thema aus: an der Decke *Leda und der Schwan* und an den Wänden, in raffinierten Spiegelungen, reichverzierte bunte Krüge mit kleinen sich aufbäumenden Pferden.

Mit Francesco Loredan neigte sich der Glanz der Familie dem Ende zu. Der letzte weibliche Nachkomme, Caterina Pisani, geborene Loredan, verkaufte den Palast an einen Möbelhändler, der ihn im Jahre 1805 der österreichischen Regierung übergab. Ein Jahr später, nach der Machtübernahme der Franzosen, wurde er Wohnsitz des ersten Gouverneurs. In den darauffolgenden Jahren beherbergte er verschiedene Behörden, bis er 1891 das Istituto Veneto di Scienze, Lettere ed Arti aufnahm, das die Säle so einrichtete, wie wir sie heute sehen.

Angeli représenta Apollon, avec *L'Aurore, l'Eternité et le Temps,* d'une recherche d'effets vive et lumineuse, qui rappelle sur le plan de la composition la leçon de Piazzetta et, sur les murs, les cadres de stuc attribuables sans doute à Abbondio Stazio et représentant les *Quatre Saisons,* remontent à l'époque du second doge Loredan, vers 1760.

Dans un boudoir voisin, le même peintre et les mêmes stucateurs élaborèrent un thème plus frivole : sur le plafond *Léda et le cygne* et aux murs, à l'intérieur de panneaux élaborés, de riches pots colorés qui contiennent des petits chevaux rampants.

Avec Francesco Loredan prennent fin les bonnes fortunes de la famille. La dernière descendante, Caterina Pisani née Loredan, vendit le palais à un marchand de meubles qui le céda à son tour, en 1805, au gouvernement autrichien ; en 1806, avec l'arrivée des Français, le palais devint la demeure du premier gouverneur et il accueillit divers bureaux au cours des années suivantes, jusqu'à ce qu'en 1891, l'Institut Royal Vénitien des Sciences, Lettres et Arts qui veilla à meubler les salles comme elles nous apparaissent aujourd'hui, y soit transféré.

Palazzo Loredan

69 The Assembly Hall. The imposing portal with Corinthian columns is probably the work of Girolamo Grapiglia, whereas the Mercury on the keystone is attributed to the 16th-century sculptor Girolamo Campagna. It is worth noting the Venetian *terrazzo* flooring with geometrical bands.

71 King Umberto's room. This room takes its name from the great portrait of the king hanging over the fireplace. It is furnished with bookshelves designed at the end of the 19th century by Federico Berchet, whereas the little table dates from the mid-19th century and was probably part of the furnishings belonging to the Institute when it was still in the Palazzo Ducale, before it moved to Palazzo Loredan.

73 The Assembly Hall. On the far wall, between the two windows, is the altar-piece by Jacopo Tintoretto with the *Madonna and Child with Four Senators*. The furniture in the hall dates back to the last years of the 19th century, when the palace became the home of the Venetian Institute of Sciences, Letters and the Arts.

74 An 18th-century room. The stucco decorations are probably the work of Abbondio Stazio and are allegorical representations of the *Four Seasons*.

75 An 18th-century room. Detail of the corner of the stucco decoration with the Loredan family's coat-of-arms.

69 Versammlungssaal. Das imposante Portal mit korinthischen Säulen schuf vermutlich Girolamo Grapiglia. Der Merkur unter dem Portalarchitrav wird einem Bildhauer des 16. Jahrhunderts, Girolamo Campagna, zugeschrieben. Bemerkenswert ist der venezianische Terrazzo-Bodenbelag mit geometrischen Bändermotiven.

71 Saal des Königs Umberto. Das große Königsbildnis über dem Kamin gab diesem Raum seinen Namen. Die Bücherschränke entwarf Federico Berchet gegen Ende des 19. Jahrhunderts. Der kleine Tisch stammt aus der Mitte des 19. Jahrhunderts und gehörte vermutlich zu der Einrichtung des Istituto Veneto, als es noch vor seinem Umzug in den Palazzo Loredan im Palazzo Ducale (Dogenpalast) untergebracht war.

73 Versammlungssaal. An der Stirnwand zwischen den beiden Fenstern befindet sich das Altarbild *Madonna mit Kind und vier Senatoren* Jacopo Tintorettos. Die Einrichtung des Saals stammt aus den letzten Jahren des 19. Jahrhunderts, als der Palast Sitz des Istituto Veneto di Scienze, Lettere ed Arti wurde.

74 Saal aus dem 18. Jahrhundert. Die Stukkaturen, die vermutlich Abbondio Stazio schuf, zeigen allegorische Darstellungen der *Vier Jahreszeiten*.

75 Saal aus dem 18. Jahrhundert. Eckstukkatur mit dem Wappen der Familie Loredan.

69 Salle des Réunions. La grande porte d'accès aux colonnes corinthiennes est probablement de Girolamo Grapiglia ; le Mercure sur la clef de voûte est du sculpteur du XVIème siècle, Girolamo Campagna. A noter : la terrasse à la vénitienne et ses bandes à motifs géométriques.

71 Salle du Roi Umberto. La salle doit son nom au grand portrait du Roi placé au-dessus de la cheminée. Elle est meublée de bibliothèques réalisées à la fin du XIXème siècle par Federico Berchet. La table date du milieu du XIXème siècle ; elle faisait probablement partie de l'ameublement de l'Institut quand celui-ci avait son siège dans le Palais ducal avant son transfert au Palais Loredan.

73 Salle des Réunions. Sur le mur du fond, entre les deux fenêtres, le retable de Jacopo Tintoretto avec *La Madone, l'Enfant et quatre sénateurs*. La décoration de la salle remonte aux dernières années du XIXème siècle, quand le palais devint le siège de l'Institut Vénitien des Sciences, des Lettres et des Arts.

74 Salle du XVIIIème siècle. Les décorations en stuc, sans doute l'œuvre de Abbondio Stazio, sont une illustration allégorique des *Quatre Saisons*.

75 Salle du XVIIIème siècle. Détail de la décoration en stuc avec le blason de la famille Loredan.

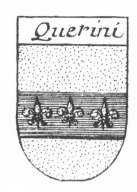

PALAZZO QUERINI STAMPALIA

QUERINI STAMPALIA

PALAZZO QUERINI STAMPALIA

The oldest chronicles, which often fade into legend suggest that the Querinis are descendants of the *Gens Sulpicia* of Rome, that they left Rome to establish themselves in Padua, from whence, to escape the barbarian invasions, they took refuge on the island of Torcello, moving to Rialto at the time of the origins of Venice.

Historically, the family is first mentioned as being in the city in the 12th century and seems to have been divided into various branches, including one in Santa Maria Formosa which appears to have resided in that district ever since 1238 and was already considerably involved in the political life of the city.

Tradition has it that the second surname, Stampalia, was added later, on the purchase by one of the Querini family of one of the Sporades islands bearing this name, when he was banished from the city for having taken part in Baiamonte Tiepolo's conspiracy in 1310. In truth, one Iseppo Querini of Santa Maria Formosa was banished, though much later, for having conspired with Marin Falier, the traitor doge who lost his head on the gallows in 1355. The purchase of Stampalia took place many years later still, in 1413. The Querini made a vain attempt to populate the island, transferring a group of settlers there to defend it from pirates. When Stampalia fell to the Turks in 1537, the Venetian family was left with nothing but the boast of a double-barreled surname.

In the 15th century, however, the Querinis invested in landed property and through their trading in the East considerably increased a fortune which was already conspicuous.

Though they had lived in Santa Maria Formosa from 1238 onwards, the building of their palace may be dated between 1513 and 1523. The plan of Venice drawn up by Jacopo de'Barbari in 1500 bears no trace of it, but in 1514 there is a record of the purchase of the buildings that clearly occupied the area where the stately home was to be. The palace was already inhabited by 1522, when items were bought for the residence. Two years

Antiken Überlieferungen zufolge, die allerdings häufig die Grenzen zur Legende überschreiten, stammen die Querini von der römischen *Gens Sulpicia* ab. Nachdem sie Rom verlassen hatten, ließen sich die Querini in Padua nieder. Von dort flüchteten sie wegen der Barbareneinfälle nach Torcello, um schließlich seit der ersten Besiedelung Venedigs im Bezirk Rialto ansässig zu werden.

In der Stadtgeschichte Venedigs wird die Familie zum ersten Mal im 12. Jahrhundert erwähnt. Die Querini waren eine weitverzweigte Familie. Die Querini von Santa Maria Formosa, die seit 1238 in dem gleichnamigen Stadtteil wohnten, nahmen am politischen Leben der Lagunenstadt regen Anteil.

Laut einer Überlieferung soll der zweite Familienname, Stampalia, angenommen worden sein, als ein Querini, der wegen seiner Teilnahme an der Verschwörung Baiamonte Tiepolos im Jahre 1310 aus Venedig verbannt worden war, die gleichnamige Insel der Sporaden erwarb. Es wurde zwar ein gewisser Iseppo Querini di Santa Maria Formosa aus der Lagunenstadt verbannt, das war allerdings später im Zusammenhang mit der konspirativen Verbindung, die zu dem verräterischen Dogen Marin Falier, der 1355 hingerichtet wurde, bestand. Der Kauf der Insel Stampalia erfolgte erst 1413. Die Querini siedelten auf der Insel eine Gruppe von Kolonen an, die das Eiland vor Pirateneinfällen schützen sollten. Diese Maßnahme war aber umsonst, denn 1537 fiel Stampalia in die Hände der Türken. Der venezianischen Familie blieb nur noch die Ehre des Doppelnamens.

Im Quattrocento investierten die Querini in Grundbesitz und vergrößerten durch den Handel im östlichen Mittelmeer ihr schon beachtliches Vermögen erheblich.

Obwohl die Familie seit 1238 in Santa Maria Formosa wohnte, wurde ihr Palast erst zwischen 1513 und 1523 erbaut. Auf dem Venedig-Plan von Jacopo de'Barbari aus dem Jahre 1500 ist er nämlich noch nicht eingezeichnet. Der Erwerb der offensichtlich vormals dort befindlichen Gebäude, auf deren Grund das herrschaftliche Haus errichtet

La tradition la plus ancienne, qui prend parfois des aspects légendaires, veut que les Querini descendent de la *Gens Sulpicia* de Rome, ville qu'ils auraient abandonnée pour s'établir à Padoue, d'où, pour échapper aux invasions barbares, ils se seraient réfugiés à Torcello et ensuite à Rialto à l'époque des origines de Venise.

Historiquement, cette famille apparaît dans la ville au XIIème siècle et elle est divisée en plusieurs branches, parmi lesquelles celle de Santa Maria Formosa qui semble avoir vécu en cet endroit depuis 1238 et qui participait déjà activement à la vie politique de la ville.

La tradition veut que le deuxième nom, Stampalia, ait été ajouté après l'achat de l'île des Sporades qui porte ce nom par un Querini, banni de la ville en 1310 pour sa participation à la conspiration de Baiamonte Tiepolo. En réalité, Iseppo Querini de Santa Maria Formosa fut banni, mais plus tard, pour avoir conspiré avec le doge traître Marin Falier, décapité en 1355. L'achat par Stampalia eut lieu des années plus tard, en 1413. Les Querini tentèrent en vain de peupler l'île en y transférant un groupe de colons censés la défendre contre les attaques des pirates, mais en 1537, elle tomba aux mains des Turcs et il ne resta à la famille vénitienne que la fierté de son double patronyme.

Au XVème siècle, les Querini investirent en propriétés terriennes et accrurent de manière importante un patrimoine déjà conséquent grâce au commerce en Méditerranée orientale.

La construction de leur palais, même s'ils habitaient à Santa Maria Formosa depuis 1238, a été réalisée entre 1513 et 1523. Vu qu'on n'en trouve aucune trace sur le plan de Venise de Jacopo de'Barbari de 1500, mais qu'en 1514 l'achat des bâtiments est enregistré, cela prouve la préexistence de ce qui deviendra ensuite la maison de la famille. Elle est déjà habitée en 1522 car on trouve des dépenses faites pour la demeure où, deux ans plus tard, une Querini fêtera ses noces.

On ignore qui a conçu le palais, dont la disposition est traditionnelle avec une façade animée de deux fenêtres multiples avec des

later, the marriage of one of the Querini girls was celebrated there.

The palace has no precise paternity from the point of view of its design. It has a traditional layout and a façade animated by two rows of mullioned windows with balconies on the first and second floors. The building impresses one as the dignified residence of a family of the mercantile nobility which did not indulge in self-glorifying architectural pomp.

The history of the palace and its extensions reflects the progressive consolidation of the Querini Stampalia's public image during the first half of the 16th century.

In fact the building was improved, but there was no single original project: additions were made, with partial interventions dictated by convenience and pragmatism, always responding to the needs of solid economy; the palace was decorated with paintings by Bonifacio de'Pitàti and Palma il Vecchio.

New additions and further extensions were also made to the palace in the first half of the 17th century, to emphasise the family's prestige. But this was also the most troubled time for the Querinis and for the palace: it became the scene of obscure disturbances, the starting point for the departure of punitive expeditions in the surrounding district, the meeting place for gangs of thugs.

The Querini brothers Polo and Francesco committed all sorts of crimes both here and in their properties in Cologne, but Francesco fell in 1659 to the hand of Vettore Grimani Calergi (for whom he had attempted to lay a trap, animated by deep-seated enmity).

But moral disapproval and the resulting legal battles did not distract them from taking part in Venetian public life. Polo Querini became Procurator of St. Mark against the payment of twenty thousand five hundred ducats, and the family image acquired a new respectability as a result of the marriage of his daughter Elisabetta to Silvestro Valier, the future doge. In an official ceremony of 1694, Elisabetta rose to the highest position of the State, thus satisfying a long-cherished wish of the noblemen of the Querini household.

At the same time, the palace at Santa Maria Formosa continued to spread out, so that in the 18th century it was apparently connected by means of an overhead passage over the canal to the opposite house on the square. This was then placed in communication with the church, which could thus be reached directly from the palace.

werden sollte, wurde im Jahre 1514 in das Stadtregister eingetragen. 1522 war das Haus bereits bewohnt, denn in diesem Jahr erfolgten belegte Ausgaben für den Wohnsitz. Zwei Jahre später fand im Palast die Hochzeit einer Querini statt.

Wer den Palast entworfen hat, ist nicht bekannt. Die Fassade der traditionellen Anlage wird im ersten und zweiten Obergeschoß von jeweils einem mehrbögigen Fensterband mit Balkon belebt. Das Gebäude wirkt wie der würdevolle Wohnsitz einer adligen Kaufmannsfamilie, die nichts von selbstverherrlichendem Architekturprunk hält.

Die Geschichte des Palastes und seiner Anbauten geht einher mit dem allmählich wachsenden öffentlichen Ansehen der Querini Stampalia, vor allem in der ersten Hälfte des 16. Jahrhunderts.

Der Palazzo wurde zwar baulich verbessert, es ist jedoch kein einheitlicher, ursprünglicher Plan überliefert. Die An- und Umbauten erfolgten aus Gründen der Vernunft und der Zweckmäßigkeit und wurden stets auf der Basis einer soliden Wirtschaftlichkeit ausgeführt. Bonifacio de'Pitàti und Palma il Vecchio schmückten die Säle mit Malereien.

Weitere Um- und Anbauten erfolgten in der ersten Hälfte des 17. Jahrhunderts, um das Ansehen der Familie zu vergrößern. Jene Zeit war allerdings auch die düsterste für die Querini und ihren Palast, der Zentrum finsterer Umtriebe und Schlupfwinkel von Räuberbanden wurde sowie Ausgangspunkt für Strafexpeditionen in die Umgebung war.

Die Brüder Polo und Francesco Querini begingen unzählige Verbrechen, auch in ihren Besitztümern in Köln. Francesco fiel im Jahre 1659 seinem Erzfeind Vettore Grimani Calergi zum Opfer. Er hatte ihm eigentlich eine Falle stellen wollen, in der er sich aber selbst verfing.

Trotz des moralischen Drucks und der folgenden Gerichtsprozesse nahmen die Querini weiterhin rege am öffentlichen Leben Venedigs teil. Für die Zahlung von 20 500 Dukaten wurde Polo Querini Prokurator von San Marco. Das Ansehen der Familie kam wieder zu Ehren, als sich seine Tochter Elisabetta mit Silvestro Valier, dem zukünftigen Dogen, vermählte. Im Jahre 1694 wurde Elisabetta durch ein offizielles Staatsbankett in das höchste Amt Venedigs berufen. So erfüllte sich für die Edelleute aus dem Hause Querini endlich ein langgehegter, doch bisher unerfüllter Traum.

Gleichzeitig wurde der Palast in Santa Maria Formosa wieder vergrößert und ausge-

balcons au premier et au deuxième étage; mais dans l'ensemble, l'édifice est la résidence digne d'une famille de l'aristocratie commerçante qui ne cherche pas à chanter sa gloire par le biais d'un déploiement de fastes architecturaux.

L'histoire du palais et de ses propriétaires reflète l'affirmation progressive de l'image publique des Querini Stampalia, en constante ascension au cours de la première moitié du XVIème siècle.

On procéda à des améliorations sur le plan de la construction, mais il n'existe pas un plan d'ensemble au départ, par ajouts, par interventions partielles dictées par des impératifs d'économie et d'opportunité, toujours en accord avec une solide gestion. Les espaces intérieurs furent décorés avec des peintures de Bonifacio de'Pitàti et de Palma le Vieux.

L'édifice fut rénové et agrandi au cours de la première moitié du XVIIème siècle, pour affirmer une fois de plus le prestige de la famille. Mais cette période fut aussi la plus sombre pour les Querini et pour le palais qui devint le théâtre de désordres et troubles, le point de départ d'expéditions punitives aux alentours, le repaire de bandes de voleurs.

Les frères Polo et Francesco Querini commirent toutes sortes de délits y compris dans leur propriété de Cologne, mais Francesco tombera en 1659 sous les coups de Vettore Grimani Calergi qu'il haïssait, et à qui il avait tendu une embuscade.

La pression morale et les vicissitudes judiciaires qui suivirent, ne les écartèrent pas de la vie publique vénitienne. Polo Querini devint Procurateur de San Marco après avoir déboursé 20 500 ducats, et à la même époque, la famille put redorer son blason, après qu'Elisabetta Querini eut épousé Silvestro Valier, le futur doge. En 1694, Elisabetta sera installée au poste suprême de l'Etat avec une cérémonie officielle, réalisant un désir resté insatisfait pour les hommes de la maison Querini.

Pendant ce temps, le palais de Santa Maria Formosa continua de s'étendre. Ainsi au XVIIIème siècle, il est relié par un passage aérien au-dessus du canal, à la maison se trouvant en face, laquelle à son tour fut reliée à l'église qui devint donc accessible à partir de la demeure.

Ces aménagements sont à mettre, bien sûr, en relation avec le nouveau prestige que la Dogaresse procurait à la famille. Mais cela faisait aussi partie de la ligne de conduite normale des Querini, qui à la fin du XVIIIème siècle, quand ils figurent parmi les famil-

These alterations were certainly linked with the new prestige that the Dogaressa had brought to the family, but they were also typical of the normal Querini line of conduct. At the end of the 18th century they were among the richest families in the city, and started further horizontal and vertical extensions of the palace.

The interiors were also updated from the point of view of their distribution and furnishings, but the façade (inasmuch as it was the reflection of lasting power and prestige) was not touched. Thus it remained in its 16th-century form to bear witness to centuries-old political and social traditions at a time when life in the Venetian Republic was on the decline.

In the 18th century, three of the Querinis – Polo and his two sons – became Procurators of St. Mark. But Polo's second son Girolamo was to rise to even higher honours: he entered the Benedictine order and progressively became a prelate of high rank by the name of Angelo Maria. He maintained contacts with the intellectual elite of the time, including Voltaire, Fénelon, Newton, Malebranche, Montesquieu, and Muratori.

First Archbishop of Corfù and then Bishop of Brescia, Prefect of the Vatican and founder of the Queriniana library at Brescia, he was a man of considerable talent and vast learning – a scholar, translator, editor and collector, as well as a theologian. Nonetheless, he maintained the principal features of his family – pride, ambition, and self-satisfaction.

He added to the fame of the Querini family and also of the Venetian Republic, to such a degree that he was counted among the *sommi tre geni patrizi* (three leading characters) together with Doge Marco Foscarini and the abbot and philosopher Antonio Conti.

Such vicissitudes are unfortunately no longer apparent from the present condition of the palace, which retains the layout of the end of the 18th century, when the last distributional alterations of the spaces were made and the furnishings were renewed.

The home underwent a "modern" renovation, according to the new principles of practicality adopted first by the rich bourgeois families and then followed by the nobility. In Palazzo Querini, the *portego* on the second floor was shortened and decorated with more simple ornamentation. The walls were divided into regular sections with classic-style stucco work on a green background and animated by refined cameos inserted

baut. Im Settecento war er sogar durch eine Brücke über dem Kanal mit dem gegenüberliegenden Haus verbunden. Dieses Gebäude hatte wiederum eine Verbindung zur Kirche, so daß man vom Palazzo aus direkt in das Gotteshaus gelangen konnte.

Die Bauveränderungen gründeten sicherlich auf dem neuen Ansehen, das die Familie durch die Dogaressa erworben hatte. Ende des Settecento gehörten die Querini zu den reichsten Familien Venedigs und veranlaßten weitere Palastumbauten.

Zu jener Zeit wurden auch Raumfolge und Ausstattung der Säle verändert. Die Fassade aber blieb unangetastet, da sie die lang während Macht und das Ansehen der Familie widerspiegelte. Mit ihrem Cinquecento-Formengut war sie Zeugin jahrhundertealter politischer und gesellschaftlicher Traditionen – und dies zu einer Zeit, als sich die venezianische Republik dem Ende neigte.

Im 18. Jahrhundert wurden drei Familienmitglieder der Querini, Polo und seine beiden Söhne, Prokuratoren von San Marco. Der zweitgeborene Sohn Polos, Girolamo, stieg jedoch zu noch weit höherer Würde auf. Nachdem er in den Benediktinerorden eingetreten war, wurde er unter dem Namen Angelo Maria ein hochgestellter Prälat. Darüber hinaus stand er mit der geistigen Elite der Zeit in Verbindung, mit Voltaire ebenso wie mit Fénelon, Newton, Malebranche, Montesquieu und Muratori.

Girolamo wurde Erzbischof von Korfu, Bischof von Brescia, Präfekt des Vatikans und gründete die Biblioteca Queriniana in Brescia. Wachen Geists und umfassend gebildet, war er ein Gelehrter, der als Literat, Übersetzer, Herausgeber, Sammler und natürlich Theologe in Erscheinung trat. Die Hauptwesenszüge der Querini – Stolz, Ehrgeiz und Selbstgefallen – legte er jedoch nie ab.

Er trug zum Ruhm der Querini und auch der Republik Venedig bei, und so kam es, daß er neben dem Dogen Marco Foscarini und dem Abt und Philosophen Antonio Conti zu den »sommi tre geni patrizi«, zu den höchsten drei Patriziern, gezählt wurde.

Die heutige Einrichtung des Palastes, die aus dem späten 18. Jahrhundert stammt, erinnert leider nicht mehr an die verschiedenen Begebenheiten aus der Familiengeschichte.

Im Settecento wurde die Raumaufteilung verändert und das Mobiliar erneuert. Gemäß den neuen Prinzipien der Funktionalität, die zuerst die wohlhabenden Familien bürgerlicher Abstammung und später das

les les plus riches de la ville, commencent de nouveaux agrandissements de l'édifice.

L'intérieur fut alors également modernisé à la fois du point de vue de la disposition des pièces que de l'ameublement, mais la façade, symbole de pouvoir et de prestige ne fut pas modifiée ; ses formes du XVIème siècle représentaient une image politique et sociale aux traditions séculaires au moment où la vie de la Sérénissime amorçait son déclin.

Au cours du XVIIIème siècle, trois des Querini devinrent Procurateurs de San Marco, Polo et ses deux fils. Mais le fils cadet de Polo, Girolamo, accéda à des honneurs bien plus élevés. En effet, entré dans l'ordre des bénédictins, il devint un prélat de haut rang du nom d'Angelo Maria. En outre, il entretenait des relations avec l'élite intellectuelle de son époque, avec Voltaire comme avec Fénelon, Newton, Malebranche, Montesquieu et Muratori.

Archevêque de Corfoue et ensuite évêque de Brescia, préfet de la Vaticana et fondateur de la Biblioteca Queriniana à Brescia, c'était un homme très intelligent et d'une grande culture : non seulement théologien, bien sûr, mais aussi écrivain, traducteur, éditeur et collectionneur. Cependant il conserve intacts les traits de caractère de la famille : l'orgueil, l'ambition et le narcissisme.

Il contribua lui aussi à la gloire des Querini et de la Sérénissime et fut cité comme l'un des « trois plus grands patriciens » de la ville avec le doge Marco Foscarini et l'abbé philosophe Antonio Conti.

Ces aspects, aussi glorieux soient-ils, de l'histoire de la famille Querini n'apparaissent malheureusement pas dans l'aménagement actuel du palais qui présente l'aspect qui lui a été donné à la fin du XVIIIème siècle, lorsque la distribution des pièces fut modifiée et le mobilier renouvelé pour la dernière fois.

La demeure subit une restructuration dans le sens « moderne », suivant les nouvelles règles de fonctionnalité adoptées en premier lieu par les riches familles d'origine bourgeoise, et suivies ensuite par l'aristocratie. Dans le Palais Querini, le *portego* du deuxième étage fut raccourci et décoré plus sobrement. Les murs sont divisés en compartiments réguliers avec des chandeliers de style classique en stuc vert pâle. Ils sont agrémentés par des camées dans les décorations au-dessus des portes. Les bustes en marbre, autre citation antique, rythment l'espace de la pièce. A l'instar des *porteghi* vénitiens, celui-ci est aussi meublé avec simplicité. Les fresques sont moins exubérantes et leurs motifs sont inspirés de l'Antiquité classique.

over the doors. A further memory of antiquity came from the marble busts regularly placed around the hall, which is fitted, as was typical of the Venetian *portego,* with a modest amount of furniture. Even the illusionistic effects of the frescoes were less exuberant and taken from models of classic antiquity.

As regards the furniture, the Querini home offers a typical example of the taste of the end of the century: divans, chairs and console tables become plainer, losing the redundant ornamentation that the virtuoso art of the carver had produced a few years previously.

When the last of the Querini Stampalia died in 1869, he willed the palace and all its contents, including the well-stocked library, the collection of paintings, the medals and all the other works of art, to become the home of a Foundation that would be open for use by scholars.

The "leitmotif" of the palace's history, the renovation and restoration which were repeatedly carried out over the course of the centuries (without altering its identity), has been picked up again in the present day. In fact, it was only a few years ago that the project by Carlo Scarpa was drawn up, principally to restore the ground floor of the building and the rear garden. The Venetian architect's intervention consisted of a "restoration, in modern terms, of those inalienable values of colour and light which have characterized and personalized the Venetian spatial environment".

The ground floor of the palace (which had been neoclassical in the previous century) has now been restored to the original form of the *portego* and has finally been repaired and protected from the insidious high tides. Moreover, the building has been connected to the little square opposite by a bridge which "undoubtedly represents the lightest and fastest linking arch to have been made in Venice in the past few centuries".

The little garden, completely restructured, includes the vestiges of the old palace, a well-curb and a Gothic lion inserted in the foliage and surrounded by the spray of the fountains which overflow into a mosaic tank. Once again, the dialectic relationship between ancient and modern structures has been emphasized, simultaneously exalting the original architectural values and pinpointing the functions to which the building is delegated.

Patriziat verinnerlichten, erfolgten Umbauten im »modernen« Sinne. So wurde der *portego* im zweiten Obergeschoß verkürzt und mit schlichteren Ornamenten ausgeschmückt. Die Wände zierten nun gleichmäßig angebrachte klassische Stuckarbeiten auf grünem Grund, und in den Sopraporten glänzten erlesene Kameen. Ein weiteres Antikenzitat waren auch die Marmorbüsten, die die Weite des Saals rhythmitisierten. Wie üblich für den venezianischen *portego* wurde auch dieser nur spärlich möbliert. Die Fresken wurden schlichter gestaltet und ihre Motive antiken Vorbildern entlehnt.

Die Einrichtung des Palazzo Querini Stampalia spiegelt den typischen Geschmack der Jahrhundertwende wider: Sofas, Stühle und Konsoltische sind linear gestaltet und verzichten auf den überladenen Schnitzdekor der Jahre zuvor.

Das letzte Familienmitglied der Querini Stampalia, Giovanni, starb im Jahre 1869. Er bestimmte, daß der Palast mit all seinen Kostbarkeiten, der reichen Bibliothek, der Gemäldesammlung, den Medaillen und allen anderen Kunstwerken zum Sitz einer Stiftung für Gelehrte werden sollte.

Die im Laufe der Jahrhunderte erfolgten zahlreichen baulichen Eingriffe, die jedoch nie die Identität des Gebäudes veränderten, prägen die Geschichte des Palazzo Querini Stampalia. Dies läßt sich bis in unsere Tage verfolgen. Carlo Scarpa wurde mit der Renovierung des Erdgeschosses und der Umstrukturierung des rückseitigen Gartens betraut. Erst vor wenigen Jahren sind seine Pläne verwirklicht worden. Bei der Neugestaltung der Räume legte der Architekt besonderen Wert darauf, daß die typische Farbgebung und Lichtführung berücksichtigt wurden, die so charakteristisch für die venezianischen Palasträume sind.

Das Erdgeschoß des Palastes, das im vorigen Jahrhundert noch klassizistisch war, erhielt seine ursprüngliche Anlage zurück, wurde grundsaniert und vor dem regelmäßigen Hochwasser geschützt. Außerdem wurde das Gebäude durch eine Brücke, die »zweifellos leichteste und schnellste Verbindung, die in den letzten Jahrhunderten in Venedig verwirklicht wurde«, mit dem kleinen Platz bei der Kirche Santa Maria Formosa verbunden.

In dem umstrukturierten kleinen Garten sind Spuren des alten Palastes zu entdecken, etwa eine Brunneneinfassung und ein gotischer Löwe, die in das Grün eigebettet sind und von der gelungenen Symbiose zwischen Alt und Neu künden.

En fait d'ameublement, la demeure des Querini offre un exemple typique du goût fin-de-siècle : divans, chaises et consoles deviennent plus linéaires et renoncent aux surcharges décoratives en vogue les années précédentes.

Le dernier des Querini, Stampalia Giovanni, mourut en 1869, stipulant que le palais avec tous les biens qu'il contenait, c'est-à-dire la riche bibliothèque, la collection de peintures, les médailles et toutes les autres œuvres d'art, deviendrait le siège d'une fondation destinée aux érudits.

Les interventions partielles, les restructurations et les récupérations qui ont été effectuées au cours des siècles n'ont jamais modifié l'identité de l'édifice ; un véritable fil conducteur s'est transmis jusqu'à nos jours. C'est en effet récemment que l'on a réalisé le projet de Carlo Scarpa qui avait pour but de récupérer le rez-de-chaussée du Palazzo Querini Stampalia et le jardin situé à l'arrière. L'intervention de l'architecte vénitien consistait en « un rétablissement en termes actuels des valeurs inaliénables de couleur et de lumière qui ont caractérisé et personnalisé l'espace et l'environnement vénitien ».

Le rez-de-chaussée du palais transformé dans un style vaguement néoclassique au siècle dernier, a été ramené à sa forme originale, et il a été restauré complètement et préservé des attaques des marées hautes. En plus, l'édifice a été relié à la petite place située en face, près de l'église Santa Maria Formosa, par un pont qui représente sans aucun doute l'arc de communication le plus léger et le plus rapide réalisé à Venise au cours des derniers siècles.

Le petit jardin, complètement restructuré, contient les vestiges de l'ancien palais, une margelle de puits et un lion gothique dans un cadre verdoyant et couverts par le bruit de l'eau des fontaines qui se déverse dans un bassin en mosaïques.

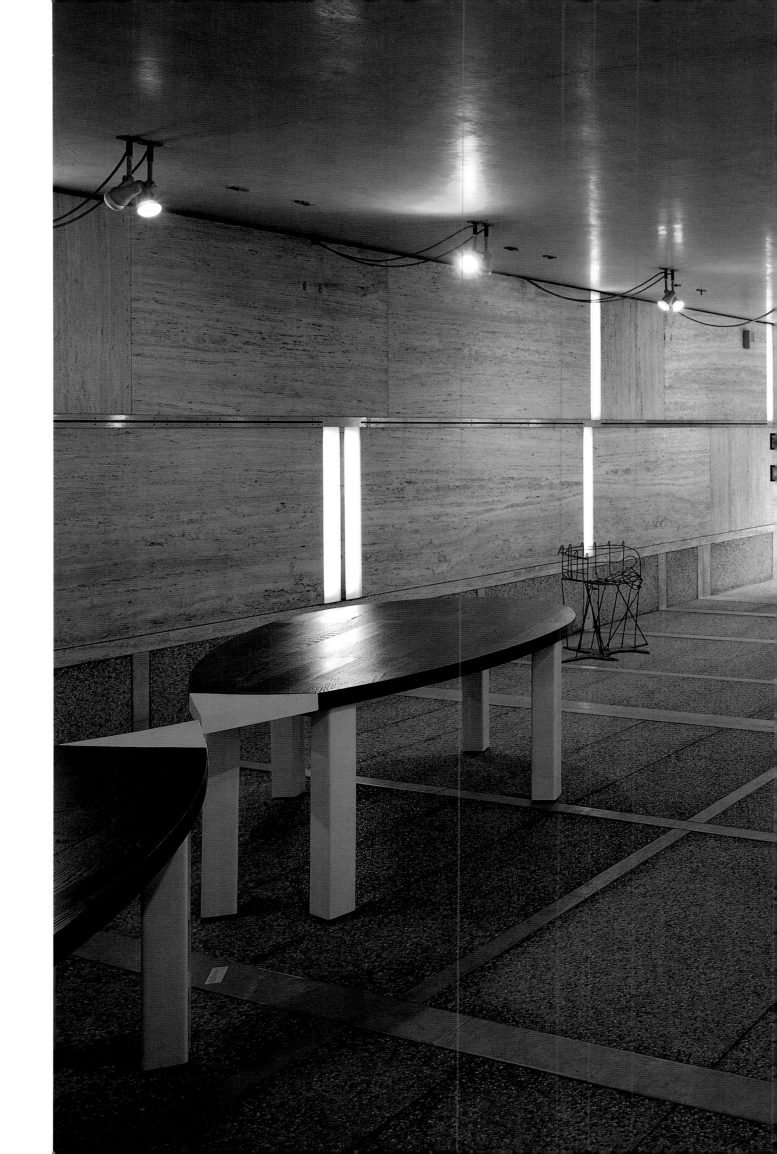

81 The Red Drawing-Room. The room takes its name from the wall covering, some of which is original and dates from the end of the 18th century. The great painting by Bartolomeo Nazzari represents the most famous member of the Querini household, Cardinal Angelo Maria. From the ceiling, there hangs a branching chandelier with floral decorations, made in Murano at the end of the 18th century.

82/83 The *portego* on the ground floor leading to the garden, as restored by Carlo Scarpa. The panels lining the walls are made of slabs of travertine separated by luminous pilasters that lie flush with the wall.

84 The Green Drawing-Room. The furniture, like the mirror, dates back to the end of the 18th century. The wall is hung with a painting representing Daniele IV Dolfin, Provveditore Generale da Mar, by Francesco Zugno. On the ceiling is an allegorical fresco enclosed in a stucco illusionist moulding with solid foliage scrolls, a pattern which was very popular during this period.

85 Jacopo Guarana (?), *Nuptial Allegory.* The fresco decorates the ceiling of the green drawing-room and may have been ordered for the marriage of Alvise Maria Querini to Maria Teresa Lippomano in 1790. The stucco oval which encloses the composition has decorations taken from the world of archaeology.

86 The *portego* on the second floor with its double portal. The simple decor, the decoration on the walls, which is divided into regular sections by delicate panels of pale green stucco, and the insertion of cameos over the doors are typical of the late 18th century.

87 The garden at the rear of the *portego* on the ground floor, with the pool of water and the palace entrance.

87 Detail of the ground floor.

81 Roter Saal. Dieser Salon verdankt seinen Namen den Tapeten, die zum Teil noch original aus dem späten 18. Jahrhundert sind. Das großformatige Gemälde Bartolomeo Nazzaris zeigt die berühmteste Persönlichkeit aus dem Hause Querini – Kardinal Angelo Maria. Von der Decke hängt ein großer Kronleuchter mit Blütendekor, der Ende des 18. Jahrhunderts auf Murano entstand.

82/83 Der von Carlo Scarpa umstrukturierte *portego* im Erdgeschoß, der zum Garten weist. Die Wandverkleidung besteht aus Travertinplatten und aus Leuchtstoffröhren, die Milchglas abschirmt und die vollkommen plan in die Steinverkleidung integriert sind.

84 Grüner Saal. Das Mobiliar und der Wandspiegel stammen aus dem späten 18. Jahrhundert. An der Wand hängt ein Gemälde von Francesco Zugno, auf dem Daniele IV. Dolfin, Generalinspekteur zur See, dargestellt ist. Die Decke schmückt ein Fresko mit allegorischer Darstellung, das eine Stuckdekoration mit dichten Pflanzenvoluten einfaßt – ein in jener Epoche weitverbreitetes Motiv.

85 Jacopo Guarana (?), *Allegorie der Hochzeit.* Dieses Fresko schmückt die Decke des Grünen Saals und wurde wohl anläßlich der Vermählung von Alvise Maria Querini und Maria Teresa Lippomano im Jahre 1790 ausgeführt. Die Stuckarbeiten, die das Oval umgeben, zeigen antike Motive.

86 *Portego* des zweiten Obergeschosses mit Doppelportal. Die schlichte Raumausstattung, die die Wand unterteilenden zarten Stuckverzierungen auf grünem Grund und die erlesenen Kameen in den Sopraporten sind typisch für den Geschmack des späten 18. Jahrhunderts.

87 Der Garten hinter dem *portego* im Erdgeschoß mit Wasserbecken und Eingang zum Palast.

87 Detail der Eingangshalle im Erdgeschoß.

81 Salon rouge. Il doit son nom à la tapisserie qui date en partie de la fin du XVIIIème siècle. La grande toile de Bartolomeo Nazzari représente le personnage le plus célèbre de la maison Querini, le cardinal Angelo Maria. Au plafond, un grand lustre aux bras décorés de fleurs, fabriqué à Murano à la fin du XVIIIème siècle.

82/83 *Portego* du rez-de-chaussée, côté jardin, dans la restructuration de Carlo Scarpa. Les panneaux recouvrant les murs sont en plaques de travertin où sont intégrées des lampes-colonnes en verre opalin .

84 Salon vert. Le mobilier comme la coiffeuse datent de la fin du XVIIIème siècle. Sur le mur, la peinture représentant Daniele IV Dolfin, inspecteur général des mers, exécutée par Francesco Zugno. Au plafond on peut admirer une fresque allégorique entourée par un cadre en stuc à volutes de végétaux, motif très courant en Europe à cette époque.

85 Jacopo Guarana (?), *Allégorie Nuptiale.* La fresque orne le plafond du Salon vert, elle aurait été exécutée à l'occasion des noces d'Alvise Maria Querini et Maria Teresa Lippomano en 1790. La forme ovale en stuc qui entoure la composition présente des décorations inspirées de l'Antique.

86 *Portego* du deuxième étage avec double porte. La décoration murale répartie en sections régulières par des chandeliers en stuc vert pâle, et l'ajout de camées sur les bas-relief au-dessus des portes est significatif de la tendance des goûts à la fin du XVIIIème siècle.

87 Jardin à l'arrière du hall au rez-de-chaussée avec le bassin et l'entrée du palais.

87 Détail du rez-de-chaussée.

PALAZZO   MALIPIERO

a S. Samuele   Sopra   Canal   Grande

PALAZZO MALIPIERO

a S. Samuele Sopra Canal Grande

68

Luca Carlevarys del. et inc.

PALAZZO CAPPELLO, MALIPIERO, BARNABÒ

The original body of the palace, which stands on the right bank of the Grand Canal in Campo San Samuele, was probably Byzantine, as suggested by the great portal on the façade facing the square, decorated with an elegant frieze of branches.

At the beginning of the 15th century, it was apparently purchased by the branch of the large Cappello family which had taken up residence in the parish of San Samuele, and it was then that a new floor was added to the building.

The purchase and extension of the building were due to Pancrazio II Cappello, head of the San Samuele branch of the family. He kept the two floors of the palace for himself and his relations, renting out the mezzanine floors.

The Cappellos were one of the most active and productive families in the city, where they resided until the 19th century. They were involved in political life as tribunes, doge's counsellors, magistrates, ambassadors, men of arms and, above all, procurators.

Pancrazio II was also a personality in the public eye; although the events of his life have not yet been fully studied, we know that he was appointed Procurator after acting as the governor of Trebizond. Despite their prestigious positions and services to the state, the Cappellos could never boast of having a doge in the family.

Their wealth and social position had led to a whole series of marriages, especially on the female side of the family, with members of equally prestigious Venetian noble families, which gave rise to very strong alliances.

The famous Bianca (who belonged to the Cappello family, but to the Sant'Aponal branch and not to the San Samuele branch) fell in love with a Florentine called Pietro Bonaventuri, fled with him and then was abandoned by him. But in Florence, this Venetian noblewoman met Francesco, the son of Cosimo de'Medici; the relationship between the two aroused a great scandal, but once consecrated by marriage after Francesco's wife had died and he had taken his father's place as Grand Duke, Bianca re-

Der ursprüngliche Baukörper des Palastes, der am rechten Ufer des Canal Grande am Campo San Samuele steht, stammt vermutlich aus byzantinischer Zeit, wovon das große, mit raffiniertem Rankenwerk geschmückte Portal an der Fassade zum Campo hin zeugt.

Anfang des 15. Jahrhunderts erwarben die Cappello das Gebäude, und zwar jener Zweig der großen Familie, der im Gemeindegebiet von San Samuele wohnte.

Der Käufer des Palazzo war Pancrazio II. Cappello, der Stammvater des Familienzweiges von San Samuele. Er ließ auf das Gebäude ein weiteres Stockwerk setzen. Die beiden Obergeschosse behielt er für sich und seine Angehörigen. Die Halbgeschosse hingegen vermietete er.

Die Cappello waren eine der aktivsten Familien der Lagunenstadt, in der sie bis zum 19. Jahrhundert lebten. Sie nahmen am politischen Leben als Tribunen, Berater des Dogen, Magistratsherren, Botschafter, Militärs und vor allem als Prokuratoren rege teil. Auch Pancrazio II. war sehr prominent. Zwar weist seine Vita einige Lücken auf, man weiß jedoch, daß er zum Prokurator ernannt wurde, nachdem er Vogt in Trabzon gewesen war. Trotz der bedeutenden Ämter, die sie bekleideten, und trotz ihrer Dienste für den Staat konnten sich die Cappello keines Dogen in ihrer Familie rühmen.

Ihr Reichtum und ihre hohe gesellschaftliche Stellung führten, vor allem bei den weiblichen Familienmitgliedern, zu einer Reihe von Vermählungen mit Angehörigen ebenso angesehener venezianischer Familien. So wurden feste Bündnisse geschaffen.

Zur Familie der Cappello, wenn auch nicht zum Zweig von San Samuele sondern zu dem von Sant'Aponal, gehörte auch die berühmte Bianca, die sich in einen gewissen Pietro Bonaventuri aus Florenz verliebte, mit ihm durchbrannte und dann von ihm verlassen wurde. In der Stadt am Arno lernte die venezianische Adlige Francesco de'Medici, den Sohn Cosimos, kennen und lieben. Ihr Verhältnis sorgte für einen Skandal. Nach dem Tod von Francescos Ehefrau heirateten die beiden jedoch. Anstelle seines Vaters war inzwischen Francesco Großherzog gewor-

Le premier noyau du palais qui se dresse sur la rive droite du Grand Canal, à Campo San Samuele, fut probablement byzantin, comme en témoigne le grand portail de la façade donnant sur la place, orné d'une frise raffinée à motifs ornementaux en vrilles végétales.

Il semble qu'au début du XVème siècle il ait été acheté par cette branche de la grande famille Cappello qui s'était établie dans la paroisse de San Samuele, et ce fut à ce moment-là que l'édifice fut surélevé d'un étage.

L'auteur de l'achat et de l'agrandissement fut Pancrazio II Cappello, l'aïeul de la branche de San Samuele qui conserva pour lui-même et pour ses proches les deux étages du palais, donnant les entresols en location.

Les Cappello furent l'une des familles les plus actives et productives de la ville lagunaire, où ils se révèlent être présents depuis le XIXème siècle, engagés dans la vie politique en qualité de tribuns, conseillers du doge, magistraux, ambassadeurs, hommes d'armes et surtout procurateurs.

Pancrazio II fut lui aussi un personnage très en vue ; bien que les vicissitudes de sa vie n'aient pas encore toutes été éclaircies, on sait qu'il fut investi de la dignité de Procurateur après avoir été bailli à Trébizonde. Malgré les charges prestigieuses et les services rendus à la patrie, les Cappello ne purent toutefois jamais se vanter de la présence d'un doge dans leur famille. Leur richesse et leur position sociale affirmée avaient déterminé toute une série de mariages, surtout dans le camp familial féminin, avec des membres de familles vénitiennes aussi prestigieuses, créant des alliances extrêmement solides.

A la souche des Cappello, même s'il s'agissait de la branche de Sant'Aponal et non de San Samuele, appartint la célèbre Bianca qui, s'enticant d'un certain Pietro Bonaventuri, florentin, se résolut à fuir avec celui-ci qui ensuite l'abandonna. Mais à Florence, la grande dame vénitienne rencontra Francesco de Médicis, fils de Cosimo ; leur relation suscita évidemment un grand tapage, mais une fois qu'elle fut consacrée par le mariage, après la mort de l'épouse de Francesco, devenu

ceived all due honours from her own family and from the Venetian seignory, which made her the gift of a splendid diamond necklace.

The sudden death of Bianca and Francesco due to a mysterious disease within days of each other was sufficient to arouse the suspicion of poisoning, but to please the new Grand Duke of Florence, the matter was allowed to drop and the family in Venice was even forbidden any outward show of mourning.

In 1507, the considerable and well-consolidated wealth of the Cappello family and a partnership with another Venetian nobleman, Luca Vendramin, a relative of the Doge Andrea enabled them to open a bank at Rialto which was so highly reputed as to be selected for the Treasury's operations for payments outside the state.

The bank was closed on the death of Vendramin, but the Cappellos would not give it up and, with an imposing ceremony, it was soon opened again with Andrea as the family's representative. In 1537, when the Venetian Republic was involved in the war against the Turks and in considerable economic difficulties, it was he who made a donation to the state of twenty thousand ducats, in acknowledgement of which he was appointed Procurator of St. Mark.

At the end of the 16th century, the marriage of Elisabetta Cappello to Cattarino Malipiero prevented the splitting of the fortune of the Cappello family (which was at risk of dying out for lack of male heirs) and laid the foundations for the future restoration of the palace.

The Malipieros were another ancient Venetian family and were among those who had remained in the Major Council after the lockout of 1297.

The extensive Malipiero family had divided into various branches, which derived their wealth from trading of various kinds and from ship-building.

It would seem that the Malipiero family also included Lauro, who had taken Ottone (the third son of Barbarossa) prisoner at the naval battle of Salvore and had conducted him to Venice. It was to commemorate this occasion that they were allowed to add the clawed foot of the imperial eagle to the family's coat-of-arms.

In 1457, the family had also given Venice a doge, in the person of Pasquale, the "dux pacificus" as Sanudo defined him, who had succeeded to government of the state at the age of sixty-five after holding very important civilian and military positions.

den. Der verstoßenen Bianca wurde nun seitens ihrer Familie wie auch seitens der Signoria von Venedig, die ihr ein herrliches Brillantkollier schenkte, alle Ehre zuteil.

Als Bianca und Francesco im Abstand von nur wenigen Tagen an einer mysteriösen Krankheit starben, kam der Verdacht auf, daß sie vergiftet worden seien. Auf Wunsch des neuen Großherzogs von Florenz wurde der Vorfall allerdings mit Schweigen bedacht, und in Venedig verbot man den Angehörigen sogar jede Art von Trauerbekundungen.

Aufgrund ihres großen Reichtums, der auf soliden Anlagen basierte, eröffneten die Cappello im Jahre 1507 zusammen mit einem anderen venezianischen Patrizier, Luca Vendramin, Angehöriger des Dogen Andrea, eine Bank im Bezirk Rialto. Das Geldinstitut war so angesehen, daß es die finanziellen Auslandstransaktionen der Staatskasse übernehmen durfte.

Nach dem Tod Vendramins wurde die Bank zunächst geschlossen. Aber schon bald darauf erfolgte ihre Wiedereröffnung durch Andrea Cappello mit einer eindrucksvollen Feier. Andrea Cappello schenkte im Jahre 1537, als sich die venezianische Republik durch den Krieg gegen die Türken in großen finanziellen Schwierigkeiten befand, dem Staat 20 000 Dukaten, der ihn daraufhin als Anerkennung zum Prokurator von San Marco ernannte.

Als Ende des 16. Jahrhunderts Elisabetta Cappello Cattarino Malipiero heiratete, war der drohende Untergang der Familie gebannt, die ohne Nachkommen zum Aussterben verurteilt war. Gleichzeitig wurde die Basis für die zukünftige Restaurierung des Palastes geschaffen.

Auch die Malipiero gehörten zu den alten venezianischen Familien, die bei der »Serrata« (Schließung) des Großen Rates im Jahre 1297 Ratsmitglieder geblieben waren. Die weitverzweigte Familie gründete ihren Reichtum auf den Handel mit unterschiedlichsten Waren sowie auf den Schiffbau.

Den Malipiero gehörte angeblich auch jener Lauro an, der bei der Seeschlacht von Salvore den dritten Sohn Barbarossas, Otto, gefangengenommen und nach Venedig gebracht hatte. Zum Andenken an dieses Ereignis durfte er das Familienwappen um die Klauen des Kaiseradlers bereichern.

1457 stellten die Malipiero den Dogen. Pasquale, den Sanudo »dux pacificus« nannte, sollte, nachdem er wichtige zivile wie auch militärische Ämter bekleidet hatte, fünfundsechzigjährig den Staat führen.

Sechs Söhnen und vier Töchtern hatte Elisabetta Cappello das Leben geschenkt, als

entre temps Grand-duc à la place de son père, tous les honneurs furent réservés à Bianca aussi bien de la part de sa famille que de la part de la Signoria de Venise, qui lui offrit un splendide collier de brillants.

Atteints d'une mystérieuse maladie, Bianca et Francesco moururent soudainement à quelques jours l'un de l'autre, ce qui fit soupçonner un empoisonnement ; mais pour complaire au nouveau Grand-duc de Florence, on étendit un voile de silence sur l'événement, à tel point qu'à Venise on interdit une quelconque manifestation de deuil aux membres de la famille.

Les richesses considérables et solides des Cappello permirent en 1507, en association avec un autre patricien vénitien, Luca Vendramin, neveu du doge Andrea, l'ouverture d'une banque à Rialto, à tel point considérée qu'elle fut désignée pour effectuer les transactions financières du Trésor Public à l'étranger.

La banque fut d'abord fermée à la mort de Vendramin, mais les Cappello n'y renoncèrent pas et elle fut bientôt rouverte avec une imposante cérémonie par Andrea en représentation de la famille. Ce fut justement lui qui en 1537, quand la Sérénissime, engagée dans la guerre contre les Turcs, se trouvait dans de graves difficultés économiques, fit à l'Etat une donation de 20 000 ducats, qui lui valut, à titre de reconnaissance, la nomination de Procurateur de San Marco.

A la fin du XVIème siècle, les noces d'Elisabetta Cappello et de Cattarino Malipiero conjurèrent la dispersion de la richesse des Cappello dont la descendance était en train de s'éteindre, et jetèrent les bases du futur aménagement du palais.

Les Malipiero étaient eux aussi l'une des vieilles familles vénitiennes, et ils faisaient partie de ceux qui étaient restés au Grand Conseil durant le coup d'Etat de 1297.

La souche principale, numériquement accrue, s'était ensuite divisée en plusieurs branches, dont la richesse provenait des commerces les plus divers et de la construction navale.

Il semble que ce Lauro qui, dans la bataille navale de Salvore avait fait prisonnier Otton, troisième fils de Barberousse, et l'avait conduit à Venise, appartînt aux Malipiero. En mémoire de l'événement, il lui aurait été accordé d'apposer les serres de l'aigle impérial sur l'écusson de la maison.

En 1457, la famille donna un doge à Venise, en la personne de Pasquale – Sanudo l'appelait le « dux pacificus » – lequel fut

After giving birth to six male and four female offspring, Elisabetta Cappello died in 1609, leaving her husband and, after him, her sons as her heirs. This fortune was increased in a little over a year by the inheritance of her father's goods (which he had almost certainly willed to his grandson, son of Elisabetta and Cattarino, who bore his own name – Silvano).

In the course of the next twenty years, it was the constant concern of Cattarino, who was known to be a shrewd businessman, to increase his ancestral patrimony and match the amounts that his wife and father-in-law had brought by their death into the Malipiero fortune. Moreover, he established a trust which forbade any heirs to single out any part of the palace at San Samuele for sale. In the case of extreme necessity, the palace could only be sold as a whole and with the consent of the various parties concerned.

Having restored the Malipiero fortunes, Cattarino then saw to it that his other children would also share in the palace at San Samuele, which the grandfather had willed to Silvano alone. This he did by purchasing in his own right the entire first floor plus two-thirds of another floor and the adjacent land.

In his will of 1631, he states: "I purchased two-thirds of San Samuel below and all of it above and entirely rebuilt it." This means that the reconstruction of the outside of the palace dates from the first years of the 17th century, though in the 16th century it had already been renovated on parts of the mezzanine floors. This is demonstrated by a relief (placed over the door towards the church) where, in addition to the family coat-of-arms with the eagle's claws, there are the initials K M (Kavalier Malipiero), with the date 1622.

After taking care of the consolidation of the oldest part of the building towards the Grand Canal and the part behind it, Cattarino began to work on the façade. It received classic-style windows instead of the previous triple-mullioned windows and two new doors on the canal side. On the second floor, rectangular windows replaced the loggia, and the façade was ultimately decorated with balconies and columns.

The reconstruction was attributed to Baldassare Longhena and there is a theory that it could be considered one of his younger works, inspired by Monopola and Vittoria.

The reconstruction of the outside corresponded to the renovation of the interior, which reflects the magnificence and luxury of the home and was completed around the sixteen-sixties.

sie im Jahre 1609 starb. Das Vermögen fiel an ihren Ehemann und nach seinem Tod an ihre Söhne. Ein gutes Jahr später vergrößerte sich das Vermögen der Adligen um das ihres Vaters, der fast alle seine Güter seinem gleichnamigen Enkel Silvano, Sohn von Elisabetta und Cattarino, vermachte.

In den folgenden zwanzig Jahren galt die ganze Sorge Cattarinos, der als kluger Geschäftsmann bekannt war, der Vermehrung des von ihm geerbten Vermögens und dem Ausgleich der Güter, die seine Frau und sein Schwiegervater bei ihrem Tode in das Vermögen der Malipiero eingebracht hatten. Darüber hinaus verbot ein Fideikommiß den Erben, Teile des Palastes zu verkaufen. Der Palazzo durfte im Falle absoluter Not nur als Ganzes und mit Zustimmung der verschiedenen Parteien veräußert werden.

Nachdem er das Vermögen der Malipiero geordnet hatte, sorgte Cattarino dafür, daß der Palazzo di San Samuele, den nach dem Willen des Großvaters allein Silvano erben sollte, auch unter seinen anderen Kindern aufgeteilt wurde. Aus diesem Grund erwarb er einen Teil des Palastes und das Nachbargrundstück.

In seinem Testament von 1631 heißt es auch: »Ich kaufte zwei Drittel von San Samuel unten und alles oben und habe es ganz neu erbaut.« Daraus wird deutlich, daß die äußere Umstrukturierung des Palastes in den ersten Jahren des 17. Jahrhunderts erfolgte. Schon im Cinquecento war bei den Halbgeschossen Hand angelegt worden. So weist ein Relief über der Tür zur Kirche hin neben dem Familienwappen mit den Klauen des Adlers die Initialen K M (Kavalier Malipiero) und das Datum 1622 auf.

Nachdem Cattarino die Verbindung des ältesten Gebäudeteils zum Canal Grande mit dem dahinterliegenden Teil veranlaßt hatte, begannen die Umbauarbeiten an der Fassade. Diese erhielt klassische Fenster anstelle der Dreipaßbögen und neue Portale an der Wasserseite. Im zweiten Stock ersetzten rechteckige Fenster eine ehemalige Loggia, und schließlich wurde die Fassade um Balkone mit Balustraden bereichert. Die Fassadengestaltung wird allgemein Baldassare Longhena zugeschrieben, wobei man davon ausgeht, daß es sich um eines seiner Jugendwerke handelt, die von Monopolo und Vittoria inspiriert waren.

Den Eingriffen an der Fassade entsprach die um die sechziger Jahre des 17. Jahrhunderts vollendete Renovierung der Säle. Sie spiegelten den Prunk und Luxus des Wohnsitzes wider.

nommé à cette charge à soixante-cinq ans, après avoir occupé de très importantes fonctions aussi bien civiles que militaires.

Ayant donné naissance à six garçons et quatre filles, Elisabetta Cappello mourut en 1609, faisant hériter son mari et après lui, ses enfants ; au patrimoine de la grande dame s'ajouta, au bout d'à peine un an, celui de son père qui léguait presque tous ses biens à son petit-fils, fils d'Elisabetta et de Cattarino, lequel portait le même prénom que lui, Silvano.

Durant les vingt années qui suivirent, le souci permanent de Cattarino, en homme d'affaire averti, fut de développer son propre patrimoine ancestral et de racheter de tout grief ce que sa femme et son beau-père avaient fait confluer, avec leur décès, dans la fortune Malipiero. En outre, par un fidéicommis, il interdisait aux héritiers d'aliéner individuellement des secteurs du palais de San Samuele ; en cas de nécessité extrême, on aurait pu vendre uniquement en bloc avec l'accord de toutes les parties.

Le patrimoine des Malipiero étant redressé, Cattarino veilla ensuite à garantir la possession d'une partie du palais de San Samuele, dont l'unique héritier devait être Silvano par la volonté du grand-père, à ses autres enfants et il le fit en achetant à son compte la totalité de l'étage noble plus les deux-tiers d'un autre étage, ainsi que le terrain attenant.

En effet, dans son testament de 1631, il affirme : « J'achetai deux-tiers de San Samuele en bas et le tout en haut et le fis refaire à neuf » ; la restructuration extérieure du palais, qui avait déjà subi des interventions dans le secteur des entresols au XVIème siècle, remonte par conséquent aux premières années du XVIIème, comme il apparaît d'après un relief placé sur la porte du côté de l'église où, à côté de l'écusson de la famille avec les serres de l'aigle, on distingue les initiales K M (Kavalier Malipiero), accompagnées de la date 1622.

Cattarino, après avoir pourvu à l'unification de la partie la plus ancienne de l'édifice du côté du Grand Canal avec la partie située derrière, débuta les travaux de la façade qui fut dotée de fenêtres classiques au lieu des trilobées, et de nouvelles portes pour l'entrée sur l'eau. Au deuxième étage, des fenêtres rectangulaires remplacèrent une ancienne loggia, et la façade fut finalement décorée de balcons à colonnes. La restructuration a été attribuée à Baldassare Longhena dont il s'agirait d'une des œuvres de jeunesse, inspirée de Monopola et de Vittoria.

A la restructuration de l'extérieur correspond la rénovation des intérieurs qui

The inventory drawn up in 1670 on the death of Gasparo, son of Cattarino, mentions a room of stucco-work (in which the beams had clearly been lost to view), a so-called Gilt Room and a so-called White Room, a reception room for the noble ladies, and so on. The stately home was also furnished with three hundred paintings, plus the tapestries and the *cuori d'oro* which, now out of fashion, had been confined to the passageways. The furniture included a great many armchairs, chairs and stools, shelves and side tables covered with damask or lined with precious stones, lapis lazuli and porphyry, with cabinets and chests.

In the *portego,* in addition to the family portraits, there was a handsome collection of weaponry, some of which bore the Malipiero coat-of-arms.

The palace was one of the richest and most hospitable in Venice, worthy of the rank of its owners.

The fortunes of the Malipieros, however, were on the decline, mainly due to the absence of male heirs. This led to the passage of all their goods into the hands of the Querini and later of the Balbi family.

Many other owners followed between the end of the 19th and the beginning of the 20th centuries, until the palace was purchased by Marco Barnabo, originally from the Cadore area. One of his 15th-century ancestors, the Consul Oliviero, had been in contact (quite by chance) with the Admiral of the Venetian Republic, Andrea Malipiero (Venice's Representative in the Cadore area), to solve a long-standing problem regarding land taxation.

The palace was restored and returned to its original splendour, preserving its layout virtually intact. The gallery and ample *portego,* with its beautiful beamed ceiling (once decorated with allegories by Padovanino) and the vast drawing-rooms to which it offers access, were provided with new furnishings and paintings of past centuries, as all the Malipiero family's goods had been dispersed.

There is a particular charm in the ample garden on the Grand Canal banks. It arose on a small piece of land, the property of the Cappello family since the 16th century, which was subsequently extended by Cattarino Malipiero in the 17th and transformed for good into a garden in the 19th. At that time a little house on the edge of the Canal was demolished and the balustrade was built. The garden was subsequently decorated by Barnabo with the coats-of-arms of the Cappello and Malipiero families.

In dem 1670 beim Tod von Gasparo, einem Sohn Cattarinos, abgefaßten Inventar werden unter anderem ein Stuckzimmer, dessen Deckenschmuck offensichtlich verloren ist, ein sogenanntes Goldenes Zimmer, ein sogenanntes Weißes Zimmer und ein Audienzsaal für die Edelfrauen erwähnt. Der Wohnsitz war außerdem mit 300 Gemälden, zahlreichen Wandteppichen und *cuori d'oro* ausgestattet, die, da sie unmodern geworden waren, in abgelegenere Räume verbannt wurden. Zur Einrichtung gehörte auch eine größere Anzahl von Sesseln, Stühlen und Lehnstühlen, Konsoltischen und mit Damast überzogenen oder mit kostbarem Lapislazuli und Porphyr verkleideten Tischchen sowie Schränkchen und Truhen.

Im *portego* befand sich außer den Familienporträts die Waffensammlung. Einige Waffen schmückt das Wappen der Malipiero.

Der Palazzo war einer der reichsten und gastfreundlichsten Wohnsitze Venedigs und dem Rang seiner Besitzer würdig.

Da männliche Erben fehlten, neigte sich das Glück der Malipiero jedoch dem Ende zu. Das gesamte Vermögen ging in den Besitz der Querini und später der Balbi über.

Zwischen dem späten 19. und dem frühen 20. Jahrhundert wechselten die Eigentümer des Palastes häufig, bis ihn schließlich Marco Barnabò aus Cadore erwarb. Dies war ein einzigartiger Zufall des Schicksal, denn dessen Ahne Konsul Oliviero stand im 15. Jahrhundert in Kontakt mit dem Admiral der Serenissima und Repräsentanten der Republik in Cadore, Andrea Malipiero, um einen Streit über die Taxierung von Land zu schlichten.

Der Palast wurde restauriert und erhielt seinen alten Glanz zurück. Die Raumaufteilung wurde beibehalten. Die Galerie, der ausgedehnte *portego*, den einst eine allegorische Deckenmalerei Padovaninos schmückte, und die großen Salons wurden mit Möbeln und Gemälden vergangener Jahrhunderte ausgestattet, denn alle Einrichtungsgegenstände der Malipiero waren verschwunden.

Am Ufer des Canal Grande liegt der ausgedehnte, hübsche Garten. Das ursprünglich nur kleine Stückchen Land, das den Cappello seit dem 16. Jahrhundert gehörte, wurde von Cattarino Malipiero im folgenden Jahrhundert erweitert und schließlich im 19. Jahrhundert in einen Garten verwandelt. Zu jener Zeit war eine alte Kate auf dem Areal am Canal Grande abgerissen worden. Barnabò schmückte den Garten mit antiken Statuen und den Wappen der Cappello und der Malipiero.

reflétaient le faste et le luxe de la demeure, presque achevée aux environs des années soixante du siècle.

L'inventaire rédigé en 1670 à la mort de Gasparo, fils de Cattarino, mentionne entre autre une chambre des stuc, dans laquelle la décoration de plafond a manifestement disparu, une chambre dite d'or et une autre dite blanche, une chambre d'audience pour les grandes dames et ainsi de suite. La demeure était en outre garnie de trois cents tableaux, plus les tapisseries et les « cœurs d'or » qui, démodés, avaient été confinés dans les zones de passage. L'ameublement comptait aussi un grand nombre de fauteuils, sièges et chaises hautes, secrétaires et bahuts, consoles et petites tables recouvertes de damas ou bien revêtues de pierres dures, lapis-lazuli et porphyre.

Dans le *portego,* en plus des portraits familiaux, on pouvait admirer la collection d'armes, dont certaines marquées de l'écusson Malipiero.

La demeure, digne du rang de ses propriétaires, était l'une des plus riches et des plus accueillantes de Venise.

La bonne fortune des Malipiero était toutefois sur la voie du déclin, surtout en raison de l'absence d'héritiers masculins, ce qui détermina le passage de tous les biens aux Querini d'abord et aux Balbi ensuite.

D'autres propriétaires se succédèrent entre la fin du XIXème et le début du XXème siècle, jusqu'à ce que le palais fût acheté par Marco Barnabò, originaire de Cadore, dont un ancêtre au XVème siècle, le consul Oliviero, par un singulier hasard, avait eu des contacts avec le capitaine de la Sérénissime Andrea Malipiero, représentant de la République en Cadore, pour mettre fin à un litige territorial qui durait depuis des années.

Le palais fut restauré et retrouva sa splendeur d'origine, en conservant presque intacte la planimétrie. Tous les objets appartenant aux Malipiero ayant été dispersés, la galerie, le *portego* aux larges proportions, avec son très beau plafond autrefois décoré des fresques allégoriques de Padovanino, et les vastes salons furent remeublés avec un mobilier et des tableaux d'époque.

Sur la rive du Grand Canal, s'étend le vaste et beau jardin, dont le noyau principal, un petit terrain, propriété des Cappello depuis le XVIème siècle, fut successivement agrandi par Cattarino Malipiero au XVIIème siècle et transformé définitivement en jardin au XIXème. A l'époque, une petite maison qui se dressait aux bords du Canal fut abattue.

Palazzo Cappello, Malipiero, Barnabò

93 Drawing-Room with a finely-carved 18th-century cabinet and looking-glasses. There is a table lamp made from a Chinese vase plus a branching chandelier of Murano glas with floral decorations.

95 18th-century, Louis Seize Drawing-Room created by J. B. Lelarge (1743–1802). The armchairs have typical features: medallion-shaped backs "à la Artois", spiral-shaped legs, and a frame carved with ribbons and flowers.

93 Salon mit einer fein geschnitzten Vitrine und einem Wandspiegel aus dem 18. Jahrhundert. Eine chinesische Vase mit Lampenschirm fungiert als Tischleuchte, und von der Decke hängt ein Kronleuchter aus Muranoglas mit Blütendekor.

95 Salon aus dem 18. Jahrhundert im Stil Ludwigs XVI. von J. B. Lelarge (1743–1802). Charakteristisch sind die Armlehnstühle mit medaillonförmigen Rückenlehnen »à la Artois«, spiralförmigen Beinen und geschnitzten Rahmen mit Band- und Blumenmotiven.

93 Salon avec « bureau-trumeau » et glaces du XVIIIème siècle finement gravées ; « abat-jour » sur vase chinois et lustre à bras de Murano avec décors floraux.

95 Salon du XVIIIème siècle style Louis XVI de J. B. Lelarge (1743–1802). Les fauteuils avec dossier à médaillon, dit « à la Artois », pieds en spirale et cadre gravé à motifs de rubans et de fleurs, sont caractéristiques.

PALAZZO MOCENIGO

a S. Stae, Sopra il Rio

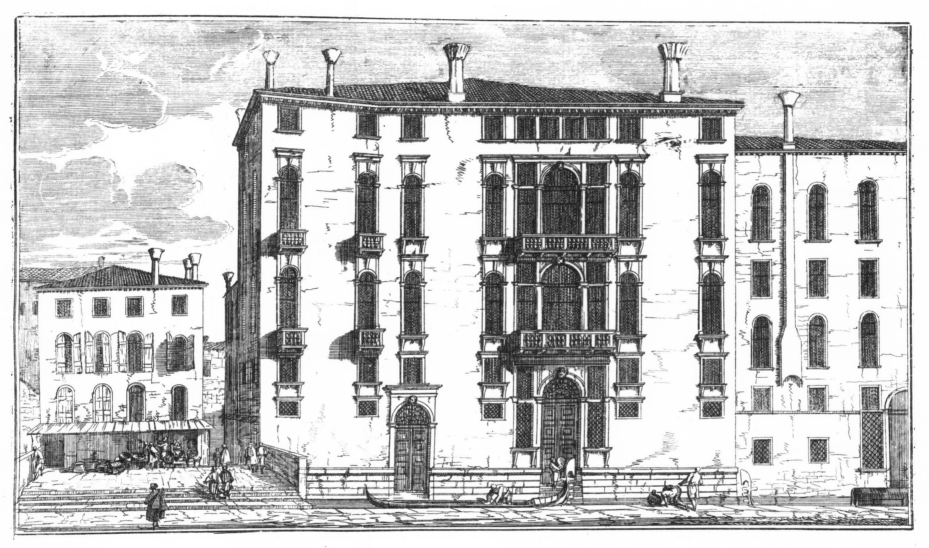

PALAZZO MOCENIGO

a S. Stae, Sopra il Rio

91

PALAZZO MOCENIGO

The Mocenigos were a family of very ancient origins, who settled in Venice around the year 1000. There is a suggestion that they were descended from the Capetian kings or from the *Gens Cornelia,* but according to the *Cronaca Altinate,* they would appear to have reached Venice from Musestre. They distinguished themselves with their particularly active role in the city's political and military life, without neglecting their patronage of the sciences and the arts.

The Mocenigos are one of the families of the Venetian nobility that provided the Republic with a considerable number of doges: in the course of four centuries, seven men belonging to various branches of the family rose to Venice's highest political rank. The first Mocenigo doges, Tommaso (elected in 1414), Piero (1474), and Giovanni (1478), had come to this position after actively contributing to the defense of the State. They had conducted successful military campaigns against the Turks in a period of wars aimed at consolidating the power of the Venetian Republic at sea.

The family grew in number and divided into separate branches, including that of San Samuele and another of San Stae (dialect form of Eustachio), taking the name of the parish where their palaces were built and distinguishing themselves by their wealth, prestige, and political offices.

The San Samuele branch of the family produced two doges. Alvise I, a fine scholar and patron of the sciences, was sent by the Republic as Captain to Cividale del Friuli and to Vicenza, then represented Venice as ambassador at the court of Charles V, and finally was elected doge in 1570. His name was linked with the defeat of the Turks in the battle of Lepanto in 1571. Alvise III was a man of arms who fought courageously against the Turks in the Peloponnesian war and was elected head of State in 1722. He dedicated himself to public works, ordering the paving of St. Mark's Square and the renovation of the decorations of the Bucentaur with sculptures by Antonio Corradini.

Alvise I was also responsible for establishing the right of primogeniture in the

Die Wurzeln der Mocenigo reichen weit zurück. Um das Jahr 1000 hatte sich die Familie in Venedig niedergelassen. Einigen Quellen zufolge stammte sie vom Königsgeschlecht der Kapetinger oder von der *Gens Cornelia* ab. Laut der *Cronaca Altinate* kamen die Mocenigo jedoch aus Musestre in die Lagunenstadt. Am politischen und militärischen Leben nahmen sie regen Anteil, ohne die Förderung von Wissenschaft und Kunst zu vernachlässigen.

Die Mocenigo zählten zu den Familien der venezianischen Aristokratie, die der Serenissima gleich mehrere Dogen stellten: innerhalb von vier Jahrhunderten wurden sieben Familienmitglieder, die verschiedenen Familienzweigen angehörten, in das höchste politische Amt berufen. Die ersten Dogen aus dem Hause Mocenigo, Tommaso (gewählt 1414), Piero (1474) und Giovanni (1478), hatten, bevor sie zu höchsten Ehren gelangten, aktiv für die Republik gestritten. In Kriegen, die die Seemacht Venedigs festigen sollten, hatten sie erfolgreiche Feldzüge gegen die Türken geführt.

Die Familie wuchs, und die zahlreichen Angehörigen teilten sich in verschiedene Zweige auf. Durch ihren Reichtum, ihr Ansehen und ihre politischen Ämter zeichneten sich die Familien von San Samuele und San Stae, eine mundartliche Form für Eustachio, besonders aus.

Zu den Mocenigo di San Samuele gehörten zwei Dogen: Alvise I. und Alvise III. Erstgenannter war Literat und Freund der Wissenschaften. Nachdem ihn die Republik als Hauptmann nach Cividale in Friaul und nach Vicenza gesandt und er Venedig als Botschafter am Hofe Karls V. vertreten hatte, wurde Alvise I. 1570 zum Dogen gewählt. Seinen Namen verband man auch mit der Niederlage der Türken in der Schlacht bei Lepanto im Jahre 1571. Alvise III. war ein Schlachtenführer, der seine Tapferkeit im Peloponnesischen Krieg gegen die Türken bewiesen hatte und 1722 in das Dogenamt aufsteigen sollte. Alvise III. ließ auch notwendige öffentliche Arbeiten durchführen. So wurde der Markusplatz gepflastert und der *bucintoro* (Prunkschiff des Dogen) mit

Les Mocenigo, une famille de très vieille souche, se sont installés à Venise aux environs de l'an 1000. Selon les archives, ils descendent des rois capétiens ou de la *Gens Cornelia.* Selon la *Cronaca Altinate,* ils seraient arrivés dans la cité lagunaire, venant de Musestre, et ils se distinguèrent par une participation souvent active à la vie politique et militaire, sans jamais oublier de protéger les sciences et les arts.

Les Mocenigo sont cités parmi les familles du patriciat vénitien qui donnèrent un grand nombre de doges à la cité. De fait, au cours de quatre siècles, sept personnes appartenant aux différentes branches de la famille furent portées au plus haut niveau de la classe politique. Les premiers doges des Mocenigo, Tommaso, élu en 1414, Piero, en 1474 et Giovanni, élu en 1478, avant de s'élever au principat, avaient mené des campagnes militaires victorieuses contre les Turcs en vue de renforcer la puissance navale de la République.

La famille s'agrandit et se répartit en plusieurs branches, parmi lesquelles celle de San Samuele et celle de San Stae, forme dialectale de Eustachio, se distinguèrent pour leur richesse, leur prestige et leurs charges politiques.

Deux doges appartinrent à la branche de San Samuele, Alvise Ier, homme de lettres et amateur des sciences qui, après avoir été envoyé par la République en tant que capitaine à Cividale du Frioul et à Vicence, puis comme ambassadeur auprès de Charles Quint, fut élu doge en 1570 et son nom est toujours relié à la défaite infligée aux Turcs lors de la bataille de Lépante en 1571. Alvise III, homme d'armes qui combattit valeureusement les Turcs lors de la guerre de Morée, arriva à la plus haute charge politique de l'Etat en 1722. Il se consacra aussi à des œuvres publiques, en faisant paver la place Saint-Marc et remplacer les décorations du Bucentaure (la galère de parade dorée) par des sculptures d'Antonio Corradini.

On doit aussi à Alvise Ier l'instauration de la primogéniture dans sa famille, avec un legs de 20 000 ducats et l'obligation pour l'aîné de s'appeler Alvise. Cette règle provo-

family, with a legacy of twenty thousand ducats and the obligation for the first son to be named Alvise. This gave rise to a number of cases of Mocenigos with the same name, especially in the second half of the 18th century, so the situation was facilitated by the use of nicknames.

The San Stae branch was established by Nicolò (1512 – 1588), brother of Doge Alvise I, who came into possession of the San Stae property as a result of the sharing of their father's inheritance. He left this to his sons Marcantonio and Tommaso, who were already living in the palace in the early years of the 17th century and enlarged it soon afterwards by incorporating a neighbouring house.

This branch of the Mocenigo family produced two more doges in Venice. Alvise II (1700 – 1709) had previously held some of the most important positions in the Venetian magistrature and had spent twenty thousand ducats for the building of the façade of the church of San Stae (organizing a competition which was won by the architect Domenico Rossi). Alvise IV, elected in 1763, had represented Venice on various occasions as ambassador to foreign states. In the city, among other positions, he had been the librarian of St. Mark's, patronizing literature and the arts and increasing the contents of the Library.

Architecturally, the palace at San Stae seems to date back to the end of the 16th or the beginning of the 17th centuries; in fact there are no reliable reports of its construction and subsequent alterations. The plan of Venice by Jacopo de' Barbari in 1500 indicates a sizeable, square building with a central courtyard, placed between the Salizzada di San Stae and the Rio Mocenigo. This was subsequently enlarged, incorporating adjacent properties and taking on its present appearance at the start of the 17th century.

The palace has two façades, one onto the *salizzada* and the other onto the Rio, which are virtually the same. They are characterized in the central block by large windows (two on the street side and three on the canal side) articulated in three sections, with lintels at the sides and an arch at the centre. The canalside façade has an ashlar-worked skirting panel.

The distribution of the spaces inside the building retains the typical features of the Venetian home, with a central *portego* used simultaneously for state reception purposes and for access to the other rooms.

The Mocenigos of San Stae continued to live in the palace until 1954, when the last

Skulpturen von Antonio Corradini neu verziert.

Alvise I. führte das Erstgeburtsrecht ein, das mit einem Legat von 20 000 Dukaten und der Verpflichtung verbunden war, den erstgeborenen Sohn Alvise zu nennen. Vor allem in der zweiten Hälfte des Settecento führte dies zu zahlreichen Fällen von Namensgleichheit. Durch ihren jeweiligen Beinamen lassen sich die einzelnen Familienmitglieder der Mocenigo allerdings voneinander unterscheiden.

Stammvater der Mocenigo di San Stae war Nicolò (1512 – 1588), Bruder des Dogen Alvise I. Nicolò kam infolge der Aufteilung des väterlichen Vermögens in den Besitz des Gebäudes in San Stae, das er seinen Söhnen Marcantonio und Tommaso hinterließ. Sie bewohnten den Palast bereits in den ersten Jahren des 17. Jahrhunderts und vergrößerten ihn wenig später durch Eingliederung eines Nachbarhauses.

Aus diesem Zweig der Mocenigo stammten zwei weitere Dogen Venedigs: Alvise II. (1700 – 1709) hatte vor seiner Wahl die wichtigsten Ämter der venezianischen Magistratur bekleidet und 20 000 Dukaten für den Bau der Kirchenfassade von San Stae bereitgestellt. Alvise IV. wurde 1763 zum Dogen gewählt. Er hatte Venedig mehrmals als Botschafter im Ausland vertreten und in der Stadt selbst zuvor neben anderen Ämtern auch das des Bibliothekars von San Marco bekleidet. Außerdem hatte er die Literatur und Kunst gefördert und die Bibliothek um zahlreiche Bände erheblich erweitert.

Der Palast von San Stae wurde Ende des 16. oder zu Beginn des 17. Jahrhunderts erbaut. Für seine Errichtung und die folgenden Umbauten gibt es keine gesicherten Belege. Auf Jacopo de' Barbaris Stadtplan von Venedig aus dem Jahre 1500 ist zwischen der Salizzada von San Stae und dem Rio Mocenigo ein großes Gebäude mit quadratischem Grundriß und Innenhof zu erkennen. Dieser Palast wurde später durch Eingliederung von Nachbarhäusern vergrößert und erhielt Anfang des 17. Jahrhunderts seine heutige Form.

Die beiden Fassaden des Palastes, die eine zeigt auf die *salizzada,* die andere zum Kanal hin, sind fast identisch gestaltet. Kennzeichnend ist der zentrale Baukörper mit dreiteiligen Fenstern, von denen sich zwei an der landseitigen Fassade befinden und drei an der Wasserseite mit bossiertem Sockel.

Die Raumaufteilung behält die dem venezianischen Wohnhaus eigenen Besonderheiten bei. Wie bei fast allen Palästen Vene-

qua de nombreuses confusions entre les Mocenigo, surtout au cours de la deuxième moitié du XVIIIème siècle, que l'on résolut en faisant appel à des surnoms.

La branche de San Stae descendait de Nicolò (1512 – 1588), frère du doge Alvise Ier. Après la répartition des biens paternels, il entra en possession des propriétés de San Stae qu'il laissa à ses fils Marcantonio et Tommaso, lesquels habitaient déjà au cours des premières années du XVIIème siècle le palais qui s'agrandit peu après en annexant une maison voisine.

Cette branche de Mocenigo donna deux autres doges à Venise, Alvise II (1700 – 1709) qui avait couvert avant son élection les charges les plus importantes de la magistrature vénitienne, et qui affecta 20 000 ducats à la construction de la façade de l'église de San Stae, pour laquelle il y eut un concours remporté par l'architecte Domenico Rossi. Alvise IV, élu en 1763, avait représenté à plusieurs reprises la ville de Venise comme ambassadeur auprès d'Etats étrangers et, en ville, parmi d'autres charges, il avait repris celle de bibliothécaire de Saint-Marc, protégeant ainsi les lettres et les arts et augmentant le fonds de la Bibliothèque.

De par sa structure architecturale, le Palais de San Stae semble dater de la fin du XVIème siècle ou début du XVIIème. Il n'y a pas d'informations claires sur sa construction ni sur ses modifications successives. Le plan de Venise de Jacopo de'Barbari de 1500, met en évidence un édifice important, de forme carrée, avec une cour centrale situé entre la *salizzada* (ruelle) de San Stae et le canal Mocenigo. Par la suite, celui-ci fut agrandi en annexant des propriétés voisines, pour prendre au début du XVIIème siècle son aspect actuel.

Le palais a deux façades pratiquement identiques, une sur la *salizzada* et l'autre sur le canal, marquées par la présence dans le corps central de serliennes, grandes fenêtres en trois parties, deux sur la façade côté terre et trois sur la façade donnant sur le canal.

La distribution intérieure des pièces respecte les caractéristiques propres à la maison vénitienne avec un *portego* central qui sert à la fois pour la représentation et le dégagement des pièces qui lui font face.

Le palais a toujours été habité par des Mocenigo de San Stae jusqu'à ce qu'en 1954, le dernier descendant de la famille, Alvise Nicolò, établisse dans un geste de clairvoyance que celui-ci serait légué à la ville de Venise qui devait en avoir l'usufruit pour en faire « une galerie d'art et compléter le Museo

descendant of the family, Alvise Nicolò, determined in a far-sighted gesture that it should be donated to the Municipality of Venice for use "as a gallery of art and an annex of the Correr Museum, with all the furniture, including the paintings, the family portraits and the archives…"

The apartment on the first floor in particular, being the home of the last Mocenigos, has kept the decorations and furnishings of the 18th and 19th centuries intact. The papers in the family archives show that the interior was completely renewed towards the end of the 18th century.

In fact, when Alvise IV was elected doge, the whole family, true to tradition, moved to the apartments in the Palazzo Ducale, where they remained for fifteen years, from 1763 to 1778. Not even the marriage in 1766 of the first son Alvise, nicknamed "Primo Kavalier", caused the ancentral home to be re-opened. But extensive restoration work was carried out in time for another marriage, of the latter's son to Laura Corner, who brought with her dowry the conspicuous commendam of Treviso.

It was in her honour that the palace was redecorated, as the rooms probably still had the traditional covering of leather with gilt impressions, the famous *cuori d'oro.* The new decorations were certainly motivated by this marriage but also by certain commemorative demands, as the Mocenigos had recently had a doge elected in the family.

The task of translating the family's glories and the recent marriage into painting was entrusted to Jacopo Guarana, an artist certainly not new to such undertakings. He painted the ceiling of the Red Drawing-Room with the *Apotheosis of the Mocenigo Family,* representing the usual allegorical figures such as Justice, Peace, and Fortitude. The *Nuptial Allegory* on the ceiling of what is now called the Green Drawing-Room, which was once the married couple's bedroom, illustrates the figure of the bride about to be transfixed by the dart of Venus, with other allegorical figures symbolizing Poetry, Love, Spring, and Plenty. Both frescoes are surrounded by a hexagonal illusionist decoration by Agostino Mengozzi Colonna, son of the more famous Girolamo.

The 18th-century furniture in the red Drawing-Room is of particular interest: apart from finely carved armchairs (some of which retain their original upholstery), console tables, a characteristic three-seater divan, and a large looking-glass, there is also the portrait of Giulio Contarini (father of Polis-

digs gibt es auch hier einen sogenannten *portego,* der repräsentativen Zwecken dient und von dem man gleichzeitig in die angrenzenden Zimmer gelangt.

Die Mocenigo di San Stae bewohnten den Palast bis 1954. In jenem Jahr bestimmte der letzte Nachkomme der Familie, Alvise Nicolò, weitsichtig, daß der Palazzo der Stadtverwaltung gehören sollte, um ihn »mit dem gesamten Mobiliar, einschließlich der Gemälde, der Familienporträts und des Archivs als Kunstgalerie und Erweiterung des Museums Correr…« zu nutzen.

In den Wohnräumen des ersten Obergeschosses ist die Ausstattung aus dem 18. und 19. Jahrhundert vollständig erhalten, da dieses Stockwerk die Residenz der letzten Mocenigo war. Aus den Inventarlisten geht hervor, daß die Räume zuletzt gegen Ende des 18. Jahrhunderts renoviert wurden.

Als Alvise IV. zum Dogen gewählt wurde, zog die ganze Familie in den Dogenpalast. Dort wohnte sie 15 Jahre lang, von 1763 bis 1778. Nicht einmal die Hochzeit des erstgeborenen Sohnes Alvise, genannt »Primo Kavalier«, im Jahre 1766 führte zur Wiedereröffnung des Hauses der Vorfahren. Erst anläßlich einer anderen Vermählung, nämlich zwischen dessen Sohn und Laura Corner, deren Mitgift aus der ansehnlichen Kommende von Treviso bestand, wurde der Palast wieder hergerichtet.

Der Palast, der vermutlich die traditionelle Wandverkleidung aus Leder mit Golddrucken, die berühmten *cuori d'oro,* aufwies, wurde neu ausgeschmückt. Anlaß für die neue Ausstattung war sicherlich diese Hochzeit, aber auch das Geltungsbewußtsein der Familie Mocenigo, die schließlich kurz vorher einen Dogen gestellt hatte.

Der erfahrene Jacopo Guarana wurde beauftragt, die Ruhmestaten der Familie und die Hochzeitszeremonie bildlich festzuhalten. Die Decke des Roten Saals bemalte er mit der *Apotheose der Familie Mocenigo.* Dargestellt sind allegorische Figuren wie Gerechtigkeit, Frieden, Stärke und Tapferkeit. Die Decke des heutigen Grünen Salons, der jedoch einst das Brautgemach gewesen sein muß, schmückte er mit der *Allegorie der Hochzeit:* Neben der Braut, die vom Pfeil Amors getroffen wird, erscheinen andere allegorische Figuren wie Poesie, Liebe, Frühling und Überfluß. Beide Fresken umgeben sechseckige Rahmen von Agostino Mengozzi Colonna, dem Sohn des berühmten Girolamo.

Die Einrichtung des Roten Saals stammt aus dem 18. Jahrhundert. Neben fein geschnitzten Sesseln, die zum Teil noch ihre

Correr, avec tout le mobilier, y compris les cadres, les portraits de famille et les archives… »

L'appartement du premier étage, qui servit de résidence aux derniers Mocenigo, a gardé dans leur intégrité les décors et l'ameublement des XVIIIème et XIXème siècles, vu que d'après les archives mêmes de la famille, il s'avère que l'intérieur fut complètement rénové vers la fin du XVIIIème siècle.

De fait, quand Alvise IV fut élu doge, toute la famille emménagea, selon la tradition, dans les appartements du Palais ducal où elle resta pendant quinze ans, de 1763 à 1778. Même les noces de l'aîné Alvise, surnommé « Primo Kavalier », en 1766 n'ont pas entraîné la réouverture de la maison. C'est à l'occasion d'un autre mariage, entre le fils d'Alvise et Laura Corner qui apportait en dot l'imposante commanderie de Trévise, que la maison subit une grande restauration.

En l'honneur de ces derniers, le palais fut redécoré ; ses pièces présentaient probablement le revêtement mural traditionnel de cuir à impressions dorées, les fameux « cœurs d'or ». Les nouvelles décorations furent certainement inspirées par cette union mais aussi par des exigences à caractère célébratif étant donné que les Mocenigo avaient eu récemment un doge dans la famille.

La tâche de traduire en peintures les gloires de la famille et le récent mariage fut confiée à Jacopo Guarana, artiste ayant l'expérience de ces entreprises. Il peignit sur le plafond du Salon rouge *L'Apothéose de la famille Mocenigo* avec la représentation des personnages allégoriques habituels, la Justice, la Paix, la Force et la Vertu Guerrière. Il réalisa *Allégorie Nuptiale* sur le plafond du Salon vert actuel qui fut sans doute à une certaine époque la chambre à coucher des époux. Dans celle-ci apparaît la mariée, sur le point d'être blessée par le dard de Vénus, en compagnie d'autres personnages qui symbolisent la Poésie, l'Amour, le Printemps et l'Abondance. Les deux fresques sont entourées d'un cadre hexagonal d'Agostino Mengozzi Colonna, fils de Girolamo qui est plus célèbre.

L'ameublement XVIIIème du Salon rouge présente aussi un intérêt particulier, en plus des fauteuils finement sculptés qui conservent encore en partie la tapisserie originale, on trouve des consoles, un divan caractéristique à trois places, une grande coiffeuse, un portrait de Giulio Contarini, père de Polissena, la femme du fils aîné du doge Alvise IV, orné d'un cadre aux sculptures raffinées, certainement l'œuvre d'Antonio Corradini qui avait décoré le bucentaure

sena, wife of the first son of Doge Alvise IV) held in a refined frame of elaborate carving. The frame is probably the work of Antonio Corradini, who had been responsible for the decoration of the Bucentaur for Alvise III a few years previously. The room is completed with 18th-century chandeliers, which may have come from the furnace of Briati, with a number of branches decorated with colourful flowers, the so-called *chioche*.

Other frescoes decorate the stately home. One of particular interest is found in the bedroom, which also contains an 18th century bed with a carved headboard, lacquered in green with an image of the Virgin at its centre. The fresco illustrates an allegory in which the winged Fame (blowing a trumpet) appears with Honour and Hymen (the nuptial symbol), with two cherubs supporting an amphora (the symbol of Plenty) and an oar (which possibly alludes to fortunate seafaring ventures). This composition by Giovanni Scagiaro (Asiago, 1726–1792), which clearly refers to family history, is surrounded by a circular frame, inscribed in an octagon interwoven with acanthus leaves, made by Giovan Antonio Zanetti.

Other artists also contributed to the pictorial decoration of the palace. In the reception room, Giambattista Canal produced four works in 1787 with putti, for fitting over the doors, which allegorically represent the *Four Seasons.* He also produced an *Allegory of the Family* which decorates what is now the dining room but was possibly once a bedroom.

Various paintings complete the interior of the palace. In the *portego* on the first floor there is a frieze under the ceiling with portraits of important members of the family, made between the 17th and 18th centuries. In various rooms around the house there are paintings celebrating special events, the so-called "Splendours of the Mocenigo Family", attributed to Antonio Stom.

Having been inhabited up until a few years ago by the last Mocenigos of San Stae, who preserved the family heritage with loving care, the palace is now one of the most significant examples of the Venetian nobleman's home. It offers a document of the final stages of a civilization which was to undergo radical changes in the course of only a few years.

originalen Bezüge haben, Konsoltischen, einem typischen dreisitzigen Sofa und einem großen Wandspiegel befindet sich in diesem Salon auch das Porträt von Giulio Contarini, dem Vater von Polissena, der Ehefrau des erstgeborenen Sohnes von Alvise IV. Das Bildnis faßt ein erlesener Rahmen mit fein gearbeiteten Schitzereien ein, vermutlich ein Werk Antonio Corradinis, der einige Jahre zuvor auch den *bucintoro* Alvises III. verziert hatte. Die Einrichtung ergänzen mehrarmige Kronleuchter aus dem 18. Jahrhundert mit polychromen Blütenornamenten, den sogenannten *chioche*. Sie stammen vermutlich aus der Glasbläserei Briatis.

Weitere Fresken schmücken den Palazzo. Besonders bemerkenswert ist dabei die Deckenmalerei im Schlafzimmer, in dem unter anderem ein Bett aus dem Settecento steht mit geschnitztem, grün lackiertem Kopfteil, das in der Mitte die Jungfrau Maria zeigt. Das Fresko thematisiert eine Allegorie. Neben dem geflügelten, Trompete blasenden Ruhm erscheinen Ehre und Hymenaeus, der Hochzeitsgott; zwei Putten tragen eine Amphore, Symbol der Üppigkeit, und ein Ruder, das vielleicht auf erfolgreiche Unternehmungen auf See verweist. Die Komposition Giovanni Scagiaros (Asiago, 1726–1792) bezieht sich offensichtlich auf familiäre Ereignisse. Sie wird von einem runden Rahmen eingefaßt, der wiederum einem von Giovan Antonio Zanetti ausgeführten Achteck mit Akanthusblätterwerk eingeschrieben ist.

Auch andere Künstler trugen zur Ausstattung des Palastes bei. Giambattista Canal führte im Jahre 1787 für den Empfangssaal vier Sopraporten mit Putten aus, die die *Vier Jahreszeiten* darstellen. Außerdem malte er eine *Allegorie der Familie,* die den heutigen Speisesaal schmückt, der früher wohl einmal als Schlafgemach diente.

Im *portego* des ersten Obergeschosses sind in einem Wandfries unter der Decke wichtige Familienmitglieder porträtiert. Die Bildnisse entstanden zwischen dem 17. und dem 18. Jahrhundert. Andere Gemälde, die nennenswerte Ereignisse darstellen, nämlich die sogenannten »Ruhmesblätter des Hauses Mocenigo«, sind auf verschiedene Räumlichkeiten des Palastes verteilt. Sie werden Antonio Stom zugeschrieben.

Gerade weil er bis vor wenigen Jahren von den Mocenigo di San Stae, die das Andenken der Familie liebevoll bewahrten, bewohnt wurde, ist dieser Palast eines der bedeutendsten Beispiele venezianischer Patrizierwohnsitze.

d'Alvise III quelques années plus tôt. Pour compléter le tout, la pièce est ornée de lustres du XVIIIème siècle, peut-être sortis des fours de Briati, munis de nombreuses branches à fleurs polychromes.

D'autres fresques décorent la demeure ; à signaler, celle de la chambre à coucher, qui contient notamment un lit du XVIIIème siècle à tête sculptée, peinte en vert avec au centre une illustration de la Vierge. Il s'agit d'une allégorie dans laquelle aux côtés de la Réputation, ailée, jouant de la trompette, on trouve la Gloire et Hyménée, symbole nuptial, avec deux amours qui portent une amphore, symbole de l'Abondance, et une rame qui fait peut-être référence aux campagnes victorieuses en mer. La composition de Giovanni Scagiaro (Asiago, 1726 – 1792), qui se rapporte évidemment à des événements survenus dans la famille, est située dans un cadre circulaire lui-même inscrit dans une forme octogonale avec des feuilles d'acanthe tressées réalisées par Giovanni Antonio Zanetti.

D'autres artistes ont également collaboré à la décoration de la demeure. Gian Battista Canal exécuta en 1787 pour le salon de réception quatre bas-reliefs au-dessus des portes, avec des putti qui représentent les *Quatre Saisons,* de même qu'une *Allégorie de la Famille* décorant aujourd'hui la salle à manger qui fut peut-être à une autre époque la chambre à coucher.

De nombreuses peintures complètent la décoration de la demeure. Dans le couloir du premier étage, une frise sous le plafond représente des portraits des personnages importants de la famille, réalisés entre le XVIIème et le XVIIIème siècle. Les diverses pièces de la maison abritent des peintures qui saluent des événements dignes d'intérêt ; ce sont les « Fastes de la maison Mocenigo » attribués au peintre Antonio Stom.

C'est parce que la demeure a été habitée jusqu'il y a peu d'années par les derniers Mocenigo de San Stae, qui ont conservé avec amour les souvenirs de la famille, qu'elle représente un des exemples les plus représentatifs des habitations patriciennes de Venise, d'autant plus qu'elle nous renseigne sur la phase finale d'une civilisation qui en l'espace de peu d'années devait subir des changements radicaux.

101 The Red Drawing-Room. The armchairs and console tables are from the 18th century, and some of the original wall covering has remained intact. The magnificent, elaborately-carved frame with figures, coats of arms, and floral decorations encloses the portrait of Giulio Contarini, father of Polissena (the wife of the first son of Doge Alvise IV).

102/103 The Red Drawing-Room. Armchairs, console tables and a large looking-glass with a carved frame, from the 18th century. The branching chandelier is particularly impressive, with its floral decorations, called *chioche*, probably made at the furnace of the Murano glass-worker Briati. The floor is Venetian *terrazzo* and contains the Mocenigo coat of arms at its centre. The carved three-seater divan dates back to the 18th century. The painting on the wall with a *Naval Battle* celebrates the clash near the isle of Sapienza between pirates and the Venetians under the command of Zaccaria Mocenigo, who did not hesitate to set fire to his ship, dying in the flames rather than fall into enemy hands.

104 Stately double door opens out into the long row of rooms.

106 Giovanni Scagiaro, *Allegory.* The fresco was done towards the end of the 18th century and alludes to an unknown event in the family's history. It shows a winged Fame, blowing a trumpet, with Honour, Hymen (the nuptial symbol), and two cherubs with an amphora and an oar, probably alluding to Plenty and to successful seafaring ventures respectively.

107 The reception room. A stucco band decorates the walls of the room. Over the doors there are more stucco works, in which Giambattista Canal painted four putti allegorically representing the *Four Seasons* in 1787. This detail shows the allegory of Winter. The 18th-century doors and neoclassical furniture are particularly noteworthy.

108/109 The *portego* on the first floor, to which access is through a double portal, topped by a split tympanum with the Mocenigo coat of arms supported by two putti. The frescoed architectural decorations of the walls are the work of the illusionist decorator Agostino Mengozzi Colonna. A frieze runs under the ceiling with 17th and 18th-century portraits of illustrious members of the Mocenigo family. Other family members are represented in the paintings on the walls.

110 Giambattista Canal, *Allegory of Mars.* The fresco was made in 1787 and decorates the ceiling of what is now the dining room but was probably originally a bedroom.

111 The palace's ground-floor *portego* is decorated with arms, busts and benches from the 18th century. The image of Lazzaro Mocenigo (1634–1665) is of particular interest in the history of the family: the admiral died when his ship caught fire.

101 Roter Saal. Sessel und Wandtische stammen aus dem 18. Jahrhundert, die Wandverkleidung ist zum Teil original. Erlesene Schnitzereien, Figuren, Wappen und Blütenmotive, schmücken den Rahmen des Porträts von Giulio Contarini, dem Vater von Polissena, Ehefrau des erstgeborenen Sohnes des Dogen Alvise IV.

102/103 Roter Saal. Sessel, Konsoltische und der große Wandspiegel mit geschnitztem Rahmen stammen aus dem 18. Jahrhundert. Besonders kostbar ist der Kronleuchter mit Blütenornamenten, genannt *chioche,* der vermutlich in der Glasbläserei Briatis in Murano angefertigt wurde. Der Bodenbelag aus venezianischem Terrazzo weist in der Mitte das Familienwappen der Mocenigo auf. Das dreisitzige Sofa mit Schnitzereien stammt aus dem 18. Jahrhundert. Das Gemälde, das eine *Seeschlacht* zeigt, erinnert an den Kampf zwischen Korsaren und Venezianern unter dem Kommando von Zaccaria Mocenigo bei der Insel Sapienza. Um nicht in die Hände der Seeräuber zu fallen, setzte Zaccaria sein Schiff in Brand, in dem er ums Leben kam.

104 Edle Flügeltüren eröffnen den Blick in die weite Saalflucht.

106 Giovanni Scagiaro, *Allegorie.* Das Fresko, das gegen Ende des 18. Jahrhunderts entstand, spielt auf ein nicht genau zu identifizierendes Familienereignis an. Zu sehen sind der geflügelte, die Trompete blasende Ruhm, Ehre und Hymenaeus, der Hochzeitsgott. Zwei Putten tragen eine Amphore und ein Ruder, die den Überfluß und die erfolgreichen Unternehmungen auf See versinnbildlichen.

107 Empfangssalon. Ein Stuckstreifen schmückt die Saalwände. Aus Stuck sind auch die Sopraporten, in die Giambattista Canal 1787 vier die *Jahreszeiten* versinnbildlichende Putten malte. Dieses Detail zeigt den Winter. Besonders edel sind die Türen aus dem 18. Jahrhundert und das Mobiliar.

108/109 *Portego* des ersten Obergeschosses. Zu diesem Saal gelangt man durch ein Doppelportal, dessen Tympanon von dem von zwei Putten gehaltenen Familienwappen der Mocenigo gesprengt wird. Die gemalten Scheinarchitekturen auf den Wänden stammen von Agostino Mengozzi Colonna. Unter der Decke verläuft ein Wandfries mit den Porträts illustrer Persönlichkeiten der Familie Mocenigo. Andere Familienmitglieder sind auf den Gemälden an der Wand dargestellt.

110 Giambattista Canal, *Allegorie des Mars.* Die 1787 ausgeführte Deckenmalerei schmückt den heutigen Speisesaal, der ursprünglich ein Schlafzimmer war.

111 Der *portego* im Erdgeschoß, der ursprünglich als Lagerstätte diente, ist mit Wappen, Büsten und Truhen aus dem 18. Jahrhundert ausgestattet. Die Büste zeigt Lazzaro Mocenigo (1634–1665), der beim Brand seines Schiffes umkam.

101 Salon rouge. Fauteuils et consoles du XVIIIème siècle avec tapisserie partiellement d'origine. Un magnifique encadrement avec sculptures, figures, armes et décorations florales pour le portrait de Giulio Contarini, père de Polissena, l'épouse du fils aîné du doge Alvise IV.

102/103 Salon rouge. Fauteuils, consoles et grande coiffeuse, avec un encadrement sculpté du XVIIIème siècle. D'une réalisation exceptionnelle, le lustre à branches avec décorations de fleurs certainement réalisé dans le four du muranais Briati. Le sol à la vénitienne de la terrasse renferme en son centre le blason des Mocenigo. Divan sculpté du XVIIIème siècle à trois places. La *Bataille Navale* sur le mur rend hommage à l'affrontement qui eut lieu près de l'île de Sapienza entre les corsaires et les Vénitiens commandés par Zaccaria Mocenigo qui, pour ne pas tomber aux mains de l'ennemi, n'hésita pas à mettre le feu à son propre navire, périssant dans l'incendie.

104 Les portes à double battant s'ouvrent sur une longue enfilade de salles.

106 Giovanni Scagiaro, *Allégorie.* La fresque réalisée vers la fin du XVIIIème siècle se réfère à un événement familial non identifié. On y trouve aussi la Réputation ailée sonnant la trompe, la Gloire, Hyménée, symbole nuptial, et deux Amours avec une amphore et une rame qui font certainement allusion à l'Abondance et aux campagnes militaires victorieuses.

107 Salon de réception. Une ceinture de stuc décore les murs de la salle. Les décorations au-dessus des portes sont également en stuc. Giambattista Canal les réalisa en 1787 ; elles représentent quatre putti symbolisant les *Quatre Saisons* : dans le cas présent, ce putto est une allégorie de l'hiver. Les portes du XVIIIème siècle et le mobilier néoclassique sont des pièces de prix.

108/109 *Portego* du premier étage auquel on accède par une double porte surmontée d'un tympan brisé par le blason des Mocenigo soutenu par deux angelots. Les décorations architecturales des murs sont des fresques réalisées par Agostino Mengozzi Colonna. Sous le plafond, une frise de portraits des XVIIème et XVIIIème siècles représente des membres illustres de la famille Mocenigo, d'autres sont représentés par les peintures murales.

110 Giambattista Canal, *Allégorie de Mars.* La fresque exécutée en 1787 orne le plafond de l'actuelle salle à manger qui était à l'origine une chambre à coucher.

111 Le *portego* du palais, au rez-de-chaussée, est décoré par des armes, des bustes et des bancs du XVIIIème siècle. Le buste de Lazzaro Mocenigo (1634–1665) est particulièrement représentatif de l'histoire de la famille ; ce dernier mourut dans l'incendie de son navire.

PALAZZO REZZONICO

PALAZZO REZZONICO ✶ PALAIS REZZONICO

Venise Joseph Kier Editeur Place S Mar N° 97

PALAZZO REZZONICO

The palace is one of the most prominent examples of Baroque architecture in Venice and was subject to a complex sequence of building activities which protracted its construction over about a century, before its final completion. Towards the middle of the 17th century, the project for the palace was entrusted by Filippo Bon, Procurator of St. Mark, to the most famous architect of the time, Baldassare Longhena.

But Longhena was unable to see his work completed: in 1682, when he died, the majestic façade onto the Grand Canal, with its triple door onto the water, had only reached the first floor. On the other hand, the rear of the building, which faced onto Campo San Barnaba, had been completed and the family had taken up residence.

However, as a result of economic problems, Filippo Bon's heirs were obliged to sell the palace, which should have become the symbol of their centuries-old activity as entrepreneurs. It was purchased in 1751 by the Rezzonico family, who originated from Lombardy and had recently acquired a noble title (in 1687) after paying a sizable sum into the exhausted coffers of the Republic. Giorgio Massari was commissioned to complete the building.

The young architect made some changes to the original project, especially in the second floor facing onto the Grand Canal. He also created an imposing entrance from the street with an impressive staircase leading up to the ballroom on the first floor. The ballroom was of unusual size and style and also in an unusual position by comparison with the traditional layout of Venetian buildings.

The work had to be done in a great hurry because the palace was to house the splendid festivities and celebrations that accompanied the election of Carlo Rezzonico, Bishop of Padua, as Pope under the name of Clement XIII in 1758.

Inventories of the goods contained in the palace illustrate what a splendid life the Rezzonico family led. Within the brief space of 50 years, they counted two cardinals (appointed by Clement XIII Rezzonico him-

Der Palazzo Rezzonico ist eines der hervorragendsten Beispiele des venezianischen Barock. Schwierigkeiten bei der Bauausführung verzögerten seine Vollendung um etwa ein Jahrhundert. Der Prokurator von San Marco, Filippo Bon, hatte Mitte des 17. Jahrhunderts den angesehensten Architekten der Zeit, Baldassare Longhena, mit der Errichtung beauftragt.

Longhena konnte die Vollendung seines Werkes nicht mehr erleben, denn als er 1682 starb, war die Prachtfassade zum Canal Grande mit dem dreifachen Tor erst bis zum ersten Obergeschoß gediehen. Der hintere Gebäudeteil zum Campo San Barnaba war jedoch fertiggestellt und die Familie bereits eingezogen.

Wegen wirtschaftlicher Schwierigkeiten sahen sich die Erben von Filippo Bon gezwungen, das Gebäude zu verkaufen, das zum Symbol ihrer jahrhundertelangen Unternehmertätigkeit hätte werden sollen. Im Jahre 1751 wurde es von den Rezzonico erworben, einer Familie lombardischer Abstammung. Ihren recht jungen Adelstitel hatten sich die Rezzonico 1687 durch die Zahlung einer ansehnlichen Summe in die leeren Staatskassen der Republik erkauft. Die Vollendung des Palastes vertrauten sie Giorgio Massari an.

Der junge Architekt nahm an dem ursprünglichen Entwurf einige Änderungen vor, insbesondere am zweiten Obergeschoß zum Canal Grande. Darüber hinaus schuf er einen eindrucksvollen Eingang von der Landseite her. Über eine imposante Freitreppe gelangte man in den Ballsaal im ersten Stock, der wegen seiner Größe und Ausstattung, aber auch wegen seiner Lage im Vergleich zur traditionellen Raumaufteilung der venezianischen Paläste recht ungewöhnlich ist.

Die Arbeiten müssen rasch vorangegangen sein, denn im Palast fanden 1758 die prunkvollen Feste und Feiern statt, die die Wahl Carlo Rezzonicos, Bischof von Padua, zum Papst (Clemens XIII.) begleiteten.

Die Kostbarkeiten, mit denen der Palast ausgestattet wurde, zeugen vom pompösen Lebensstil der Familie Rezzonico. Innerhalb von nur 50 Jahren stellten die Rezzonico auf

Le palais qui constitue l'un des épisodes marquants de l'architecture baroque vénitienne, fut exposé à de complexes vicissitudes concernant sa construction qui en prolongèrent l'édification pendant presqu'un siècle. Filippo Bon, Procurateur de San Marco, confia le projet vers le milieu du XVIIème siècle au plus célèbre architecte de l'époque, Baldassare Longhena.

Longhena ne put toutefois pas voir son œuvre achevée puisqu'en 1682, quand il mourut, la majestueuse façade sur le Grand Canal, avec la triple porte sur l'eau, n'était parvenue qu'au premier étage noble; la partie arrière, du côté de Campo San Barnaba, était achevée et la famille s'y était installée.

Suite à des échecs économiques, les héritiers de Filippo Bon furent contraints de vendre cet édifice qui aurait dû devenir l'expression de leur activité séculaire d'entrepreneur. Il fut acheté en 1751 par les Rezzonico, famille d'origine lombarde et de noblesse récente, acquise en 1687 après le versement d'une somme considérable dans les caisses vides de la République, et ceux-ci en confièrent l'achèvement à Giorgio Massari.

Le jeune architecte apporta des modifications au projet d'origine, surtout en ce qui concerne le second étage noble sur le Grand Canal, créant en outre une prestigieuse entrée côté terre avec un imposant escalier à partir duquel on accédait à la salle de bal, au premier étage, inhabituelle de par ses dimensions et ses ornements, mais également de par son emplacement même par rapport à la planimétrie traditionnelle des édifices vénitiens.

Les travaux durent être réalisés en toute hâte étant donné que le palais, en 1758, quand Carlo Rezzonico, évêque de Padoue, gravit le Saint-Siège sous le nom de Clément XIII, fut le siège des fêtes et des célébrations exceptionnelles qui accompagnèrent l'élection.

L'inventaire des biens contenus dans le palais met en évidence la vie fastueuse des Rezzonico qui, en un peu plus de cinquante ans, purent compter dans leur famille deux cardinaux, élus justement par Clément XIII Rezzonico, dont le népotisme était bien connu, et un Procurateur de San Marco.

self, who was famous for his nepotism) and also a Procurator of St. Mark.

But the family's fortunes lasted little more than half a century and in 1810 the family itself died out. From then onwards the palace passed through a number of hands, some famous like Carlo Pindemonte, relative of Ippolito Pindemonte, the poet, and Robert Barret Browning, painter and son of the poet Robert Browning. Browning jr. died in 1889, in what had once been the private apartments of Pope Clement XIII. In 1934 the palace was purchased by the Municipality of Venice for use as a Museum of the Eighteenth Century.

The Rezzonico family furniture was almost entirely sold off, but the splendid frescoes and stucco-work were preserved. They now provide a superb background to the 18th-century ornaments, paintings and furniture which have been brought together in the palace to recreate the atmosphere of a Venetian stately home of the period.

From the vast street-side entrance, an imposing staircase leads to the state apartments. The grand reception room is remarkably spacious by comparison with noble homes of the time, spanning the height of the first and second floors, which necessitated the demolition of a floor and the closing of a row of windows.

The enormous space seems even larger because of the illusionist architectural effects painted on the walls by Pietro Visconti, who collaborated in this particular case with Giovanni Battista Crosato, the painter of the fresco on the ceiling. This depicts Apollo's chariot with the four continents, Europe, Asia, America and Africa, recalling the Apollonian myths to celebrate the Rezzonico family, whose coat of arms stands out at the centre of the main wall.

Of the original furnishings in the great hall, there remain the enormous gilt metal and wood chandeliers with their floral motives, whereas the tall armchairs, vases, and statues of ebony and boxwood (sculpted by Andrea Brustolon, the most famous Veneto carver of the early 18th century) come from Palazzo Venier at San Vio.

Celebration of the family glories is a recurrent theme in the palace's pictorial decorations, some of which were the work of Giambattista Tiepolo, who worked here in the summer of 1758, together with his son Giandomenico and the illusionist Girolamo Mengozzi Colonna. Tiepolo frescoed the ceiling of the first hall leading off to the left of the ballroom with a *Nuptial Allegory* to

Empfehlung Clemens' XIII. Rezzonico, der für seinen Nepotismus bekannt war, zwei Kardinäle und einen Prokurator von San Marco.

Das Glück war der Familie jedoch nur wenig mehr als ein halbes Jahrhundert gewogen. Bereits im Jahre 1810 verstarb der letzte Familienangehörige. Den Palast bewohnten nun verschiedene Besitzer, auch bekannte Persönlichkeiten wie Carlo Pindemonte, Verwandter des Dichters Ippolito Pindemonte, und der Maler Robert Barret Browning, Sohn des englischen Dichters Robert Browning. Browning junior starb im Jahre 1889 in den einstigen Privatgemächern Clemens' XIII. 1934 erwarb die Stadtverwaltung von Venedig den Palazzo, um darin das Museo del Settecento Veneziano einzurichten.

Die Palastausstattung der Familie Rezzonico ging fast vollständig verloren. Erhalten blieben aber die herrlichen Fresken und Stukkaturen. Sie bilden heute einen würdevollen Rahmen für Nippsachen, Gemälde und Möbel aus dem Settecento, mit denen der Palast wie ein Patrizierwohnsitz des 18. Jahrhunderts eingerichtet wurde, um seinen ursprünglichen Flair wiederherzustellen.

Von der Landseite gelangt man durch das große Eingangsportal zu der imposanten Freitreppe, die zu den Repräsentationsräumen im Obergeschoß führt. Die enormen Ausmaße des großen Festsaals sind im Vergleich zu ähnlichen Räumlichkeiten in anderen Palazzi ungewöhnlich. Seine Raumhöhe umfaßt beide Obergeschosse.

Der an sich schon großzügige Saal wirkt durch die Scheinarchitekturen, die Pietro Visconti zusammen mit Giovanni Battista Crosato auf die Wände malte, noch größer. Crosato schuf auch die Deckenmalerei: Apolls Wagen mit den vier Kontinenten Europa, Asien, Amerika und Afrika. Dieses Fresko läßt die apollinischen Mythen zum Ruhm der Familie Rezzonico wiederaufleben, deren Wappen in der Mitte der größten Wand prangt.

Von der früheren Saalausstattung sind die großen Lüster aus Holz und vergoldetem Metall mit Blütenmotiven erhalten geblieben. Die Armlehnstühle, Blumenvasen und Statuen aus Eben- und Buchsbaumholz schuf Andrea Brustolon, der Anfang des 18. Jahrhunderts der berühmteste Schnitzer Venetiens war. Diese Möbel stammen ursprünglich aus dem Palazzo Venier in San Vio.

Die Verherrlichung des Familienruhms ist ein immer wiederkehrendes Thema im Bildprogramm des Palastes. Auch Giambattista Tiepolo wurde mit Ausmalungen zu diesem Thema betraut. Anläßlich der Hoch-

La bonne fortune de la famille ne dura toutefois qu'un peu plus d'un demi-siècle : en 1810 elle s'éteignait, et à partir de cette époque jusqu'en 1934, quand la Commune de Venise l'acheta, en le destinant au Museo del Settecento Veneziano, le palais passa aux mains de divers propriétaires, dont certains illustres, comme Carlo Pindemonte, neveu du poète Ippolito Pindemonte et Robert Barret Browning, peintre et fils du poète et lettré Robert Browning, qui en 1889 mourut justement dans les anciens appartements privés de Clément XIII.

Le mobilier des Rezzonico fut presque complètement disséminé, mais on conserva les splendides apparats de fresques et stucs qui servent de cadre superbe, aujourd'hui, aux bibelots, tableaux et meubles du XVIIIème siècle placés dans le palais comme dans une demeure patricienne de la même époque, ceci afin d'en recréer l'atmosphère.

Depuis la vaste entrée côté terre, l'imposant escalier introduit dans les appartements de réception, où s'ouvre la grande salle des fêtes, élément d'une singulière originalité par rapport aux édifices patriciens de l'époque, obtenue en utilisant la double hauteur des deux étages nobles, avec démolition consécutive d'un plancher et fermeture d'une rangée de fenêtres.

Le vaste espace apparaît encore agrandi en raison des fausses architectures, peintes sur les murs par Pietro Visconti en collaboration avec Giovanni Battista Crosato, auteur de la fresque du plafond qui représente le char d'Apollon, avec les quatre continents Europe, Asie, Amérique et Afrique, et se réfère aux mythes apolliniens avec des intentions commémoratives envers les Rezzonico, dont les armoiries ressortent au centre du plus grand mur.

De l'ancien ameublement du salon restent les grands lustres en bois et métal doré, à motif floral, tandis que les hautes chaises, les porte-fleurs et les statues d'ébène et de buis, sculptés par Andrea Brustolon, le plus célèbre graveur vénitien des premières années du XVIIIème siècle, proviennent du Palazzo Venier à San Vio.

La célébration des gloires familiales est un motif qui se répète dans les décorations picturales du palais : à cette tâche fut appelé également Giambattista Tiepolo qui, durant l'été 1758, avec son fils Giandomenico et le quadratoriste Girolamo Mengozzi Colonna, peignit, à l'occasion du mariage de Ludovico Rezzonico, futur Procurateur de San Marco, avec Faustina Savorgnan, la fresque du plafond de la première salle à laquelle on accède

commemorate the marriage of Ludovico Rezzonico, future Procurator of St. Mark, to Faustina Savorgnan.

The couple stands out against the intense light of the sky, on Apollo's chariot drawn by four fiery white chargers, amidst flocks of doves and putti and allegorical figures of the Virtues, while an old man (possibly Merit) with a lion symbolizing Venice at his feet, holds a flag with the two families' combined coats of arms. The dynamism of the figures, emphasised by the soft but sunny colours, and the overall unity of the composition make this fresco one of Tiepolo's masterpieces, belonging to the time just before the artist moved to Madrid.

The painter's activity was not limited to this composition, since he also created the *Allegory of Merit* for the Rezzonico family, again for commemorative purposes: Merit appears in the form of a bearded old man with a crown of laurel, ascending towards the Temple of Glory between the allegorical figures of Nobility and Virtue, while Fame blows a trumpet amidst flocks of putti.

The fresco decorates what chroniclers of the time indicated to be the bedroom of Ludovico and Faustina, but which is now known as the Throne Room because it contains the magnificent chair used by Pope Pius VI in 1782. Of particularly high quality is the rich gilt furniture, comprising chairs, chandeliers, round coffee tables and a console table, originally belonging to the noble Barbarigo family and made by Antonio Corradini, a sculptor from Este who was active in Venice until the third decade of the 18th century.

Like all the stately homes, Ca' Rezzonico could not be without a chapel, especially as the family boasted a pope and other high prelates among its members. The family chapel was built and decorated with gilt stucco work on a white background at the behest of one of the Pope's relatives called Carlo. Today it is adorned with an altarpiece by Francesco Zugno depicting the *Madonna and Saints,* with a prie-dieu from the mid-18th century which can be converted into an armchair.

Besides Tiepolo and Crosato, Gaspare Diziani was also involved in the decoration of the palace. On the ceiling of the so-called Sala dei Pastelli, where the Rezzonico family welcomed the papal nuncio with the news of the election of Clement XIII, Diziani developed about 1760 an animated allegorical composition with Poetry and Painting, Architecture, Music, and Sculpture, while a putto armed with a torch leads Ignorance to its downfall.

zeit von Ludovico Rezzonico, dem späteren Prokurator von San Marco, und Faustina Savorgnan schuf Tiepolo im Sommer 1758 zusammen mit seinem Sohn Giandomenico und Girolamo Mengozzi Colonna die Deckenmalerei des ersten Salons, zu dem man vom Ballsaal aus gelangt. Dargestellt ist eine *Allegorie der Hochzeit.*

Das Brautpaar steht zwischen Tauben, Putten und personifizierten Tugenden auf Apolls Wagen, der von vier feurigen, weißen Rössern gezogen wird. Ein alter Mann, vielleicht der Verdienst, zu dessen Füßen ein Löwe, das Symbol Venedigs, liegt, trägt das Banner mit den Wappen der beiden Familien. Das Fresko entstand, kurz bevor Tiepolo nach Madrid zog.

Tiepolo schuf weitere Werke für die Rezzonico. Ebenfalls zum Ruhm der Familie führte er die *Allegorie des Verdienstes* aus. Der Verdienst lagert als bärtiger und lorbeergekrönter alter Mann auf Wolken zwischen den Allegorien des Adels und der Tugend. Daneben wird der Tempel des Ruhms sichtbar.

Dieses Fresko schmückt, laut Inventar, das einstige Schlafgemach von Ludovico und Faustina. Heute heißt dieser Raum Sala del Trono, weil sich darin der prunkvolle, 1782 von Pius VI. benutzte Stuhl befindet. Qualitativ besonders hochwertig ist das reiche, vergoldete Mobiliar von Antonio Corradini, Bildhauer aus Este, der bis zum dritten Jahrzehnt des 18. Jahrhunderts in Venedig wirkte. Die Stühle, Kronleuchter und der Konsoltisch gehörten ursprünglich zum Besitz der Adelsfamilie Barbarigo.

Wie in allen wohlhabenden Patrizierhäusern durfte auch in der Ca' Rezzonico keine Kapelle fehlen, zumal zur Familie ein Papst und hohe Prälaten gehörten. Ein Angehöriger des Papstes, Carlo, ließ die Hauskapelle erbauen und mit vergoldeten Stuckarbeiten auf weißem Grund ausschmücken. Heute ist sie mit dem kleinen Altarbild *Madonna und Heilige* von Francesco Zugno, einem Schüler Giambattista Tiepolos, und mit einem Betstuhl aus der Mitte des 18. Jahrhunderts ausgestattet, der in einen Sessel verwandelt werden kann.

Neben Tiepolo und Crosato war auch Gaspare Diziani an der Ausschmückung des Palastes beteiligt. Für die Decke der Sala dei Pastelli, in der die Familie Rezzonico den päpstlichen Nuntius mit der Nachricht der erfolgten Wahl von Clemens XIII. empfing, arbeitete Diziani um 1760 eine lebhafte allegorische Komposition aus. Dargestellt sind Poesie, Malerei, Architektur, Musik und Bildhauerei.

par la salle de bal, sur la gauche, avec *Allégorie Nuptiale.*

Les deux époux sur le char d'Apollon traîné par quatre fougueux destriers blancs, entre vols de colombes, putti et figures allégoriques des Vertus, se détachent contre la lumière intense du ciel, tandis qu'un vieillard, sans doute le Mérite, avec à ses pieds un lion, symbole de Venise, tient le drapeau avec les armoiries réunies des deux familles. Le dynamisme des personnages souligné par les couleurs pâles mais nettes et la qualité organique de la composition font de cette fresque l'un des chefs-d'œuvre de Tiepolo, que l'on peut répertorier à un moment précédant de peu l'installation de l'artiste à Madrid.

Le peintre exécuta également pour les Rezzonico, toujours à des fins commémoratives, *Allégorie du Mérite,* lequel apparaît sous l'aspect d'un vieillard barbu et couronné de laurier, en ascension vers le temple de la Gloire entre la Noblesse, avec sa longue lance, et la Vertu, tandis que la Célébrité, entourée d'angelots, souffle dans une trompette.

La fresque orne celle qu'autrefois les chroniques indiquaient comme la chambre à coucher de Ludovico et Faustina et qui aujourd'hui est connue comme Salle du trône, puisqu'elle abrite le fastueux fauteuil utilisé par Pie VI en 1782. Sur le plan de la qualité, le riche mobilier doré, composé de chaises à dossier, lampadaires, guéridons et d'une table-applique – ayant appartenu à l'origine à la noble famille Barbarigo, œuvre de Antonio Corradini, sculpteur d'Este actif à Venise jusqu'à la troisième décennie du XVIIIème siècle – est de grande valeur.

Comme toutes les demeures patriciennes, Ca' Rezzonico se devait de posséder une chapelle, d'autant plus que la famille pouvait se glorifier de compter un pontife et de hauts prélats parmi ses membres ; un neveu du pape, Carlo, la fit construire et agrémenter de stucs dorés sur fond blanc, et elle est aujourd'hui décorée d'un petit retable de Francesco Zugno, élève de Giambattista Tiepolo, avec *La Madone et des Saints* et d'un prie-Dieu du milieu du XVIIIème siècle qui peut se transformer en fauteuil.

Aux côtés de Tiepolo et de Crosato, Gaspare Diziani fut également actif dans la décoration du palais. Sur le plafond de ce qu'on appelle la Salle des pastels, où les Rezzonico accueillirent le nonce apostolique qui portait la nouvelle de l'élection consommée de Clément XIII, il élabora vers 1760 une composition allégorique animée dans la-

The commemoration of the family is repeated yet again in the fresco illustrating *The Triumph of Virtue* that Jacopo Guarana was commissioned to create in the Sala degli Arazzi, so named because of the three great Flemish tapestries depicting stories of Solomon and the Queen of Sheba. The room contains carved and lacquered furniture of such refinement as to be considered among the most notable examples of the Rococo style. Both the furniture and the tapestries come from Palazzo Balbi Valier at Santa Maria Formosa.

In compliance with the usual layout of the Venetian palace, Ca' Rezzonico also has a *portego,* i.e. a vast elongated hall extending lengthwise and providing access to the other rooms which lead off from either side. This contains a majestic portal in the form of a triumphal arch which gives access to the staircase leading to the second floor. Over the arch is the family coat of arms with the motto "Si Deus pro nobis". The keystone bears the head of a young man, sculpted by the workshop of Giuseppe Marchiori, who frequently worked with Massari.

The second floor at Ca' Rezzonico basically repeats the layout of the first. As it was handed down to us without any furniture or decorations, a series of rooms have been recreated and furnished with antique pieces of the period, in accordance with 18th-century tradition.

The bed in the alcove of the bedroom is particularly noteworthy: it comes from Palazzo Carminati and has an ivory-coloured carved wooden headboard from the second half of the century. In the centre of the alcove is a painting of the *Holy Family with St. Anne and St. John* in tempera. A narrow corridor leads from here to the dressing-room containing wardrobes painted with tempera in pale grey, green and violet.

A particularly significant glimpse of life in this period is provided by the frescoes with which Giandomenico Tiepolo decorated a small villa purchased by his father at Zianigo, near Mirano; these were removed and reassembled in the rooms on the second floor of the palace, respecting their original arrangement as much as possible.

The story of the Rezzonico family was played out in a short space of time (less than a century), but their sumptuous palace with its ample, richly-decorated and frescoed rooms, offers a better reflection than most others in Venice of the opulence and luxury that were destined to become nothing more than memories after the fall of the Republic.

Die Verherrlichung der Familie wird in dem Fresko *Der Triumph der Tugend* von Jacopo Guarana noch einmal wiederholt. Dieses Fresko befindet sich in der wegen der drei großen flämischen Bildteppiche genannten Sala degli Arazzi. Die Tapisserien zeigen Geschichten von Salomon und der Königin von Saba. Dieser Saal ist mit erlesenen geschnitzten und lackierten Möbeln eingerichtet, die als die bemerkenswertesten Zeugnisse des Rokoko bezeichnet werden können. Sie stammen wie die Bildteppiche aus dem Palazzo Balbi Valier in Santa Maria Formosa.

Entsprechend der allgemein üblichen Raumaufteilung des venezianischen Palastes hat auch Ca' Rezzonico einen *portego,* einen großen, langen Saal, von dem man zu den angrenzenden Zimmern gelangt. Im *portego* befindet sich ein majestätisches Portal in Form eines Triumphbogens, durch das man zur Treppe gelangt, die zum zweiten Obergeschoß führt. Über dem Portal ist das Familienwappen mit dem Motto »Si Deus pro nobis« angebracht. Den Schlußstein des Portalbogens bildet der Kopf eines jungen Mannes, eine Arbeit aus der Werkstatt von Giuseppe Marchiori, der oft mit Massari zusammenarbeitete.

Das zweite Obergeschoß des Palastes wiederholt im wesentlichen die Raumaufteilung des ersten Stockwerkes. Da in dieser Etage Einrichtung und Ausschmückung fehlten, wurden mehrere Räume mit originalen Möbeln aus dem Settecento ausgestattet.

Besondere Aufmerksamkeit verdient das Bett des Schlafzimmers, das aus dem Palazzo Carminati stammt. Das Kopfteil aus elfenbeinfarbenem Holz entstand in der zweiten Hälfte des 18. Jahrhunderts. In der Mitte ist *Die Heilige Familie mit der Hl. Anna und dem Hl. Johannes* in Tempera dargestellt. Vom Schlafgemach aus führt ein enger Gang zum Ankleidezimmer mit grau, grün und lila bemalten Schränken.

Einen besonders guten Eindruck vom Leben am Ende des 18. Jahrhunderts bieten die Fresken, die Giandomenico Tiepolo für eine Villa seines Vater in Zianigo bei Mirano schuf. Diese Fresken wurden an ihrem Ursprungsort abgetragen und in den Sälen des zweiten Obergeschosses des Palazzo Rezzonico angebracht, wobei ihre ursprüngliche Anordnung soweit wie möglich erhalten blieb.

Die Geschichte der Familie Rezzonico umfaßt zwar nur ein knappes Jahrhundert, der kostbare Palazzo Rezzonico jedoch spiegelt den Prunk wider, der mit dem Untergang der Republik zur bloßen Erinnerung werden sollte.

quelle apparaissent la Poésie avec la Peinture, l'Architecture, la Musique et la Sculpture, tandis qu'un putto brandissant un flambeau se bat contre l'Ignorance.

La célébration de la famille revient une nouvelle fois dans la fresque *Le Triomphe de la Vertu* que Jacopo Guarana fut appelé à exécuter dans la salle dite maintenant des tapisseries, en raison de la présence de trois grandes tapisseries flamandes. Elle est garnie de meubles gravés et laqués avec un raffinement tel qu'on les considère comme l'un des plus remarquables témoignages du style rococo. Ils proviennent, comme les tapisseries, du Palazzo Balbi Valier à Santa Maria Formosa.

Fidèle au plan habituel du palais vénitien, Ca' Rezzonico présente aussi un *portego,* c'est-à-dire une vaste salle allongée et s'ouvrant sur les pièces qui la jouxtent ; à l'intérieur, un majestueux portail en forme d'arc de triomphe donne accès à l'escalier qui monte au second étage noble : à son faîte, les armes de la famille avec la devise « Si Deus pro nobis » et sur la clef de voûte, une tête de jeune homme, œuvre de l'atelier de Giuseppe Marchiori.

Le second étage noble du palais reprend substantiellement la planimétrie du premier. Puisqu'il était dépourvu d'ameublement et d'ornements, une série de pièces ont été garnies de meubles du XVIIIème siècle.

La chambre à coucher, ou alcôve, provenant du Palazzo Carminati, qui renferme dans une structure en bois blanc ivoire gravé de la seconde moitié du siècle, un lit à tête façonnée peinte à la détrempe et ornée au centre d'une représentation de la *Sainte Famille avec sainte Anne et saint Jean,* mérite une attention particulière. Un couloir étroit mène de la chambre à la pièce garde-robe aux armoires peintes à la détrempe en gris, vert et violet clairs.

Une impression particulièrement significative de la vie de la fin du siècle est fournie par les fresques avec lesquelles Giandomenico Tiepolo avait décoré une petite maison que son père avait achetée à Zianigo, près de Mirano, et qui une fois arrachées, furent remontées dans les salles du deuxième étage du palais, en respectant, autant que possible, leur disposition d'origine.

L'histoire des Rezzonico dura un très bref laps de temps, moins d'un siècle, mais le prestigieux palais dans lequel vécut la famille, avec ses vastes salles riches en ornements et fresques, reflète le faste et le luxe qui, avec la chute de la République, ne seront bientôt plus que des souvenirs.

Palazzo Rezzonico

117 Giambattista Tiepolo, *Nuptial Allegory.* This fresco, which gives its name to the hall, was created by the artist in 1758, with the help of his son Giandomenico and the illusionist decorator Girolamo Mengozzi Colonna, for the marriage of Ludovico Rezzonico and Faustina Savorgnan. In the detail: a bearded old man (possibly Merit), with a lion at his feet (symbolizing Venice), holds a flag with the married couple's combined coats of arms.

118/119 The ballroom. This was created by the architect Giorgio Massari using the full height of the two upper floors. It was decorated with illusionistic architectural effects painted by Pietro Visconti, who collaborated with Giovanni Battista Crosato, the painter of the fresco *The Chariot of the Sun and the Four Continents,* which decorates the ceiling. Of the original ballroom furnishings, there only remain the gilt wooden chandeliers, whereas the vases, the tall arm chairs and the ebony and boxwood statues by Andrea Brustolon all come from Palazzo Venier at San Vio.

121 The imposing staircase which leads to the great ballroom on the first floor is decorated with two putti representing Winter and Autumn, which are by the most important Baroque sculptor operating in Venice – Giusto Le Court.

122 The Sala del Parlatorio. This room is named after the famous painting *Parlour of the Nuns of San Zaccaria* by Francesco Guardi. The furniture has a yellow-green lacquered finish with a floral decoration. The chest of drawers with a marble top and the huge looking-glass with a gilt crest are particularly worthy of note.

123 The *portego* on the first floor with the great triumphal-arch portal topped with the Rezzonico coat of arms. There is a head on the keystone, the work of Giovanni Marchiori, and 16th-century sculptures on either side by Alessandro Vittoria. The *portego* furnishings include elegantly carved divans.

124 Gaspare Diziani, *The Triumph of Poetry.* This fresco decorates the so-called Sala dei Pastelli in which the walls are hung with a series of pastel portraits by Rosalba Carriera. On the ceiling, Poetry is at the centre, surrounded by Architecture, Sculpture, Music, and Painting. On the architectural illusionist frame, there are other monochromatic painted figures of the Sciences.

125 Jacopo Guarana, *The Triumph of Virtue.* This fresco decorates the ceiling of the Sala degli Arazzi and has architectural illusionist elements on the edges of the base frame with other images of the Virtues.

126 The Throne Room. This room takes its name from the carved and gilt wooden throne used by Pius VI in 1782, when he stayed at Chioggia. The rich gilt

117 Giambattista Tiepolo, *Allegorie der Hochzeit.* Dieses Fresko, dem der Saal seinen Namen verdankt, entstand 1758 anläßlich der Hochzeit von Ludovico Rezzonico und Faustina Savorgnan. Tiepolo führte es in Zusammenarbeit mit seinem Sohn Giandomenico und Girolamo Mengozzi Colonna aus. Der Ausschnitt zeigt einen bärtigen alten Mann, vielleicht der personifizierte Verdienst, mit einem Löwen, Symbol der Stadt Venedig, zu seinen Füßen. Er hält ein Banner mit den Familienwappen der beiden Brautleute.

118/119 Den Ballsaal schuf der Architekt Giorgio Massari unter Nutzung der Höhe der beiden Obergeschosse. Pietro Visconti, der mit Giovanni Battista Crosato, dem Schöpfer des Deckenfreskos *Der Wagen der Sonne und die vier Kontinente,* zusammenarbeitete, schmückte den Saal mit Scheinarchitekturen aus. Von der ursprünglichen Einrichtung sind die Leuchter aus vergoldetem Holz erhalten. Die Blumenvasen, Armlehnstühle sowie Ebenholz- und Buchsbaumholzstatuen von Andrea Brustolon stammen aus dem Palazzo Venier in San Vio.

121 Die imposante Freitreppe, die zum großen Ballsaal im ersten Obergeschoß führt, zieren zwei Putten, die den Winter und den Herbst darstellen. Sie sind ein Werk des bedeutendsten in Venedig wirkenden Bildhauers des Barock, Giusto Le Court.

122 Sprechsaal. Das berühmte Gemälde *Sprechzimmer der Nonnen von San Zaccaria* von Francesco Guardi gab diesem Saal seinen Namen. Er ist mit grüngelben Lackmöbeln mit Blütendekor eingerichtet. Besonders kostbar ist die Kommode mit Marmorplatte, über der ein großer Wandspiegel mit vergoldetem, reich verziertem Rahmen hängt.

123 *Portego* des ersten Obergeschosses mit großem Triumphbogenportal, über dem das Wappen der Rezzonico angebracht ist. Am Scheitel des Bogens befindet sich ein männlicher Kopf, der aus der Werkstatt von Giovanni Marchiori stammt. Das Portal flankieren zwei Skulpturen von Alessandro Vittoria aus dem Cinquecento. Zur Einrichtung des *portego* gehören elegant gearbeitete Sitzmöbel.

124 Gaspare Diziani, *Der Triumph der Poesie.* Dieses Fresko schmückt die sogenannte Sala dei Pastelli, in der eine Reihe von Pastellporträts von Rosalba Carriera hängen. Die Deckenmalerei zeigt in der Mitte die Poesie zwischen Architektur, Bildhauerei, Musik und Malerei. Auf dem gemalten Architekturrahmen befinden sich weitere Figuren der Wissenschaft in monochromer Farbgebung.

125 Jacopo Guarana, *Der Triumph der Tugend.* An den Ecken des Deckenfreskos in der Sala degli Arazzi sind architektonische Scheinkonsolen gemalt, auf denen sich weitere Figuren befinden.

126 Sala del Trono, so genannt nach dem geschnitzten

117 Giambattista Tiepolo, *Allégorie Nuptiale.* La fresque qui donne son nom à la salle fut réalisée en 1758 par l'artiste en collaboration avec son fils Giandomenico et avec l'encadreur Girolamo Mengozzi Colonna, à l'occasion des noces de Ludovico Rezzonico et Faustina Savorgnan. Dans la vue de détail : un vieillard barbu, peut-être l'allégorie du Mérite, porte un étendard avec les blasons des deux époux ; à ses pieds, le lion symbole de la ville.

118/119 Salle de bal. Elle fut conçue par l'architecte Giorgio Massari, qui utilisa la hauteur de deux étages, et décorée avec de faux éléments d'architecture peints par Pietro Visconti qui collabora avec Giovanni Battista Crosato, auteur de la fresque *Le char du Soleil et les quatre continents* qui orne le plafond. De l'ancien ameublement du salon, il reste les lustres en bois doré. Quant aux cache-pots, chaises hautes et statues de bois et de buis, de Andrea Brustolon, ils proviennent du Palais Venier à San Vio.

121 L'imposant escalier qui mène à la grande salle de bal du premier étage est décoré avec deux putti qui représentent l'Hiver et l'Automne, œuvre du plus grand sculpteur baroque travaillant à Venise, Giusto Le Court.

122 Salle du Parloir. Elle doit son nom à la fameuse toile de Francesco Guardi le *Parloir des nonnes de San Zaccaria* ; elle est garnie de meubles aux décorations florales. On admirera pour son intérêt particulier, la commode avec tablette en marbre, surmontée d'un grand miroir avec cimier doré.

123 *Portego* du premier étage avec grande porte à arc de triomphe surmontée du blason Rezzonico. Sur la clef de voûte, une tête, œuvre des ateliers de Giovanni Marchiori et sur les côtés, deux sculptures du XVIème siècle d'Alessandro Vittoria. La décoration se compose d'élégants divans rococo.

124 Gaspare Diziani, *Le Triomphe de la Poésie.* La fresque orne la salle dite Salle des pastels où l'on peut admirer, sur les murs, une série de portraits au pastel de Rosalba Carriera. Au plafond, la Poésie se trouve au centre entre l'Architecture, la Sculpture, la Musique et la Peinture. Sur la fausse corniche, il y a d'autres figures des Sciences, peintes en monochrome.

125 Jacopo Guarana, *Le Triomphe de la Vertu.* La fresque orne le plafond de la Salle des Tapisseries, et dans les angles on peut admirer, sur les fausses corniches, d'autres représentations des Vertus.

126 Salle du trône. On l'appelle ainsi car elle contient le trône en bois doré et sculpté utilisé par Pie VI en 1782, quand il s'arrêta à Chioggia. On admirera le riche mobilier doré se composant notamment de chaises à hauts dossiers sculptés. Le grand vase blanc avec des décorations en or est de fabrication chinoise.

furniture, including some carved tall chairs, is particularly noteworthy. The great white vase with gilt decorations is of Chinese origin.

127 The Alcove. This contains a bed, with an ivory-white carved headboard from the second half of the 18th century. The headboard is painted in tempera with an oval representing a *Holy Family with St. Anne and St. John.* Over the bed is a pastel *Madonna* by Rosalba Carriera.

128 The chapel extending from the first floor, decorated with gilt-on-white stucco work; there is a small altarpiece hanging on the wall with the *Madonna and Saints* by Francesco Zugno, one of Tiepolo's pupils. The peculiar prie-dieu can be adjusted to become an armchair.

129 The Alcove. The side door, topped by an oval with a female portrait, leads to the dressing room with the wardrobes.

129 The stuccoed dressing room on the second floor. This room has variously coloured 18th-century stucco decorations which entirely cover the walls and also form the frames of the huge looking-glasses.

130 The Green-Lacquered Room, which takes its name from the furniture, dating from around 1750–60 and comprising chests of drawers, console tables, small armchairs and looking-glasses lacquered in a dark green with gilt plaster decorations, inspired by a taste for Oriental styles.

130 The Sala del Guardi. The walls contain three frescoes by Gian Antonio Guardi inside shaped stucco frames; these represent *Venus and Love, Apollo,* and *Minerva.* The room contains green-lacquered furniture from the 18th century with coloured floral decorations. The Veronese red marble fireplace has very fine stucco work on the cowl which surrounds an image of Plenty in the centre.

131 The great Murano glass chandelier has twenty branches with coloured glass floral decorations. It was probably made towards the middle of the 18th century at the furnace of Giuseppe Briato.

132 Giandomenico Tiepolo, *The New World.* Detail of the frescoes that decorated the Tiepolo villa at Zianigo and were removed in 1909 and reassembled here, respecting the original arrangement as far as possible. The fresco represents a crowd waiting to take a peep at a magic lantern.

132 The Zianigo chapel. Re-assembled in this hall, these frescoes present religious subjects from the Old Testament and episodes from the life of San Gerolamo Miani. In the detail: Giandomenico Tiepolo, *San Gerolamo Miani Reciting the Rosary.* The furnishings of the chapel are the work of Veneto artisans of the 18th century.

133 The Sala degli Arazzi. This takes its name from the three great tapestries with Biblical subjects from the end of the 17th century. The finely-made Rococo-style furniture is of Venetian origin.

136 Giambattista Tiepolo, *Allegory of Merit.* The fresco was created by the artist at the same time as the *Nuptial Allegory* and is framed with illusionistic decorations by Girolamo Mengozzi Colonna. Merit is represented as on old man with a beard, crowned with laurel, rising to the temple of Glory. The fresco decorates the ceiling of the Throne Room.

vergoldeten Thron, den 1782 Pius VI. benutzte, als er sich in Chioggia aufhielt. Besonders wertvoll ist auch das reiche vergoldete Mobiliar, zu dem unter anderem Stühle mit hoher geschnitzter Rückenlehne gehören. Die große weiße Vase mit Goldverzierungen stammt aus China.

127 Alkoven. Hier steht ein Bett mit elfenbeinfarbenem geschnitztem Kopfteil aus der zweiten Hälfte des 18. Jahrhunderts. Das Kopfteil ist mit Temperafarben bemalt. In der Mitte ist *Die Heilige Familie mit der Hl. Anna und dem Hl. Johannes* dargestellt. Über dem Bett hängt eine *Muttergottes* in Pastell von Rosalba Carriera.

128 Die Kapelle im ersten Obergeschoß schmücken vergoldete Stuckarbeiten auf weißem Hintergrund. Das kleine Altarbild *Madonna und Heilige* schuf Francesco Zugno, ein Schüler Tiepolos. Der Betstuhl wird durch Umklappen zum Sessel.

129 Alkoven. Über der Tür, die zum Ankleidezimmer führt, ist ein ovales weibliches Porträt angebracht.

129 Stuckankleidezimmer im zweiten Obergeschoß. Dieser Raum ist vollständig mit polychromen Stuckarbeiten aus dem Settecento ausgeschmückt, die auch die Rahmen der großen Spiegel bilden.

130 Saal der grünen Lackmöbel. Dieser Name bezieht sich auf die Einrichtung von etwa 1750–60. Sie besteht aus dunkelgrünen Lacksesseln, -kommoden, -konsoltischen und -spiegeln mit von Chinoiserien inspiriertem Dekor aus vergoldeter Gipspaste.

130 Sala del Guardi. An den Wänden befinden sich in geformten Stuckrahmen drei Fresken von Gian Antonio Guardi, auf denen *Venus und Amor, Apoll* und *Minerva* dargestellt sind. Der Saal ist mit grünen Lackmöbeln mit farbigem Blütendekor aus dem 18. Jahrhundert eingerichtet. Am Rauchfang des Kamins aus rotem veronesischem Marmor befinden sich feinste Stuckarbeiten, in deren Zentrum die Allegorie des Überflusses dargestellt ist.

131 Großer Kronleuchter aus Murano mit 20 Armen und Blütendekorationen aus buntem Glas. Der Leuchter entstand vermutlich Mitte des 18. Jahrhunderts in der Glasbläserei von Giuseppe Briati.

132 Giandomenico Tiepolo, *Die Neue Welt.* Dieses Wandbild gehört zu den Fresken, die die Villa Tiepolos in Zianigo schmückten. Sie wurden 1909 abgelöst und hierher übertragen, wobei die ursprüngliche Anordnung erhalten blieb.

132 Kapelle von Zianigo. Die Fresken aus Zianigo zeigen religiöse Themen aus dem Alten Testament und Episoden aus dem Leben des Heiligen Gerolamo Miani. Detailansicht: Giandomenico Tiepolo, *Der Hl. Gerolamo Miani betet den Rosenkranz.* Die Einrichtung der Kapelle wurde im 18. Jahrhundert in Venetien gefertigt.

133 Sala degli Arazzi. Dieser Saal verdankt seinen Namen den drei großen Bildteppichen mit biblischen Geschichten, die Ende des 17. Jahrhunderts entstanden. Die fein gearbeiteten Rokoko-Möbel wurden in Venedig gefertigt.

136 Giambattista Tiepolo, *Allegorie des Verdienstes.* Dieses Fresko entstand zur gleichen Zeit wie die *Allegorie der Hochzeit.* Es wird von Malereien Girolamo Mengozzi Colonnas gerahmt. Der Verdienst ist als bärtiger, lorbeergekrönter alter Mann dargestellt, der zum Tempel der Glorie emporsteigt. Das Fresko schmückt die Decke des Thronsaals.

127 Alcôve. On y trouve dans un ensemble de bois sculpté de couleur blanc ivoire, datant de la seconde moitié du XVIIIème siècle, un lit dont la tête est sculptée et peinte à la détrempe avec un ovale qui représente une *Sainte Famille avec sainte Anne et saint Jean.* Au-dessus du lit, une *Madone,* pastel de Rosalba Carriera.

128 Chapelle du premier étage décorée de stucs dorés sur fond blanc. Sur les murs, un petit retable avec *La Madone et des Saints* de Francesco Zugno, élève de Tiepolo. Le prie-Dieu une fois renversé devient un fauteuil.

129 Alcôve. Porte latérale, surmontée d'un ovale avec un portrait de femme ; elle mène à la pièce des garde-robes.

129 Cabinet des stucs. Au deuxième étage du palais, ainsi nommé car il est entièrement décoré de stucs polychromes du XVIIIème siècle encadrant également les grandes glaces.

130 Salle des laques vertes. Doit son nom au mobilier datant de 1750–60 environ, constitué de commodes, consoles, fauteuils et miroirs, le tout laqué vert sombre avec décorations en pastille dorée, dans le style des chinoiseries.

130 Salle de Guardi. Sur les murs dans des cadres en stuc, trois fresques de Gian Antonio Guardi représentent *Vénus et l'Amour, Apollon* et *Minerve.* La salle est garnie de meubles en laque verte du XVIIIème siècle avec des décorations florales de couleurs. Sur le manteau de la cheminée en marbre rouge de Vérone, des stucs très raffinés encadrent l'Abondance.

131 Grand lustre à vingt flammes de Murano, avec des décorations florales en verre de couleur. Celui-ci fut probablement fabriqué vers le milieu du XVIIIème siècle dans le four de Giuseppe Briati.

132 Giandomenico Tiepolo, *Le nouveau monde.* Détails des fresques qui décoraient la villa des Tiepolo à Zianigo et qui, arrachées en 1909, furent recomposées en respectant le mieux possible la disposition d'origine. La fresque représente une foule qui attend de mettre son œil devant l'objectif d'une lanterne magique.

132 La chapelle de Zianigo. Dans cette salle on peut admirer des personnages de l'Ancien Testament et des épisodes de la vie de saint Gerolamo Miani. Dans la vue de détail : Giandomenico Tiepolo, *Saint Gerolamo Miani récitant le rosaire.* La décoration de la chapelle est l'œuvre d'artisans vénitiens du XVIIIème siècle.

133 Salle des Tapisseries. Cette salle doit son nom aux trois grandes tapisseries de la fin du XVIIème siècle représentant des épisodes de la Bible. L'élégant mobilier de style rococo est de fabrication vénitienne.

136 Giambattista Tiepolo, *Allégorie du Mérite.* La fresque fut réalisée par l'artiste à la même époque que celle de *Allégorie Nuptiale ;* elle est encadrée par des peintures de Girolamo Mengozzi Colonna. Le Mérite y est représenté comme un vieillard barbu couronné de lauriers qui monte vers le temple de la Gloire. Cette fresque décore le plafond de la Salle du trône.

Palazzo
Albrizzi
a S.
Appolinare

Palazzo
Albrizzi
a S.
Appolinare

P. Coronelli

PALAZZO ALBRIZZI

Palazzo Albrizzi stands on a somewhat secluded site in the city, in the parish of Sant'Aponal (a dialect form of Apollinare), far from the most popular routes. One side faces onto the Rio di San Cassiano (a secondary canal which flows into the Grand Canal) and the other side, which has now become its main façade, faces onto a peaceful little square. This square was created towards the end of the 18th century by the Albrizzi family, who purchased and demolished a number of little houses in order to add light to their home and emphasise its street-side façade.

The palace was built at the end of the 16th century for the Bonomo family; in the subsequent century it was purchased in two separate stages (in 1648 and 1692) by the Albrizzis. This was a family originally from Bergamo which had a canvas trade in Venice (in fact, when he died in 1643, Maffeo Albrizzi was remembered as the "cloth merchant residing between two anchors").

In addition to canvas, the Albrizzis also traded in oil, which they transported in their own fleet of ships. This fleet they placed at the disposal of the Venetian Republic at the time of the war of Crete, an island where the family had a trading base. In fact, Antonio Albrizzi, Maffeo's relative, is remembered for having died near Candia, in combat against the Turks. The epigraph for his brother Maffeo, who is buried in the church of Sant'Aponal, mentions the boats which supported the Venetian fleet during the conflict.

Their sacrifice of blood and money in the defense of Crete is also mentioned in the family's request for accession to the Venetian nobility, which Maffeo's sons obtained in 1667 against the payment of a hundred thousand ducats.

The considerable fortune accumulated by their trading enabled the Albrizzis to purchase the Bonomo palace "of beautiful construction and decorated with marble", as it was remembered by Sansovino-Stringa.

In fact the palace required no structural restoration nor renovation at the time of its purchase, so it retained the typical architectural features of the period spanning the 16th

Der Palazzo Albrizzi erhebt sich abseits der Hauptstraßen in einem eher abgelegenen Teil der Stadt, in der Pfarrgemeinde von Sant'Aponal (dialektische Kurzform für Apollinare). Mit einer Seite blickt der Palast auf den Rio di San Cassiano, einen Nebenkanal, der zum Canal Grande fließt, und mit der heutigen Hauptfassade auf einen ruhigen *campiello* (kleiner Platz). Dieser Platz wurde gegen Ende des 18. Jahrhunderts von den Albrizzi angelegt, die zu diesem Zweck einige zuvor erworbene kleine Häuser abreißen ließen. Ihr neuer Wohnsitz erhielt so mehr Licht und die landseitige Fassade kam besser zur Geltung.

Der Ende des 16. Jahrhunderts für die Familie Bonomo erbaute Palazzo wurde im folgenden Jahrhundert in zwei Teilkäufen, 1648 und 1692, von den aus Bergamo stammenden Albrizzi erworben. Die Albrizzi widmeten sich in Venedig dem Leinwandhandel. So wird Maffeo Albrizzi in der Sterbeurkunde aus dem Jahre 1643 als »telariol alle due Ancore« bezeichnet.

Außerdem handelten die Albrizzi mit Öl, für dessen Transport sie eigene Schiffe einsetzten. Diese Schiffe stellte die Familie der Republik Venedig im Krieg gegen Kreta zur Verfügung, wo die Albrizzi eine Handelsniederlassung unterhielten. Antonio Albrizzi starb im Kampf gegen die Türken bei Candia. Das Epigraph auf dem Grab seines Bruders Maffeo, der in der Kirche Sant'Aponal beigesetzt wurde, erinnert an die Schiffe, die im Verlauf des Konflikts der venezianischen Flotte zu Hilfe eilten.

Auch im Bittgesuch um die Aufnahme in das Patriziat, die die Söhne Maffeos im Jahre 1667 mit der Zahlung von 100 000 Dukaten erhielten, wird an die Blut- und Geldopfer bei der Verteidigung von Kreta erinnert.

Das durch den Handel erworbene enorme Vermögen ermöglichte den Albrizzi den Kauf des Palazzo der Bonomo, »einem wunderbaren Bauwerk, mit Marmor geschmückt«, wie Sansovino-Stringa bemerkt.

Da der Palast in sehr gutem Zustand war, nahmen die Albrizzi keine baulichen Änderungen oder Renovierungen vor. So

Le Palazzo Albrizzi se dresse à l'écart, loin des parcours les plus fréquentés, dans la paroisse de Sant'Aponal (forme dialectale pour Apollinare). Il expose une façade sur le canal de San Cassiano, une rivière secondaire qui conflue ensuite avec le Grand Canal, et l'autre, aujourd'hui la principale, donne sur un *campiello* tranquille, créé vers la fin du XVIIIème siècle par les Albrizzi qui firent abattre une rangée de petites maisons, achetées précédemment, dans le but de donner de la lumière à la demeure et d'en faire ressortir la façade située côté terre.

Le palais construit à la fin du XVIème siècle par la famille Bonomo fut acheté à deux reprises au cours du siècle suivant, en 1648 et en 1692, par les Albrizzi, d'origine bergamasque, qui se vouaient au commerce de la toile à Venise ; ainsi Maffeo Albrizzi est évoqué en 1643 dans son acte de décès comme « telariol alle due Ancore » (marchand de tissus habitant les Deux Ancres).

Les Albrizzi pratiquaient également le commerce de l'huile, transportée dans leurs propres bateaux qui furent mis à la disposition de la Sérénissime à l'époque de la guerre de Candie, île où la famille avait des bases commerciales ; Antonio Albrizzi, neveu de Maffeo, trouva la mort près de La Canée en combattant les Turcs ; l'épigraphe de son frère, Maffeo, enterré dans l'église de Sant'Aponal, fait allusion aux embarcations qui furent d'un grand secours à la flotte vénitienne durant le conflit.

Même dans la supplique pour l'admission au patriciat, que les fils de Maffeo obtinrent en 1667 après avoir déboursé 100 000 ducats, on évoque les sacrifices de sang et d'argent subis pour la défense de La Canée.

La consistante fortune accumulée avec la pratique du commerce permit aux Albrizzi l'acquisition du palais Bonomo « de très belle construction, orné de marbre » comme le rappelle Sansovino-Stringa.

Le palais ne nécessitait en effet ni restaurations statiques ni restructurations au moment de l'achat et conserva donc ses caractéristiques typiques de l'architecture de transition entre XVIème et XVIIème siècles :

and 17th centuries: on the first and second floors, both fronts have triple mullioned windows with side lintels and a central arch, but with no sign of any other particular formal refinement apart from the finely carved roofing over the windows.

The severe majesty of the outside is contrasted by the interior decoration on the first floor of the building, which is the richest, most exuberant and imaginative example of Rococo stuccoed art to have been created in Venice.

At the end of the 17th century, Venetian stucco decorations were exemplary not only for their technical perfection but also, and above all, for their function – which was not just ornamental but also figurative and dominated every possible space.

This is the case of the *portego* on the first floor of Palazzo Albrizzi, where a highly-elaborate arrangement of stucco work by the Ticino-born Abbondio Stazio covers every space left free by the paintings.

Though the palace required no renovation of its architectural structure, the Albrizzis took great care over the embellishment of its interior, welcoming decorative forms that were new to Venice. They were the direct outcome of Stazio's period in Rome, where he had completed his apprenticeship, but were tempered by a Venetian sense of balance.

This splendid stucco work – one of Stazio's earliest in Venice – is distributed everywhere: on the portal giving access to the monumental staircase, with the family's coat of arms supported by putti and a great angel blowing a trumpet; on the ceiling, where the three great allegorical paintings by the young Giannantonio Pellegrini are enclosed in substantial frames supported by more putti in flight, wrapped in heavy flowing drapery; over the doors, where allegorical subjects are treated with great plastic effect, to the point that the figures in the foreground seem fully rounded sculptures.

This remarkable plastic effect is repeated with the same force in the heavy frames around the vast paintings by Pietro Liberi, while it is less evident in the motives – comprising reliefs of foliage, vine branches, flowers and drapery – developed in the skirting and in the spaces between one section of the wall and the next.

Rococo divans and console tables which are more decorative than functional furnish the *portego,* which thus takes on an imaginatively sculptured appearance.

Stazio's creative inspiration is given even freer rein in the decoration of the ceiling

blieben die typischen Architekturmerkmale aus der Zeit des Übergangs vom Cinquecento zum Seicento erhalten: Beide Fassaden sind symmetrisch gestaltet. Einzig die dreiteiligen Arkadenfenster in der Mitte jedes Geschosses sind aufwendiger gestaltet.

Der strengen Majestät des Äußeren steht die reiche Innenausstattung des ersten Geschosses gegenüber. Sie zeigt das Üppigste und Phantasievollste der Rokoko-Stuckkunst in Venedig.

Gegen Ende des 17. Jahrhunderts waren die Stukkaturen der Lagunenstadt stilbildend. Nicht nur die technische Perfektion, sondern auch die neue Dekorationsart waren vorbildhaft. Stuckfiguren füllten nun in einer Art *horror vacui* jeden freien Platz.

So überlagern im *portego* des Obergeschosses Stuckfiguren jeden von Ausmalungen freigelassenen Raum. Diese hervorragenden Stukkaturen schuf der Tessiner Abbondio Stazio.

Wenn auch die Bauweise des Palastes keine Renovierungen erforderte, so sorgten sich die Albrizzi doch um die reiche Verschönerung der Innenräume mit in Venedig bis dahin ungekanntem Zierat. Die neuen Dekorationen hatten ihre Wurzeln in Rom, wo Stazio seine Lehrzeit absolviert hatte, und wurden durch den venezianischen Einfluß etwas gemäßigter.

Die herrlichen Stuckarbeiten, eines der ersten venezianischen Werke Stazios, finden sich überall: über dem Eingangstor an der monumentalen Freitreppe in Form des Familienwappens, das von Putten und einem großen Engel mit Trompete gehalten wird; an der Decke, wo drei große allegorische, von Putten gehaltene Gemälde des jungen Giannantonio Pellegrini von üppigen, fließenden Stoffdrapierungen umrahmt werden; über den Türen, wo die allegorischen Themen so gut ausgearbeitet sind, daß die vordersten Figuren wie Vollplastiken wirken.

Der plastische Effekt wiederholt sich mit derselben Kraft in den breiten Rahmen der großen Gemälde Pietro Liberis. Die Motive auf den Sockeln und den die Wände unterteilenden horizontalen Wandauflagen hingegen zeigen flachere Reliefs mit Laubwerk, Weinranken, Blumen und Stoffdrapierungen.

Eher dekorative als funktionale Rokoko-Sitzmöbel und -Konsoltische füllen den großzügigen *portego,* der so ein phantasievoll plastisches Aussehen erhält.

Noch entfesselter wirkt die Ausschmückung der Decke des großen, nahezu quadratischen Ballsaals, der Teil eines angrenzenden

les deux façades se distinguent par des fenêtres trilobées, à la hauteur des étages nobles, sans autres raffinements formels particuliers, si l'on excepte les petits toits bien découpés qui dominent les fenêtres.

A la sévérité majestueuse de l'extérieur s'oppose la décoration intérieure de l'étage noble de l'édifice qui est ce que l'art du stuc rococo a produit de plus opulent, pétulant et plein de fantaisie à Venise.

A la fin du XVIIème siècle, la décoration en stuc est exemplaire dans la ville lagunaire, non seulement en raison de sa perfection technique mais aussi et surtout à cause de la fonction dont elle s'acquitte, en revêtant des caractères non seulement ornementaux mais également figuratifs et en dominant chaque espace possible.

C'est ce que l'on peut constater dans le *portego* de l'étage noble du Palazzo Albrizzi, où un apparat de stucs très élaboré, œuvre du Tessinois Abbondio Stazio, recouvre tout espace laissé libre par les tableaux.

Si le palais n'eut point besoin d'interventions architecturales, les Albrizzi se soucièrent d'embellir les intérieurs avec des formes décoratives inédites à Venise qui, quand bien même modérées par l'équilibre de la Vénétie, prenaient leurs ascendants directs dans la région romaine où le stucateur avait accompli son apprentissage.

Les splendides stucs, l'une des premières œuvres vénitiennes de Stazio, sont réparties partout : sur le portail d'accès à l'escalier d'honneur avec l'écusson de la maison soutenu par deux putti et un grand ange qui souffle de la trompette ; au plafond où les trois grandes toiles à thème allégorique, œuvre du jeune Giannantonio Pellegrini, sont cernées de cadres volumineux soutenus par d'autres putti, enveloppés dans des draps aux plis lourds ; sur les dessus-de-porte aux sujets allégoriques traités avec un telle maîtrise que les personnages du premier plan semblent sculptés en ronde-bosse.

L'effet plastique se répète avec la même évidence dans les cadres massifs des vastes toiles de Pietro Liberi, tandis que dans les motifs qui se développent sur les socles et les espaces entre les subdivisions des murs, le relief avec feuillages, sarments de vignes, fleurs et drapés devient moins sensible.

Des petits divans et des consoles de style rococo constituent l'ameublement typique, plus décoratif que fonctionnel, du *portego* qui, dans son ensemble, revêt un aspect sculptural plein d'imagination.

Le génie créatif de Stazio apparaît encore plus déchaîné dans la décoration du pla-

over the grand, nearly square ballroom which is part of an adjacent building and was probably added to the stately home with the purchase of the second part of the palace in 1692.

Here the artist covered the ceiling with a great flowing velarium comprising a mass of folds supported by twenty-eight winged putti in various attitudes, while the corners are occupied by large male figures seated on the frame and apparently acting as caryatids to sustain the heavy drapery.

The highly elaborate ceiling decoration, with the ivory-white stucco enlivened by intense gilt effects (as in the *portego*), is contrasted by the walls of the room, which are relatively plain. Over the doors are medallions depicting mythological themes, and on the walls are large-scale portraits of the Barbarigo Procurators (inherited by the family) and of members of the Albrizzi line, held in huge, cleverly-carved gilt frames.

The armchairs, the table, and the console tables are also very finely carved and decorated with medallions bearing portraits of other members of the Albrizzi family.

The drawing-room (which leads off from the ballroom) is completely lined with looking-glasses and further stucco work that creates peculiar trompe-l'œil effects on the ceiling. The Louis Seize furniture was designed especially for this room.

The room faces onto the beautiful garden created on the site of the San Cassiano theatre, which had once belonged to the Tron family of San Benedetto. It was the first theatre in Venice and Europe to become public, by decision of the Council of Ten in 1636. San Cassiano was considered the largest theatre in the city, with a full six levels of boxes, but was little used after the fall of the Republic and was finally destroyed in 1812, the area subsequently being occupied by the garden of Palazzo Albrizzi.

Numerous members of the Albrizzi family held important political positions and some of them even became Procurators of St. Mark. But the most famous family member is Isabella Teotochi, who was married for the second time to Giuseppe Albrizzi and who animated the Venetian cultural scene between the end of the 18th and the beginning of the 19th centuries with her literary circle. In her salon at San Moisè, the noble lady welcomed personalities of great cultural and artistic standing such as Ugo Foscolo, Ippolito Pindemonte, Stendhal, Vittorio Alfieri, Lord Byron (who nicknamed her the "de Staël of Venice"), and Antonio Canova, who

Gebäudes ist. Er wurde vermutlich beim Erwerb des letzten Palastteils im Jahre 1692 hinzugefügt. Als Deckenverkleidung erdachte Stazio ein großes schwebendes Zeltdach aus dichten Falten, zwischen denen sich stützend 28 geflügelte Putten in unterschiedlichen Haltungen befinden. In den Ecken sitzen auf der Umrahmung vier große männliche Gestalten, die wie Atlanten die schwere Stoffdrapierung halten.

Im Gegensatz zu der reich gearbeiteten Deckendekoration, deren elfenbeinfarbene Stukkaturen wie auch im *portego* durch intensive Vergoldungen belebt werden, stehen die relativ schlichten Saalwände. In den Sopraporten befinden sich Medaillons mit mythologischen Themen und an den Wänden die großformatigen Bildnisse der Prokuratoren des Hauses Barbarigo, die der Familie durch Erbschaft zufielen, sowie die Porträts der Albrizzi, die große, vergoldete und schön geschnitzte Rahmen einfassen.

Die Armlehnstühle, der Tisch und die Konsoltische sind fein geschnitzt. In den Verzierungen sind Medaillons mit den Bildnissen weiterer Mitglieder des Hauses Albrizzi eingelassen.

Der durch den Ballsaal zugängliche Salon ist vollständig mit Spiegeln und Stukkaturen verkleidet, so daß an der Decke einzigartige optische Effekte entstehen. Die Einrichtung im Stil Ludwigs XVI. wurde speziell für diesen Raum entworfen.

Der Saal öffnet sich zu dem wunderbaren Garten hin. Dort befand sich einst das Theater von San Cassiano, das der Familie Tron von San Benedetto gehörte. Es war in Venedig und sogar ganz Europa das erste Theater, das durch Beschluß des Zehnerrats im Jahre 1636 für öffentlich erklärt wurde. Mit seinen sechs Logenreihen wurde es als das größte Theater der Stadt angesehen, jedoch nach dem Untergang der Republik wenig genutzt und im Jahre 1812 schließlich zerstört. Auf seinem Grund entstand dann der Garten des Palazzo Albrizzi.

Zahlreiche Angehörige der Familie Albrizzi bekleideten wichtige politische Ämter, und einige von ihnen wurden sogar Prokuratoren von San Marco. Doch das berühmteste Familienmitglied ist Isabella Teotochi, die in zweiter Ehe mit Giuseppe Albrizzi verheiratet war und zwischen dem ausgehenden 18. und dem beginnenden 19. Jahrhundert das kulturelle Leben Venedigs mit ihrem literarischen Zirkel bereicherte. In ihrem Salon bei San Moisè verkehrten berühmte Persönlichkeiten aus Kunst und Kultur, wie Ugo Foscolo, Ippolito Pindemonte, Stend-

fond de la grande salle de bal, presque carrée, qui fait partie d'un édifice adjacent et fut probablement ajoutée à la demeure avec l'achat de la dernière partie du palais effectué par la famille en 1692. L'artiste imagina en couverture du plafond un grand rideau volant à plis très épais parmi lesquels s'introduisent pour le soutenir vingt-huit putti ailés, dans des attitudes différentes, tandis qu'aux coins quatre grands personnages masculins assis sur le cadre semblent s'acquitter de la fonction d'atlantes en tenant la lourde draperie.

A la décoration très élaborée dans laquelle, comme dans le *portego,* les stucs ivoire sont rehaussés par d'intenses dorures, s'opposent les murs de la salle, relativement sobres, si l'on excepte les dessus-de-porte ornés de médaillons à thème mythologique, sur lesquels se placent les grands portraits des Procurateurs de la maison Barbarigo, parvenus à la famille par héritage, et ceux de la maison Albrizzi, dotés de grands cadres dorés et habilement gravés. Les fauteuils, la table et les consoles dans les frises desquelles s'insèrent des médaillons avec des portraits d'autres membres de la maison Albrizzi sont aussi d'une gravure très fine.

Le salon, auquel on accède par la salle de bal, est entièrement revêtu de miroirs et encore de stucs qui créent de singuliers effets optiques au plafond. L'ameublement de style Louis XVI a été expressément conçu pour cette pièce.

La pièce donne sur le très beau jardin créé là où se dressait le théâtre de San Cassiano, appartenant à la famille Tron de San Benedetto, et qui fut le premier à Venise et en Europe à devenir public après délibération du Conseil des Dix en 1636. Considéré comme le plus grand théâtre de la ville avec ses six rangées de loges, il fut peu utilisé après la chute de la Sérénissime, et finalement détruit en 1812. C'est sur le terrain où il se trouvait que s'étendit le jardin de Palazzo Albrizzi.

De nombreux membres de la maison Albrizzi occupèrent d'importantes charges politiques, certains devinrent même Procurateurs de San Marco ; mais le plus célèbre est Isabella Teotochi, qui épousa en secondes noces Giuseppe Albrizzi et qui anima entre la fin du XVIIIème et le début du XIXème siècles, la vie culturelle vénitienne avec son salon littéraire où se donnaient rendez-vous, dans le pavillon de la grande dame à San Moisè, des personnages de premier plan du monde de la culture et de l'art, tels qu'Ugo Foscolo, Ippolito Pindemonte, Stendhal,

made her the famous Bust of Helena, which is still kept in the house, together with other heirlooms concerning Isabella.

As a result of Alessandro Albrizzi's marriage in 1783 to Alba Zenobio (the last descendant of her family and therefore sole heiress), all the Zenobio family's wealth, including properties in the Alto Adige, were handed over to the Albrizzis, thus increasing an already considerable fortune.

The palace, with its perfectly preserved furnishings and decorations, is one of the most remarkable examples of Venetian Baroque and has been inhabited by the Albrizzi family without interruption ever since it was bought.

hal, Vittorio Alfieri, Lord Byron, der sie »die Staël Venedigs« nannte, und Antonio Canova. Letzterer schuf für sie die Büste der Helena, die sich zusammen mit anderen Erinnerungsstücken an Isabella noch heute im Palazzo befindet.

Nach der Heirat im Jahre 1783 von Alessandro Albrizzi und Alba Zenobio, letztes Mitglied ihrer Familie und daher Alleinerbin, gingen die gesamten Güter der Zenobio, einschließlich der Besitztümer in Südtirol, in das bereits beträchtliche Vermögen der Albrizzi über.

Die Albrizzi bewohnten den Palazzo fortwährend. Seine perfekt erhaltene Einrichtung und dekorative Ausstattung sind eines der beachtlichsten Zeugnisse des Barock in Venedig.

Vittorio Alfieri, Lord Byron, qui la surnomma la « Madame de Staël de Venise » et Antonio Canova qui exécuta pour elle le fameux Buste d'Hélène, conservé encore aujourd'hui dans la demeure, parmi les autres souvenirs d'Isabella.

Suite au mariage célébré en 1783 entre Alessandro Albrizzi et Alba Zenobio, dernière descendante de cette famille et par conséquent héritière universelle du patrimoine, tous les biens des Zenobio, les propriétés du haut Adige incluses, fusionnèrent avec la Maison Albrizzi, dont la fortune était déjà considérable.

Le palais qui, avec ses ameublements et ses ornements, constitue l'un des plus considérables témoignages du baroque à Venise, n'a cessé d'être habité par la famille Albrizzi.

141 The *portego* on the first floor, entirely coated with ivory and gold stucco work. The frames around the paintings on the ceiling and walls and over the doors, the skirting and the wall sections are some of Abbondio Stazio's most elaborate creations. They are animated by mythological and allegorical subjects, foliage, and flights of putti wrapped in flowing folds of drapery.

143 The great portal leading into the *portego* on the first floor, with allegorical decorations over the doors and the great family coat of arms supported by putti and an angel blowing a trumpet. The stucco decorations are the work of the Ticino-born Abbondio Stazio, the most impressive stucco worker of 18th-century Venice, who created them towards the end of the 17th century. They are one of the artist's first works in the lagoon city.

145 The square ballroom. The walls have been left relatively smooth to contrast with the highly-elaborate ceiling and are hung with carved and gilt frames containing the huge portraits of the Procurators (not only the Albrizzis, but also the Barbarigo family) which became the property of the Albrizzis on the marriage of Giovanni Battista Albrizzi to Teresa Barbarigo in 1740. On the left-hand wall is a portrait of the famous admiral Angelo Emo, who is also related to the Albrizzis and whose great galley lamp is preserved in the *portego* on the ground floor.

146/147 The square ballroom. The ceiling is completely covered with a closely-folded velarium of stucco supported by twenty-eight winged putti and by four male figures arranged like caryatids at its four corners. The technical perfection and creative inspiration of the ceiling make it a remarkable example of artistic stucco work.

148 The square ballroom. Detail of a stucco medallion with a mythological subject, supported by putti and decorated with elements of foliage over one of the doors. Like the frames for the paintings, the furniture also has elegant carved decorations. Medallions in the console tables contain portraits of members of the Albrizzi family.

149 The drawing-room lined with mirrors and large stucco panels. The Louis Seize furniture was designed especially for this room, which faces onto the beautiful garden created by the Albrizzis on the site of the San Cassiano theatre, destroyed in 1812 (the first public theatre in Venice and Europe).

151 The stucco ceiling in the Louis Seize Drawing-Room. There are remarkable trompe-l'œil effects in the composition, which depicts a great cupola enclosed in festoons of foliage supported by putti.

PALAZZO ZENOBIO
SOPRA IL RIO DEL CARMINE

PALAZZO ZENOBIO SOPRA IL RIO DEL CARMINE

Architettura di Antonio Gaſpari

Luca Carleuarijs del: et inc: 93

PALAZZO ZENOBIO

Far from the famous tourist routes, Ca' Zenobio faces onto the quiet Rio dei Carmini on a site that is not spectacular, like the Grand Canal, but rather is characterised by serene intimacy, unchanged by time.

Ca' Zenobio was built towards the end of the 17th century on the site where the Gothic Palazzo Morosini had stood until a few years before. Because there are few other contemporary buildings in the city with a similarly broad layout, Palazzo Zenobio is one of the most important examples of Venetian late-Baroque style, not only architecturally but also for the decoration of the interior.

The building takes its name from the family who owned it up until the mid-19th century and had it built in the form in which we see it today, according to the design of the architect Antonio Gaspari.

The Zenobio family were rich landowners originally from Verona, where they had lived since the mid-15th century. In the first fifty years of the 17th century, they had enormously increased their wealth, to the degree that when the Republic of Venice offered accession to the Venetian nobility in exchange for appropriate sums of money (in order to finance the war of Crete) in 1645, Pietro Zenobio was quick to pay the necessary hundred thousand ducats. In 1646 he became a patrician of St. Mark "con posteri in perpetuo".

A few years later, the Zenobios acquired the title of Counts of the Empire from the Archduke Ferdinando Carlo, Count of the Tyrol, having already been invested with the four castles of Monreale, Salorno, Enna and Caldivo in the Tyrol.

They continued to stay in Verona, however. It was only after the marriage of one of Pietro's granddaughters, Margherita, to a member of the Donà family that the Zenobios purchased a large property in Este from Marco and Tommaso Corner and the Gothic palace in Venice from Elena Morosini, the first of a long series of real-estate investments in the lagoon city.

The reconstruction of the old Palazzo Morosini began in the early sixteen-eighties and was entrusted by Verità Zenobio and her

Weitab von den bekannten Pfaden der Touristen steht der Palazzo Zenobio, der auf den stillen Rio dei Carmini blickt. Die Lage des Palastes kennzeichnet eine im Laufe der Zeit unverändert gebliebene heitere Vertrautheit.

Ca' Zenobio wurde gegen Ende des 17. Jahrhunderts auf dem Areal des gotischen Palazzo Morosini erbaut. Da es recht wenige zeitgenössische Paläste mit einem ähnlich breitgelagerten Baukörper gibt, ist der Palazzo Zenobio eines der wichtigsten Gebäude des späten venezianischen Barock. Auch die Ausstattung der Innenräume ist bemerkenswert.

Die Zenobio, deren Name der Palazzo trägt, ließen das Gebäude, so wie es sich heute noch zeigt, nach dem Entwurf des Architekten Antonio Gaspari erbauen. Bis Mitte des 19. Jahrhunderts blieb der Palast im Besitz der Familie.

Die Zenobio waren sehr wohlhabende Großgrundbesitzer, die seit Mitte des 15. Jahrhunderts in Verona ansässig waren. In der ersten Hälfte des 17. Jahrhunderts hatten sie ihr Vermögen um einiges vergrößert. So fiel es Pietro Zenobio auch nicht schwer, als die Republik Venedig im Jahre 1645 zur Finanzierung des Kreta-Krieges gegen Zahlung von 100 000 Dukaten den Zugang zur venezianischen Aristokratie öffnete, den erforderlichen Betrag unverzüglich zu entrichten. 1646 war Pietro Patrizier von San Marco »con posteri in perpetuo«.

Ein paar Jahre später erwarben die Zenobio von Erzherzog Ferdinand Karl, Graf von Tirol, den Grafentitel, nachdem sie bereits in die vier Burgen von Monreale, Salorno, Enna und Caldivo in Tirol investiert hatten.

Die Familie lebte zunächst weiterhin in Verona. Erst nach der Vermählung einer Enkelin Pietros, Margherita, mit einem Mitglied der Familie Donà erwarben die Zenobio von Marco und Tommaso Corner große Liegenschaften in Este und den gotischen Palast von Elena Morosini. Dies war nur der Beginn für viele weitere Immobilienkäufe in der Lagunenstadt.

Anfang der achtziger Jahre des 17. Jahrhunderts begann der Bau des Palazzo Zeno-

Loin des parcours touristiques bien connus de la ville, Ca' Zenobio donne sur le paisible canal des Carmini dans un endroit que caractérise moins son aspect scénographique spectaculaire, comme c'est le cas du Grand Canal, que son intimité sereine inchangée dans le temps.

Construit vers la fin du XVIIème siècle là où peu d'années auparavant s'élevait le palais gothique des Morosini, le Palazzo Zenobio est l'un des rares à son époque à posséder cette structure allongée, il représente donc sur le plan architectural, mais pas moins par la décoration des intérieurs, l'un des plus importants épisodes de la période finale du baroque vénitien.

L'édifice porte le nom de la famille qui le posséda jusqu'à la moitié du XIXème siècle et le fit construire sur le projet de l'architecte Antonio Gaspari, sous la forme que nous lui connaissons aujourd'hui.

Riche famille de propriétaires terriens d'origine véronaise, les Zenobio, qui résidaient à Vérone depuis le milieu du XVème siècle, avaient démesurément accru leur patrimoine au cours des premiers cinquante ans du XVIIème siècle, à tel point qu'en 1645, quand la Sérénissime, pour financer la guerre de Candie, ouvrit l'accès au patriciat vénitien en échange d'une forte somme d'argent, Pietro Zenobio n'eut aucune difficulté à débourser les 100 000 ducats obligatoires, devenant en 1646 Patricien de San Marco « con posteri a perpetuo » (avec ses descendants à perpétuité).

Quelques années plus tard, les Zenobio acquièrent de l'archiduc Ferdinando Carlo, comte du Tyrol, le titre de comtes de l'Empire, ayant déjà reçu l'investiture des quatre châteaux de Monreale, Salorno, Enna et Caldivo au Tyrol.

Toutefois, ils continuèrent de vivre à Vérone ; ce fut seulement après le mariage d'une descendante de Pietro, Margherita, avec un membre de la famille Donà que l'achat par Marco et Tommaso Corner d'une grande propriété à Este et du palais gothique d'Elena Morosini à Venise fut effectué, avant une longue série d'investissements immobiliers dans la ville lagunaire.

younger brother Pietro to Antonio Gaspari, one of Baldassare Longhena's pupils. Gaspari drew up a project which was unusual for Venice: a building with a very broad façade of Istrian marble facing onto the canal, with two wings surrounding an inner garden. The pavilion designed by Tommaso Temanza was erected at the bottom of the garden in the 18th century as a scenographic enclosure, used by the Zenobios for the family archives and library.

The compact rectangular palace façade is given rhythm by a number of windows concentrated mainly at the centre, thus accentuating the chiaroscuro effects and the interior room arrangement. The great ballroom faces onto the first-floor balcony.

The convergence of attention at the centre of the façade is a motive new to Venice and more reminiscent of architecture on dry land. The balconies were topped by a pediment (formerly set with the great family coat of arms extending above the roofline) intended to give the composition an upward thrust.

From the ample entrance hall on the ground floor, there is an ornate staircase of modest size leading to a not particularly high, rather narrow, elongated *portego* which faces onto the inner garden on one side and through an arch onto the vast ballroom on the other. Like a handful of other similar examples still preserved today, the ballroom has pictorial and stucco decorations which make it one of the most remarkable examples of late Baroque interior design.

The project for the decoration of the great hall (which reaches the height of two floors) and of the little *portego* leading into it, forming a "T", was certainly worked out by Gaspari. The frescoes were entrusted to Louis Dorigny (1654–1742), a French painter who had spent some years in Rome and Umbria and had then moved to Venice where he was highly successful. He was commissioned to do a number of works up until his departure for Verona in 1688. For the stucco work the Zenobios called in Abbondio Stazio, an artist from the Ticino region, born in 1663, who was to become the most important stucco-worker in Venice during the first half of the 18th century.

The decoration of the interior of Ca' Zenobio therefore involved three young artists working together in remarkable harmony, as is demonstrated by the exemplary fusion between architecture, painting and sculptural effects.

Dorigny's composition is on the ceiling of the great ballroom, with an elaborate

bio, den Verità Zenobio und ihr jüngerer Bruder Pietro dem Schüler Baldassare Longhenas, Antonio Gaspari, anvertrauten. Gaspari entwarf ein für Venedig ungewöhnliches Gebäude mit einer breitgelagerten Fassade aus istrischem Marmor zum Kanal und mit zwei Flügeln, die den Garten begrenzen. Im 18. Jahrhundert wurde im Garten ein von Tommaso Temanza entworfener Pavillon errichtet, den die Zenobio als Archiv und Hausbibliothek nutzten.

Die kompakte rechteckige Fassade des Palastes wird von zahlreichen Fenstern rhythmisiert, die sich merklich im Zentrum der Front konzentrieren, um die Helldunkelkontraste zu betonen und die Raumanordnung im Innern hervorzuheben. Hinter dem Balkon des ersten Obergeschosses liegt der große Ballsaal.

Ein völlig neues Motiv in Venedig war die Konzentration der aufwendigen Bauteile auf das Fassadenzentrum. Über den Balkonen erhebt sich der Giebel, an dem einst das große Familienwappen über die Dachlinie hinaus prangte, um der Komposition eine aufsteigende Wirkung zu verleihen. Dieses Motiv erinnert eher an die Architektur des Festlandes.

Von der großzügigen Eingangshalle im Erdgeschoß führt eine zwar verzierte, aber bescheidene Treppe zu einem nicht besonders hohen, ziemlich engen und langen *portego*. Von dort blickt man von der einen Seite auf den Garten im Innenhof. Auf der anderen Seite gelangt man durch einen Bogen zum großen Ballsaal, dessen Ausstattung mit Malereien und Stuckarbeiten eines der außergewöhnlichsten Zeugnisse des Spätbarock darstellt.

Der Plan für die Ausstattung des großen Saals, der die Raumhöhe zweier Stockwerke einnimmt, und des kleinen *portego,* der zu ihm führt, wurde sicherlich von Gaspari ausgearbeitet. Die Ausführung der Fresken wurde Louis Dorigny (1654–1742) anvertraut. Der französische Maler hatte einige Jahre in Rom und in Umbrien verbracht, bevor er nach Venedig kam, wo er große Erfolge verzeichnen konnte und bis zu seiner Weiterreise nach Verona im Jahre 1688 zahlreiche Aufträge erhielt. Die Stukkaturen führte Abbondio Stazio aus. Der 1663 im Tessin geborene Künstler sollte der bedeutendste Stukkateur der ersten Hälfte des 18. Jahrhunderts in der Lagunenstadt werden.

Mit der Ausstattung der Innenräume waren also drei junge Künstler beschäftigt. Sie arbeiteten in einmaliger Harmonie zusammen, wie die beispielhafte Verschmel-

La reconstruction du vieux palais Morosini débuta durant les premières années quatre-vingt du siècle et fut confiée par Verità Zenobio et son plus jeune frère, Pietro, à Antonio Gaspari, élève de Baldassare Longhena, qui élabora un projet inhabituel pour Venise : un édifice à la façade en pierre d'Istrie très allongée donnant sur le canal avec deux ailes délimitant le jardin intérieur, au fond duquel, au XVIIIème siècle, fut dressé le pavillon conçu par Tommaso Temanza, que les Zenobio utilisèrent comme archives et bibliothèque familiale.

La compacte façade rectangulaire du palais est ponctuée de nombreuses fenêtres qui, en se concentrant de façon sensible dans la partie centrale, accentuent les effets de clairs-obscurs et mettent en évidence la présence de la grande salle de bal qui donne sur le balcon de l'étage noble.

La convergence de l'attention au centre de la façade avec les balcons et le fronton, sur lequel on posait autrefois le grand écusson de la famille qui dépassait de la ligne du toit, dans l'intention de conférer un développement ascensionnel à la composition, est un nouveau motif à Venise et rappelle plutôt l'architecture continentale.

Depuis la grande entrée du rez-de-chaussée, un escalier décoré, mais de dimensions modestes, introduit dans un *portego* pas très haut, plutôt étroit et long qui donne d'un côté sur le jardin de la cour intérieure et de l'autre, à travers un arc, sur la très vaste salle de bal qui, par ses décorations picturales et ses stucs, constitue, avec peu d'autres exemples similaires encore conservés aujourd'hui, l'un des témoignages les plus extraordinaires de la fin du baroque.

Le projet des ornements de la grande salle, qui atteint la hauteur des deux étages, mais également du petit *portego* qui mène à elle, formant un « T », fut certainement étudié par Gaspari, mais l'exécution des fresques fut confiée à Louis Dorigny (1654–1742), peintre français qui, après avoir passé quelques années à Rome et en Ombrie, arriva à Venise, où il obtint un grand succès et reçut de nombreuses commandes jusqu'au moment de son départ pour Vérone en 1688 ; pour les stucs, les Zenobio engagèrent Abbondio Stazio, un artiste tessinois, né en 1663, qui deviendra le plus important stucateur de Venise durant la première moitié du XVIIIème siècle.

L'aménagement intérieur de Ca' Zenobio fut donc confié à trois jeunes artistes qui travaillèrent en singulière harmonie, comme il ressort de la fusion exemplaire entre l'architecture, la peinture et l'art plastique.

frame of pilasters enriched with foliage and animated with male and female figures incarnating the Sciences and the Arts. It depicts a great central figure, Aurora, her wings unfurled as she is carried by the wind, who precedes the Sun-god's chariot drawn by fiery chargers; over her head there are two putti in flight, carrying a torch and a container of dew, which represent the dawn.

The sequence of the seven windows opening onto the canal is virtually continued in those of equal size illusionistically painted on the upper part of the three inner walls. These are separated by thirteen female figures, nine of which represent the Muses. The only bizarre element in this elaborate composition is the image of a dwarf smoking a pipe, just beside the balcony over the majestic entrance arch which was intended to house the orchestra.

The lower part of the hall is lined with mirrors which are certainly of French inspiration, framed with elaborate stucco work. There are two ovals on the short walls, representing *The Fall of Phaethon* and *The Death of the Children of Niobe*. In the corners of the hall, there are two coats of arms and two monograms, probably standing for Verità Zenobio, to indicate the person who commissioned the work.

The layout of the various episodes in this iconographic scheme, centred on Apollo, god of light and order and inspiration of the Muses, is based on the rich arrangement of white and gold stucco work. The frames and military trophies, putti and pilasters around the lacunar doors harmonize so perfectly with the paintings that there is no doubt they were planned together. In fact, even the four medallions in gilt stucco over the doors are linked with the Apollonian theme, representing Apollo with Daphne, Apollo with Marsyas, Marsyas being skinned, and Apollo with Chione.

Louis Dorigny and Abbondio Stazio were also responsible for the decoration of other rooms in the palace, for example the small, low *portego* with its typical iconographic subjects illustrating the theme of Virtue conquering Vice.

The lower vaulted ceiling of the *portego* gives rise to a different pictorial style, which is narrower and more descriptive by comparison with the great hall. Here again, there are highly refined stucco frames around the pictures, including those over the doors, which contain groups of cherubs representing the Fine Arts. On the walls hang three landscapes created by Luca Carlevarijs, an-

zung von Architektur, Malerei und Plastik zeigt.

An der Decke des großen Ballsaals, gerahmt von einem sorgfältig ausgearbeiteten Architekturprospekt, den Blumenbuketts schmücken und männliche und weibliche die Wissenschaften und die Künste verkörpernde Figuren beleben, befindet sich die Komposition Dorignys: die große, zentrale Figur mit geöffneten Flügeln, die vom Wind getragen wird, ist Aurora. Links neben der Göttin der Morgenröte sieht man den Sonnenwagen, den feurige Rösser ziehen. Oberhalb von Aurora flüchten zwei Putten mit Fackel und Taubehälter. Sie stellen die Morgendämmerung dar.

Die sieben Fenster zum Kanal finden ihre Entsprechung in den gleichgroßen gemalten Fenstern oben an den drei Innenwänden. Zwischen ihnen wurden dreizehn weibliche Gestalten eingefügt, von denen neun Figuren die Musen darstellen. Die einzige bizarre Note in der durchdachten Komposition ist der pfeiferauchende Zwerg in der Nähe des Orchesterbalkons über dem würdevollen Eingangsbogen.

Die Wände des Saals sind mit französisch anmutenden Spiegeln ausgestattet. Sie werden von feinsten Stukkaturen gerahmt. Über den Spiegeln, in einer schmalen Wandzone, befinden sich zwei ovalförmige Darstellungen, die *Den Sturz des Phaethon* und *Den Tod der Niobiden* zeigen. An den Saalecken bezeichnen zwei Wappen und zwei Monogramme, wahrscheinlich von Verità Zenobio, den Auftraggeber.

Die verschiedenen Malereien, in deren Zentrum Apoll, der Gott des Lichts und der Ordnung und Herr der Musen, steht, befinden sich zwischen reich gestalteten weißen und vergoldeten Stuckarbeiten. Diese harmonieren mit ihren Rahmen, Waffentrophäen, Putten und Wandpfeilern, die die Kassettentüren rahmen, perfekt mit den Malereien und zeugen von einer einheitlichen Planung. Auch die Darstellungen in den vier Medaillons aus vergoldetem Stuck über den Türen beziehen sich auf den apollinischen Mythos. Auf ihnen sind Apoll und Daphne, Apoll und Marsyas, der enthäutete Marsyas und Apoll und Chione dargestellt.

Louis Dorigny und Abbondio Stazio arbeiteten auch bei der Ausschmückung anderer Räume des Palastes zusammen. So stellten sie in dem kleinen und niedrigen *portego* ein typisches ikonographisches Thema dar, die Tugend besiegt das Laster.

Die niedrigere Gewölbedecke des *portego* forderte im Vergleich zu dem großen Saal

La grande salle de bal, au plafond encadré d'un appareil élaboré à piliers, enrichi d'éléments végétaux et animé de personnages masculins et féminins qui incarnent les Sciences et les Arts, présente la composition de Dorigny : une grande figure centrale aux ailes déployées transportée par les vents, l'Aurore, précède le char du soleil traîné par de fougueux destriers, tandis qu'au-dessus d'elle, deux putti en fuite qui tiennent une torche et un vase contenant de la rosée, représentent le crépuscule du Matin.

Les sept fenêtres qui surplombent le grand fenêtrage sur le canal trouvent leur propre continuité dans celles, de dimensions égales, peintes en trompe-l'œil sur la partie supérieure des trois murs intérieurs. Treize personnages féminins y sont intercalés, dont neuf représentent les Muses ; unique note bizarre dans une composition si élaborée, le nain qui fume la pipe près du balcon destiné à l'orchestre, au-dessus du majestueux arc d'entrée.

Les parois de la salle sont revêtues de miroirs d'inspiration française encadrés de stucs très élaborés, avec deux ovales, sur ceux des murs étroits, qui représentent *La Chute de Phaéton* et *La Mort des Niobides ;* aux angles de la salle, deux écussons et deux monogrammes, probablement de Verità Zenobio, indiquent le commanditaire.

Les diverses représentations centrées sur le thème de la divinité de la Lumière et de l'Ordre, Apollon, inspirateur des Muses, sont confiées au riche apparat de stucs blancs et dorés, avec cadres, trophées d'armes, putti et parastates qui encadrent les portes à caissons. Il s'harmonise si parfaitement avec les tableaux que cela révèle une claire homogénéité de programmation. En effet, même les quatre médaillons en stuc doré, sur les portes, se réfèrent au mythe apollinien avec les représentations d'Apollon et Daphné, Apollon et Marsyas, Marsyas écorché et Apollon et Chioni.

Louis Dorigny et Abbondio Stazio décorèrent également d'autres pièces du palais et surtout le *portego* petit et bas avec des sujets d'iconographie courante pour illustrer le thème de la Vertu qui vainc le Vice.

Le plafond à voûte basse du *portego* détermine un style pictural différent, moins large et plus descriptif. Ici encore, des stucs très raffinés encadrent les tableaux, ceux des dessus-de-porte inclus, dans lesquels apparaissent des groupes de petits amours qui représentent les Beaux-Arts. Les trois paysages du mur sont l'œuvre de Luca Carlevarijs,

other young artist born in Udine in 1663, who came to Venice in 1679 and was under the patronage of the Zenobio family (so he was not surprisingly known as Luca di Ca' Zenobio).

In fact the great wealth they had accumulated enabled the Zenobio family to patronize a number of artists working in Venice between the end of the 17th and the beginning of the 18th centuries. Among others, these included Gregorio Lazzarini (who painted a ceiling in the palace in 1700, depicting *Ceres and Bacchus*) and Giambattista Tiepolo (whose biographer Da Canal recalls him having supplied a whole series of paintings for various rooms in the palace).

Unfortunately, many of these works of art have since disappeared. After the fall of the Venetian Republic, the last of the Zenobios, Alvise, abandoned the city for London, where he died in 1815. The palace went to his sister Alba and was sold to Count Salvi of Vicenza, who began an extensive restoration programme which produced many changes, though the ballroom and *portego* were fortunately left intact.

In 1850, the palace was purchased by the Community of Armenian Fathers and is now the home of the Armenian College.

einen weniger breiten und eher beschreibenden Malstil. Auch hier rahmen kostbare Stukkaturen die Malereien. In den Sopraporten stellen Amoretten die schönen Künste dar. An den Wänden hängen drei Landschaftsbilder von Luca Carlevarijs. Der 1663 in Udine geborene Künstler kam 1679 nach Venedig und arbeitete unter dem Schutz der Zenobio, weshalb er auch als Luca di Ca' Zenobio bekannt wurde.

Ihr unermeßlicher Reichtum ermöglichte es den Zenobio, zwischen dem Ende des Seicento und dem Beginn des Settecento zahlreiche in Venedig wirkende Künstler zu unterstützen. Unter anderem protegierten sie Gregorio Lazzarini, der um 1700 für ihren Palast eine Deckenmalerei mit *Ceres und Bacchus* schuf, und Giambattista Tiepolo, dessen Biograph Da Canal daran erinnert, daß er zahlreiche Säle des Wohnsitzes ausgemalt hat.

Heute sind viele dieser Kunstwerke leider verloren. Nach dem Untergang der Republik Venedig verließ der letzte Zenobio, Alvise, die Lagunenstadt und begab sich nach London, wo er 1815 verstarb. Den Palast erbte dessen Schwester Alba, die ihn an den Grafen Salvi aus Vicenza verkaufte. Dieser veranlaßte umfangreiche Restaurierungsarbeiten, die zum Glück den Ballsaal und den *portego* nicht betrafen.

Im Jahre 1850 wurde der Palast von der Armenischen Katholischen Bruderschaft erworben. Heute ist er Sitz des Armenischen Kollegs.

un autre jeune artiste, né à Udine en 1663 et arrivé à Venise en 1679, que les Zenobio protégeaient, et ce n'est pas un hasard si le peintre était alors connu sous le nom de Luca de Ca' Zenobio.

Les grandes richesses accumulées par la famille permirent en effet aux Zenobio de protéger de nombreux artistes actifs à Venise entre la fin du XVIIème et le début du XVIIIème siècle : entre autres Gregorio Lazzarini qui, en 1700, peignit pour le palais un plafond avec *Cérès et Bacchus* et Giambattista Tiepolo, dont son biographe Da Canal mentionne qu'il a fourni des toiles pour plusieurs pièces de la demeure.

Aujourd'hui, hélas, nombre de ces œuvres d'art ont disparu : en effet, après la chute de la République de Venise, le dernier des Zenobio, Alvise, abandonna la ville lagunaire pour Londres, où il mourut en 1815 ; transmis en héritage à sa sœur Alba, après la mort de celui-ci, le palais fut vendu au comte Salvi de Vicence. Ce dernier débuta un vaste programme de restauration qui apporta de nombreux changements, laissant heureusement intacts le salon et le *portego*.

En 1850, le palais fut acheté par la Communauté des Pères Arméniens Catholiques et il est aujourd'hui le siège du Collège Arménien.

157 The small *portego* leading into the ballroom. It is decorated with stucco work by Abbondio Stazio and frescoes by Louis Dorigny, who illustrated the theme of Virtue conquering Vice. There are three landscapes on the walls: these are the work of Luca Carlevarijs, one of the artists under the patronage of the Zenobio family. The *portego* has one side facing onto the inner garden and the other leading through a majestic arch to the ballroom.

158/159 The ballroom. The fresco decorations on the ceiling and walls are by Louis Dorigny and illustrate the theme of Apollo, god of light and order and inspiration of the Muses; these appear between the painted windows in the upper part of the walls, where there is also a great balcony for the orchestra. The painted episodes are set in stucco work by Abbondio Stazio.

161 The ballroom seen from the small, low and narrow *portego* with which it forms a "T".

162 Louis Dorigny, *Aurora, Goddess of the Dawn.* This fresco is in the centre of the ballroom ceiling and contains a great winged figure, Aurora, before the chariot of the sun. Over her head are two putti in flight, representing the dawn.

163 The ballroom. The walls are lined with great mirrors of French inspiration, framed with very elaborate stucco work; there are two ovals on the shorter walls representing *The Fall of Phaethon* and *The Death of the Children of Niobe.*

157 Kleiner *portego* zum Ballsaal. Diesen Raum schmücken Stukkaturen von Abbondio Stazio und Fresken von Louis Dorigny. Dargestellt ist das Thema der Tugend, die das Laster besiegt. An den Wänden befinden sich drei Landschaften von Luca Carlevarijs, den die Zenobio wie andere junge Künstler förderten. Der *portego* öffnet sich auf einer Seite zum Garten, auf der anderen gelangt man durch einen majestätischen Bogen zum Ballsaal.

158/159 Ballsaal. Die Fresken an der Decke und an den Wänden, die Louis Dorigny schuf, zeigen Begebenheiten aus dem Leben Apolls, Gott des Lichts und der Ordnung. Er war auch der Herr der Musen, die zwischen den gemalten Fenstern im oberen Teil der Wände sitzen. Die einzelnen Episoden rahmen Stukkaturen von Abbondio Stazio.

161 Der Ballsaal vom kleinen, niedrigen und schmalen *portego* aus gesehen, der zusammen mit dem großen Saal eine T-Form bildet.

162 Louis Dorigny, *Aurora, Göttin der Morgenröte.* Dies ist das Hauptfresko an der Ballsaaldecke. Die große geflügelte Hauptfigur – die Morgenröte – schwebt rechts neben dem Sonnenwagen, während zwei flüchtende Putten über ihr die Morgendämmerung darstellen.

163 Ballsaal. Den größten Teil der Wände verkleiden große, französisch anmutende Spiegel mit fein ausgearbeiteten Stuckrahmen. Oberhalb der Spiegel an den beiden Schmalseiten befinden sich zwei ovale Darstellungen mit *Dem Sturz des Phaethon* und *Dem Tod der Niobiden.*

157 Petit *portego* d'accès à la salle de bal. Il est décoré de stucs d'Abbondio Stazio et de fresques de Louis Dorigny qui illustrent la victoire de la Vertu sur le Vice. Sur les murs on découvre trois paysages de Luca Carlevarijs qui bénéficia comme d'autres jeunes artistes du mécénat des Zenobio. Le *portego* donne d'un côté sur le jardin intérieur, de l'autre sur la salle de bal en passant sous un arc majestueux.

158/159 Salle de bal. Les fresques au plafond et sur les murs sont de Louis Dorigny et elles traitent du dieu de la Lumière et de l'Ordre, Apollon, inspirateur des Muses qui se trouvent entre les fausses fenêtres dans la partie supérieure des murs. Des stucs d'Abbondio Stazio encadrent les différents épisodes.

161 Salle de bal vue du petit *portego,* bas et étroit qui forme avec la grande salle un dessin en « T ».

162 Louis Dorigny, *L'Aurore.* Il s'agit de la fresque centrale du plafond de la salle de bal. Le grand personnage ailé au centre, Aurore, précède le char du soleil ; au-dessus d'elle, deux putti en fuite représentent le crépuscule matinal.

163 Salle de bal. La partie inférieure des murs est couverte de grands miroirs d'inspiration française et encadrés de stucs très élaborés. Sur les petits murs, deux illustrations ovales de *La Chute de Phaéton* et *La Mort des Niobides.*

PALAZZO PISANI

ā S. Stefano

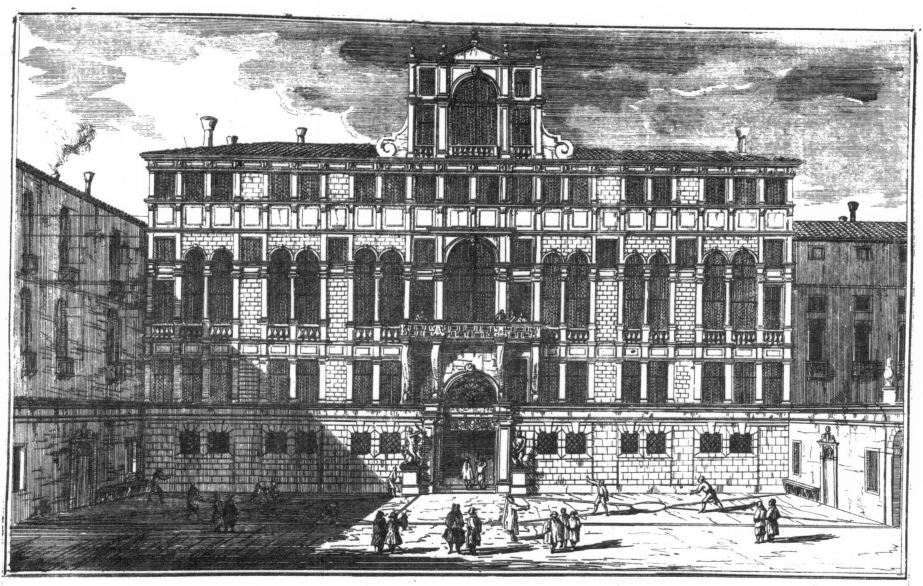

PALAZZO PISANI
ā S. Stefano

PALAZZO PISANI

With dimensions that make it one of the most imposing in the whole city of Venice, this palace belonged to one of the richest and most respected families in the city. The Pisani had been known since the 14th century for their properties purchased in Venice and on the mainland with the profits they made by trading.

Towards the end of the 16th century, Alvise Pisani, who belonged to the so-called "dal Banco" branch of the family (because it owned a bank at Rialto) and was considered one of the four pillars of Venetian finance, left his home in Santa Maria del Giglio and built the grandiose palace at Santo Stefano, in the parish of San Vidal. Here his descendants continued to live, being known from then onwards as the Pisani di Santo Stefano.

The palace was constructed in the first twenty years of the 17th century on land previously occupied by a house Alvise had inherited and other neighbouring buildings he had purchased and then demolished to make way for this grand construction (in the history of which there are still various gaps). According to chroniclers of the time, there was never a single project by one architect; there were only various suggestions and indications that Alvise Pisani himself supplied.

Many of Alvise's descendants went into public service: two of his grandsons, Alvise and Almorò (a Venetian dialect form of Ermolao), were elected Procurators of St. Mark, in 1647 and 1656 respectively. The latter became the sole owner of the palace and other goods, which he had bound by a trust establishing that everything – including the works of art – should be inalienable and subject to the right of male primogeniture, the heir being under an obligation to be called Almorò.

One of his sons also rose to the dignity of Procurator, but preferred to live in the apartments placed at his disposal by the State in the Procuratie Nuove of Piazza San Marco rather than in the palace of Santo Stefano. The palace became the particular concern of one of Almorò's grandsons instead. He commissioned Girolamo Frigimelica to add a second floor to the palace, which early 18th-

Seiner gewaltigen Ausmaße wegen gilt der Palazzo Pisani als eines der imposantesten Bauwerke der Stadt. Er gehörte einer der angesehensten und reichsten Familien Venedigs, den Pisani, die Händler waren und seit dem 14. Jahrhundert zahlreiche Ländereien auf dem Festland und in Venedig erworben hatten.

Alvise Pisani, der zum Familienzweig mit dem Beinamen »dal Banco« gehörte (so genannt wegen der Bank, die der Clan im Bezirk Rialto besaß) und als eine der Stützen der venezianischen Finanzwelt galt, verließ gegen Ende des 16. Jahrhunderts seinen Wohnsitz in Santa Maria del Giglio. Bei Santo Stefano, im Gemeindegebiet von San Vidal, ließ er den Palast erbauen, in dem seine Nachkommen wohnen sollten. Sie wurden daher Pisani di Santo Stefano genannt.

In den ersten beiden Jahrzehnten des 17. Jahrhunderts wurde der Palazzo auf dem Areal eines geerbten Gebäudes und anderer Nachbargebäude errichtet. In der Baugeschichte des Palastes klaffen allerdings noch zahlreiche Lücken. So hatte es laut zeitgenössischer Chroniken nie einen einheitlichen Architektenplan gegeben, sondern lediglich Vorschläge und Anleitungen von Alvise Pisani selbst.

Viele Nachkommen Alvises schlugen eine Beamtenkarriere ein: Zwei seiner Enkel, Alvise und Almorò (mundartlich für Ermolao), wurden 1647 bzw. 1656 zu Prokuratoren von San Marco gewählt. Nachdem Almorò Alleinerbe des Palastes und anderer Güter geworden war, vinkulierte er das gesamte Vermögen mit einem Fideikommiß. Fortan wurden alle Vermögenswerte einschließlich der Kunstwerke unveräußerlich und konnten nur an den erstgeborenen Sohn vererbt werden, der zudem obligatorisch Almorò heißen mußte. Auch einer seiner Söhne wurde Prokurator. Dieser zog es jedoch vor, Wohnung in den Räumlichkeiten zu nehmen, die ihm der Staat in den Neuen Prokuratien am Markusplatz zur Verfügung stellte, als im Palast bei Santo Stefano.

Ein Enkel Almoròs hingegen widmete dem Palazzo besondere Aufmerksamkeit. So ließ er den Palast, der auf Stichen aus den ersten Jahren des 18. Jahrhunderts mit nur

Le palais, l'un des édifices les plus imposants de la ville, appartient à une des familles les plus prestigieuses et les plus fortunées de Venise, les Pisani, connus depuis le XIVème siècle pour leurs propriétés sur la terre ferme et les biens immobiliers à Venise acquis avec les gains provenant de la pratique du commerce.

Vers la fin du XVIème siècle, Alvise Pisani qui appartenait à la branche de la famille dite « dal Banco » (de la banque), parce que propriétaire d'une Banque à Rialto, considérée comme l'une des quatre colonnes portantes de la finance vénitienne, quitta sa demeure de Santa Maria del Giglio et construisit à Santo Stefano, dans la paroisse de San Vidal, le palais grandiose dans lequel habitèrent ses descendants connus depuis lors comme Pisani de Santo Stefano.

Le palais fut édifié durant les premières vingt années du XVIIème siècle sur le terrain d'une maison héritée et d'autres voisines, achetées et ensuite démolies, pour faire place à la majestueuse construction dont l'histoire est encore bien lacunaire; si l'on s'en tient aux chroniques de l'époque, il n'y eut jamais de projet homogène de la part d'un architecte, mais plutôt des suggestions et des indications fournies par Alvise Pisani en personne.

Des descendants d'Alvise, nombreux furent ceux qui entrèrent au service de l'Etat: deux de ses petits-fils, Alvise et Almorò, forme dialectale pour Ermolao, furent élus respectivement en 1647 et 1656 Procurateurs de San Marco; le second, devenu unique propriétaire du palais et des autres biens, les bloqua, en instituant un fidéicommis sur la base duquel toute chose, œuvres d'art incluses, devenait inaliénable et sujette à la primogéniture masculine, avec l'obligation pour l'héritier de s'appeler Almorò. Un de ses fils parvint également à la dignité procuratoire, mais tous préférèrent vivre dans les appartements mis à leur disposition par l'Etat dans les Nouvelles Procuraties de Piazza San Marco plutôt que dans le palais de Santo Stefano. C'est un neveu d'Almorò qui lui consacra une attention particulière. Le palais, qui dans les gravures des premières années du XVIIIème siècle apparaît caractérisé par un

century engravings depict with only one floor above ground. Frigimelica also extended the building with two new wings beyond the old court, enlarging it to add the ballroom and the library.

These renovations took place in the first two decades of the 18th century and Almorò was supported by his brothers, some of whom had taken up a military career, while others had gone into politics. One of the latter was Alvise, the first member of the family to be elected to the highest rank in the State, becoming doge in 1735. The event fulfilled a long-cherished Pisani wish, as demonstrated by the popular verses which resounded through Venice on the occasion: "El primo dei Pisani alfin xe dose / la desditta una volta xe finia. / El tempo xe vegnù de buttar via / l'oro e l'argento come tante nose." (The first Pisani is at last a Doge, / the old baseness is over. / The time is come / to squander gold and silver coins as though they were nuts.)

But the Pisanis' enormous wealth was destined to grow even further as a result of the marriages of the doge's sons and grandsons to heiresses of the Venetian nobility such as Isabella Correr (who brought as part of her dowry the famous numismatic museum created by Girolamo Correr) and Giustiniana Pisani di Santa Maria del Giglio (that branch of the family died with her, so her family's fortune was united with that of the Pisanis of Santo Stefano).

But such a vast fortune, with collections of coins and medals, a library famous for its comprehensiveness, and a collection of one-hundred-and-fifty-nine paintings, including works by Titian, Tintoretto, and Veronese, was not sufficient to satisfy the princely demands of the last of the Pisanis. They became burdened with debts in the course of the 19th century and were forced to sell off all their goods, including the palace. The building was purchased in lots by the Municipality of Venice, and since 1940 it has been the home of the Benedetto Marcello musical conservatory.

Despite all the squandering and pillaging, the palace's general layout and decorations still bear witness to the pomp and opulence stressed by Venetian chroniclers in their descriptions of the ceremony held in honour of Gustav III of Sweden on May 5th 1784, when "all the spacious rooms were not only richly and gracefully adorned, but also illuminated by numerous chandeliers… as were the other apartments, the main gallery, full of paintings by the most renowned artists… and the lengthy staircase leading to the library…"

einem Obergeschoß dargestellt ist, von Girolamo Frigimelica um ein Stockwerk erhöhen. Der Architekt baute außerdem neben dem alten Innenhof zwei Flügel an und vergrößerte den Palast um einen zusätzlichen Ballsaal und die Bibliothek.

Als Almorò diese Umbauten in den ersten zwei Jahrzehnten des 18. Jahrhunderts durchführen ließ, unterstützten ihn seine Brüder, von denen einige die militärische, andere die politische Laufbahn eingeschlagen hatten. Zu letzteren gehörte Alvise, der als erstes Familienmitglied im Jahre 1735 Doge wurde. Nun endlich hatte sich der langgehegte Wunsch der Pisani erfüllt. Die mundartlichen Verse, die bei dieser Gelegenheit in Venedig kursierten, sprechen für sich: »El primo dei Pisani alfin xe dose / la desditta una volta xe finia. / El tempo xe vegnù de buttar via / l'oro e l'argento come tante nose.« (Endlich ist der erste Pisani Doge / die Schmach von einst ist vorbei. / Die Zeit ist gekommen, / mit Gold und Silber um sich zu werfen als seien es Nüsse.)

Das gewaltige Vermögen der Pisani sollte noch weiter anwachsen, dank der ehelichen Verbindungen, die die Söhne und Enkel des Dogen mit reichen Erbinnen des venezianischen Adels schlossen: mit Isabella Correr, deren Mitgift das berühmte, von Girolamo Correr eingerichtete Münzmuseum war, und mit Giustiniana Pisani di Santa Maria del Giglio, die das Vermögen ihres aussterbenden Familienzweigs mit der der Pisani di Santo Stefano vereinte.

Doch trotz kostbarer Münz- und Medaillensammlungen, trotz einer renommierten, sehr umfassenden Bibliothek und trotz einer wertvollen Gemäldesammlung, die 159 Bilder zählte und zu der unter anderem Werke von Tizian, Tintoretto und Veronese gehörten – all dies reichte nicht aus, um die fürstlichen Ansprüche der letzten Pisani zu erfüllen. Völlig überschuldet mußten sie im 19. Jahrhundert ihr gesamtes Hab und Gut verkaufen. Die Gemeinde Venedig erwarb nach und nach den Palast, der seit 1940 Sitz des Konservatoriums Benedetto Marcello ist.

Trotz Verschwendung und Enteignung bewahrt das Gebäude im Hauptbau und in der Ausstattung noch immer den üppigen Prunk, den die venezianischen Chronisten in ihren Schilderungen des Festes zu Ehren von Gustav III. von Schweden am 5. Mai 1784 beschreiben: »all die prachtvollen Zimmer waren nicht nur reich und anmutig ausgestattet, sondern wurden auch von unzähligen Lüstern beleuchtet… wie auch die anderen Wohngemächer und die Hauptgalerie mit

unique étage noble, fut alors surélevé et en acquit un second grâce à l'architecte Girolamo Frigimelica, qui veilla en outre à le prolonger de deux ailes latérales en plus de la vieille cour et à l'agrandir avec l'adjonction de la salle de bal et de la bibliothèque.

Dans ces interventions, qui eurent lieu durant les deux premières décennies du XVIIIème siècle, Almorò fut secondé par ses frères, dont certains avaient entrepris la carrière des armes, d'autres celle de la politique : parmi ces derniers, Alvise, pour la première fois dans l'histoire de la famille, atteignit la plus haute charge de l'Etat, en devenant doge en 1735. L'événement concrétisa une aspiration depuis longtemps caressée par les Pisani comme le soulignent les vers populaires qui coururent à Venise à cette occasion : « El primo dei Pisani alfin xe dose / la desditta una volta xe finia. / El tempo xe vegnù de buttar via / l'oro e l'argento come tante nose. » (Le premier des Pisani finalement devient doge / la déveine d'autrefois est terminée. / Le temps est venu de distribuer l'or et l'argent comme autant de noix.)

L'énorme richesse des Pisani devait encore croître, en vertu des mariages que les descendants du doge contractèrent avec des héritières du patriciat vénitien comme Isabella Correr, qui apporta en dot le célèbre musée numismatique formé par Girolamo Correr, et Giustiniana Pisani de Santa Maria del Giglio par laquelle le bien de cette branche, qui s'éteignit avec sa personne, fut uni à celui des Pisani de Santo Stefano.

Un patrimoine aussi vaste avec des collections de monnaies et de médailles, une bibliothèque renommée pour son intégralité et une collection de tableaux riche de 159 toiles, parmi lesquelles des œuvres de Titien, de Tintoret et de Véronèse, ne suffit pas à satisfaire les exigences princières des derniers Pisani qui, accablés de dettes, vendirent tous leurs biens au cours du XIXème siècle. Le palais fut acheté petit à petit par la Commune de Venise et est depuis 1940 le siège du conservatoire musical Benedetto Marcello.

Malgré les gaspillages et les expropriations, l'édifice conserve encore dans son corps principal et dans ses ornements des témoignages du faste et de l'opulence que les chroniqueurs vénitiens soulignent dans leurs descriptions de la fête donnée en l'honneur de Gustave III de Suède, le 5 mai 1784 quand « toutes les chambres magnifiques étaient non seulement richement et gracieusement ornées, mais illuminées de nombreux lustres… comme l'étaient les autres appartements et la galerie principale parés des ta-

That the Pisanis had concentrated so much of their efforts on the construction and embellishment of the palace is demonstrated by the two statuary groups from the beginning of the 17th century on the threshold. These can be traced back to the hand of the sculptor Girolamo Campagna and represent the first and last of the twelve labours of Hercules: *The Slaying of the Nemean Lion* and *The Capture of Cerberus,* the three-headed guard dog of Hades.

The vast entrance hall, which faces sideways onto the inner courtyard, still preserves the great triple poop-light, called the *fanò,* which stood over the quarterdeck of the galley of Andrea Pisani. He was the admiral who fought numerous successful battles against the Turks between 1716 and 1718, only to die in the explosion of the powder-magazine of the fortress on Corfù.

This is one of the most important examples of a Venetian *fanò* from the start of the 18th century, with rich and elegant carving in the horns of plenty that support the embossed copper lanterns. The lanterns are decorated with statuettes of the Virtues and a base bearing the family coat of arms with a lion rampant.

Some of the rooms on the ground floor have stucco decorations from the second half of the 18th century, and the two inner courtyards are animated by 18th-century statues, including busts of the twelve Caesars, a popular subject in Venetian stately homes.

Two statues from the same period stand at the foot of the stairs, the first flight of which leads to the mezzanine floor where, in addition to stucco work depicting the *Myth of Apollo,* there is also a painting of the *Aurora* by Sebastiano Ricci (Belluno 1659–Venice 1734) and another by Gregorio Lazzarini (Venice 1655 – Villabona 1730) of *Psyche Borne to Olympus by Mercury.*

Access to the spacious and well-lit *portego* on the first floor is through a monumental portal decorated not only with pillars but also with great putti which are so elegantly made as to recall the hand of the most famous stucco-worker of 18th-century Venice, Abbondio Stazio.

The walls of the *portego* were once decorated with the portraits of seven illustrious Pisani personalities, but now there are only two: Andrea (the admiral) and Alvise (the Procurator of St. Mark). But the ceiling still preserves the green chiaroscuro work of Jacopo Guarana (Verona 1720 – Venice 1808) with the three times of day: Aurora, Apollo

Gemälden der renommiertesten Maler… sowie die lange Treppe, die zur Bibliothek führt…«

Die beiden Statuengruppen aus dem frühen 17. Jahrhundert an der Türschwelle können dem Bildhauer Girolamo Campagna zugeschrieben werden; sie stellen die erste und die letzte der zwölf »Arbeiten« des Herkules dar: *Die Tötung des Nemeischen Löwen* und *Die Gefangennahme von Cerberus,* dem dreiköpfigen Höllenhund.

In der weitläufigen Eingangshalle, von der man seitlich auf den ersten Innenhof blickt, hängt auch heute noch eine große Schiffslaterne mit drei Lichtern, auch *fanò* genannt. Sie stammt vom Achterdeck der Galeere Andrea Pisanis. Der Admiral gewann zwischen 1716 und 1718 zahlreiche Schlachten gegen die Türken, kam aber bei der Explosion der Pulverkammer der Festung von Korfu ums Leben.

Dieses bedeutendste Beispiel eines venezianischen *fanò* aus dem frühen Settecento zieren reiche und elegante Schnitzereien an den Füllhörnern, die die Laternen aus getriebenem Kupfer tragen. Auf den Laternen sind die Tugenden dargestellt, und an der Basis prangt das Familienwappen mit dem sich aufbäumenden Löwen.

Einige Räume im Erdgeschoß sind mit Stukkaturen aus der zweiten Hälfte des 18. Jahrhunderts ausgestattet. In den beiden Innenhöfen stehen Statuen aus dem Settecento, wie die für adlige Wohnsitze typischen Büsten der zwölf Cäsaren.

Zwei Statuen aus der gleichen Epoche erheben sich zu Füßen der großen Freitreppe. Die erste Rampe führt zum Halbgeschoß, wo sich neben den Stukkaturen zum *Mythos des Apoll* auch die Gemälde *Aurora* von Sebastiano Ricci (Belluno 1659 – Venedig 1734) und *Psyche wird von Merkur zum Olymp geführt* von Gregorio Lazzarini (Venedig 1655 – Villabona 1730) befinden.

Zum großzügigen und hellen *portego* des ersten Obergeschosses gelangt man durch ein monumentales Portal, das mit Säulen und Putten verziert ist. Ihre feine Ausführung erinnert an den berühmtesten Stukkateur im Venedig des 18. Jahrhunderts, Abbondio Stazio.

Die Wände des *portego* schmückten einst Porträts von sieben illustren Familienangehörigen. Heute sind nur noch das Bildnis von Andrea, dem Admiral, und das von Alvise, dem Prokurator von San Marco, zu sehen. An der Decke jedoch kann man noch die kontrastreichen, in Grüntönen gehaltenen Malereien von Jacopo Guarana

bleaux des peintres les plus renommés… et le très long escalier conduisant à la bibliothèque… »

Que les Pisani eussent fait converger une bonne partie de leurs efforts sur la construction et l'embellissement du palais, la présence sur le seuil de deux groupes statuaires du début du XVIIème siècle, qu'il faut relier à l'art du sculpteur Girolamo Campagna en témoignent ; ils représentent le premier et le dernier des douze travaux d'Hercule : *L'Abattage du lion de Némée* et *La Capture de Cerbère.*

Le vaste porche, qui donne de côté sur la première cour, conserve encore la grande lanterne à trois lumières, appelée également *fanò,* qui se dressait sur le gaillard d'arrière de la galère d'Andrea Pisani, le capitaine qui mena d'heureuses batailles contre les Turcs entre 1716 et 1718 et mourut dans l'explosion de la poudrière de la forteresse de Corfou.

Il s'agit d'un des exemplaires les plus significatifs de *fanò* vénitiens du début du XVIIIème siècle par la richesse et l'élégance des gravures ornant les cornes d'abondance qui soutiennent les lanternes de cuivre bosselé décorées de statuettes représentant les Vertus, tandis que sur le socle revient l'écusson de la famille avec le lion rampant.

Certaines des pièces du rez-de-chaussée présentent des ornements en stuc de la seconde moitié du XVIIIème siècle, tandis que les deux cours sont animées par la présence de statues datant du même siècle, parmi lesquelles les bustes des Douze Césars, thème qui se répète dans les demeures patriciennes.

Deux statues de la même époque se dressent au pied du grand escalier, qui avec sa première rampe conduit à l'entresol où, outre les stucs avec le *Mythe d'Apollon,* on conserve également une toile de Sebastiano Ricci (Belluno, 1659 – Venise, 1734), *L'Aurore,* et une autre de Gregorio Lazzarini (Venise, 1655 – Villabona, 1730), *Psyché conduite sur l'Olympe par Mercure.*

On accède au spacieux et lumineux *portego* du premier étage noble par un portail monumental orné, en plus des colonnes, de grands putti dont l'exécution raffinée semble proche des procédés du plus célèbre stucateur du XVIIIème à Venise, Abbondio Stazio.

Autrefois, les murs du *portego* étaient décorés des portraits de sept personnages illustres de la famille : aujourd'hui il n'en reste que deux, ceux d'Andrea, capitaine général de mer, et d'Alvise, Procurateur de San Marco ; mais le plafond conserve encore les clairs-obscurs verts de Jacopo Guarana (Vérone, 1720 – Venise, 1808) représentant les trois

on his chariot of the sun with the Hours, and Apollo descending from his chariot at the end of the day.

The rooms on the first floor, i.e the palace's state apartments, were obviously the most ornate. It was here that Francesco Zugno (Venice 1708–1787), the best of Tiepolo's pupils, created the great allegorical fresco, probably for the marriage of Alvise and Giustiniana Pisani in 1775.

The scene depicts Religion (near the altar), Justice (with the Roman magistrate's fasces) and Charity. Eternal Felicity rests on the celestial vault (to the left), while a warrior with a crown of laurel (at the bottom) stamps on the weapons to signify Patriotism. The two central figures indicate Generosity (the female) and Valour (the male caressing the lion). There is also a refined elegance in the monochromatic yellow scenes of nymphs and satyrs which surround the ceiling.

The same artist frescoed other rooms on this floor, including the chapel, where his hand is recognizable in the grisaille with the *Presentation of Jesus at the Temple,* featuring the painter's typical tenderness and piety, similar to the style of Tiepolo.

The altar and the chapel were very probably designed by Bernardino Maccaruzzi, who saw to the modernizing of part of the interior only a few years prior to the fall of the Republic. The small altarpiece with the *Holy Family and St. John* which stands over the tabernacle is the work of Piazzetta's pupil Giuseppe Angeli.

On the opposite side of the *portego,* towards the canal, there was once a gallery full of paintings by the most famous artists of Venice and the Veneto region. These had to be sold by the last Pisanis and are now preserved, at least in part, in foreign museums. This was also the fate of the vast painting by Antonio Pellegrini (Venice 1675–1741) which decorated the ceiling of the great ballroom (now a concert hall) built between 1717 and 1720.

The second floor housed the library, the richest and most comprehensive of those belonging to the Venetian nobility, which was opened to the public two days a week. It included a set of six thousand Venetian coins and an admirable ceiling with five paintings by Pellegrini, now at Newport in a Vanderbilt villa called Marble House.

Despite losing such a vast fortune and the ups and downs it suffered, the palace still bears witness to the pomp and prestige of its past, with those works of art which still remain.

(Verona 1720 – Venedig 1808) bewundern. Thematisiert sind die drei Tageszeiten, die durch Aurora, Apoll auf dem Sonnenwagen mit den Stunden, und Apoll, der am Ende des Tages vom Wagen steigt, personifiziert werden.

Da die Zimmer des Obergeschosses die Repräsentationsräume des Hauses waren, weisen sie die reichsten Verzierungen des Palastes auf. Hier schuf Francesco Zugno (Venedig 1708 – 1787), der talentierteste Schüler Tiepolos, vermutlich anläßlich der Hochzeit von Alvise und Giustiniana Pisani im Jahre 1775, ein großformatiges Fresko mit allegorischem Inhalt (S. 175). Dargestellt sind oben rechts die personifizierte Religion, die Justiz mit dem Liktorenbündel und die Barmherzigkeit. Links auf dem hellblauen Gewölbe befindet sich das ewige Glück, unten sieht man einen Krieger mit Lorbeerkranz, der die Waffen mit Füßen tritt: er symbolisiert die Heimatliebe. Die zentrale weibliche Figur verkörpert die Großzügigkeit, während die zentrale männliche die Tapferkeit personifiziert. Von erlesener Eleganz sind auch die monochrom gelb gehaltenen Szenen mit Nymphen und Satyren, die die Decke rahmen.

Derselbe Maler schuf auch in anderen Sälen dieses Stockwerkes Fresken. In der Kapelle ist seine Hand in der Grisaille *Die Darbringung Jesu im Tempel* erkennbar. Seine Ausführung charakterisieren Sanftheit und Andacht, ähnlich dem Stil Tiepolos.

Die Kapelle und der Altar wurden vermutlich von Bernardino Maccaruzzi entworfen, der nur wenige Jahre vor dem Untergang der Republik einige Säle modernisierte. Das kleine Altarbild *Die Heilige Familie und der Hl. Johannes* über der Mensa schuf Giuseppe Angeli, ein Schüler Piazzettas.

Gegenüber dem *portego,* zum Kanal hin gelegen, befand sich die reiche Gemäldegalerie, zu der Werke der berühmtesten venezianischen Künstler gehörten. Die letzten Pisani mußten jedoch die Gemälde verkaufen. So gelangte das große Bild Antonio Pellegrinis (Venedig 1675–1741) ins Ausland. Es schmückte einst die Decke des großen Ballsaals, der heute als Konzertsaal dient und zwischen 1717/20 erbaut wurde.

Das zweite Obergeschoß beherbergte die umfangreichste Bibliothek des venezianischen Adels. Zweimal wöchentlich war sie für Publikum geöffnet. Hier wurde auch die Münzsammlung aufbewahrt, die 6 000 Exemplare zählte. An der Decke konnte man die fünf Gemälde Pellegrinis bewundern, die sich heute in Newport in einer Villa der Vanderbilt, dem Marble House, befinden.

moments du jour : L'Aurore, Apollon sur le char du soleil avec les Heures, Apollon qui en fin de journée descend du char.

Les pièces de l'étage noble, où l'on recevait, étaient évidemment les plus décorées du palais et c'est en effet ici que Francesco Zugno (Venise, 1708 – 1787) exécuta une grande fresque allégorique, probablement à l'occasion des noces d'Alvise et de Giustiniana Pisani en 1775.

Sur cette fresque apparaissent la Religion, près de l'autel, la Justice, avec le faisceau des licteurs et la Charité ; sur la voûte céleste, à gauche, pose le Bonheur éternel, tandis qu'en bas un guerrier avec une couronne de laurier, esquissant le geste de fouler les armes du pied, signifie l'Amour de la Patrie. Les deux personnages centraux indiquent, pour le féminin, la Générosité et pour le masculin qui caresse le lion, la Bravoure. Les scènes en camaïeu jaune avec des nymphes et des satyres qui servent d'encadrement au plafond sont également d'une élégance raffinée.

Le même artiste peignit des fresques dans d'autres salles de l'étage, la chapelle incluse, où il faut reconnaître sa main dans la « grisaille » de la *Présentation de Jésus au temple,* caractérisée par l'habituelle inclination à la douceur et au recueillement propres au peintre et semblables au style de Tiepolo. L'autel et la chapelle furent selon toute probabilité dessinés par Bernardo Maccaruzzi qui, quelques années avant la chute de la République, veilla à moderniser une partie des intérieurs, tandis que le petit retable avec *La Sainte Famille et saint Jean* qui domine la Sainte Table est l'œuvre de l'élève de Piazzetta, Giuseppe Angeli.

Du côté opposé au *portego,* sur le canal, se trouvait la riche galerie de tableaux des plus célèbres artistes vénitiens et de la Vénétie. Vendus par les derniers Pisani , ils sont conservés aujourd'hui, du moins en partie, dans des musées étrangers ; la grande toile d'Antonio Pellegrini (Venise, 1675 – 1741) qui ornait le plafond de la grande salle de bal, aujourd'hui salle des concerts, construite entre 1717 et 1720, gagna l'étranger de la même façon.

Au second étage noble se trouvait la bibliothèque, sans doute la plus riche parmi celles des patriciens vénitiens, qui était ouverte au public deux jours par semaine ; on y conservait aussi la collection de monnaies qui comptait bien 6 000 exemplaires. Au plafond, on pouvait admirer les cinq toiles de Pellegrini qui se trouvent désormais à Newport dans une villa des Vanderbilt, la Marble House.

169 View of the first loggia-lined courtyard from the *portego* on the ground floor. In the first two decades of the 18th century, the palace was extended by the architect Girolamo Frigimelica, who raised the building by an extra floor to add the second-floor state apartments.

171 The ground-floor *portego.* On the rear wall is the great triple poop lamp, called the *fanò* in Venetian dialect, which stood over the quarterdeck of the galley of Andrea Pisani, the admiral who fought successful battles against the Turks between 1716 and 1718. It is one of the most significant examples of a Venetian *fanò* from the early 18th century, with rich and elegant carving. There are two statues from the second half of the 18th century standing on either side of the staircase leading to the first floor.

172 The chapel on the second floor. Both the chapel and the altar were probably designed by Bernardino Maccaruzzi, who modernized part of the palace's interior not long before the fall of the Venetian Republic. Over the altar is a small altarpiece by Giuseppe Angeli, the *Holy Family and St. John.*

173 A door to one of the second-floor rooms, inlaid with ivory, ebony, and other precious materials and topped by a stucco oval representing Faith. The room has a twin door, with a stucco image of Charity.

175 Francesco Zugno, *Allegory of Virtues with Generosity and Valour.* This frescoed ceiling decorates one of the rooms on the first floor. It was probably created for the marriage of Alvise and Giustiniana Pisani in 1775. It depicts Religion, Justice, and Charity; the two central figures are Generosity and Valour.

169 Blick in den ersten Arkadenhof vom *portego* des Erdgeschosses aus. In den ersten beiden Jahrzehnten des 18. Jahrhunderts wurde der Palast von dem Architekten Girolamo Frigimelica erweitert, indem er ihn um ein weiteres Obergeschoß erhöhte.

171 *Portego* im Erdgeschoß. An der Stirnwand befindet sich die große Schiffslaterne mit drei Lichtern, *fanò* genannt, die das Achterdeck der Galeere von Andrea Pisani bekrönte. Der Admiral schlug zwischen 1716 und 1718 erfolgreiche Schlachten gegen die Türken. Die Schiffslaterne aus dem frühen 18. Jahrhundert zeichnet sich durch besonders feine und reiche Dekorationen aus. Den Aufgang zur Treppe zum ersten Obergeschoß flankieren zwei Statuen aus der zweiten Hälfte des 18. Jahrhunderts.

172 Kapelle im zweiten Obergeschoß. Sowohl die Kapelle als auch den Altar entwarf vermutlich Bernardino Maccaruzzi, der nur wenige Jahre vor dem Untergang der Serenissima einige Räume des Palastes modernisierte. Über dem Altar befindet sich das kleinformatige Bild *Die Heilige Familie und der Hl. Johannes* von Giuseppe Angeli.

173 Tür eines Saals im zweiten Obergeschoß mit Einlegearbeiten aus Elfenbein, Ebenholz und anderen wertvollen Materialien, über der sich ein Stuckoval mit der Darstellung des Glaubens befindet. In diesem Saal gibt es eine ähnliche Tür, über der die Barmherzigkeit dargestellt ist.

175 Francesco Zugno, *Allegorie der Tugenden mit Großzügigkeit und Tapferkeit.* Diese Deckenmalerei schmückt ein Zimmer im ersten Obergeschoß. Sie wurde wahrscheinlich anläßlich der Hochzeit von Alvise und Giustiniana Pisani im Jahre 1775 ausgeführt. Dargestellt sind Religion, Gerechtigkeit und Barmherzigkeit; die beiden Hauptfiguren personifizieren Großzügigkeit und Tapferkeit.

169 Vue de la première cour à arcades depuis le *portego* du rez-de-chaussée. Au cours des deux premières décennies du XVIIIème siècle, le Palais fut agrandi par l'architecte Girolamo Frigimelica qui ajouta un second étage à l'édifice.

171 *Portego* du rez-de-chaussée. Sur le mur du fond, le grand fanal à trois feux qui s'élevait sur le gaillard d'arrière de la galère d'Andrea Pisani, lequel remporta des grandes batailles contre les Turcs entre 1716 et 1718. C'est l'un des exemplaires les plus intéressants de fanaux du début du XVIIIème siècle pour la richesse et l'élégance de ses gravures. Des deux côtés de l'escalier menant au premier étage, on peut admirer deux statues de la seconde moitié du XVIIIème siècle.

172 Chapelle au deuxième étage. La chapelle comme l'autel furent certainement dessinés par Bernardino Maccaruzzi qui, quelques années seulement avant la chute de la Sérénissime, modernisa quelques pièces du palais. Sur l'autel, un petit retable avec *La Sainte Famille et saint Jean,* œuvre de Giuseppe Angeli.

173 Porte d'une salle du deuxième étage marquetée en ivoire, ébène et autres matériaux précieux ; elle est surmontée d'une illustration en stuc de la Foi. Dans la salle on peut découvrir une autre porte semblable mais surmontée de la Charité.

175 Francesco Zugno, *Allégorie de la Vertu autour de la Générosité et de la Bravoure.* La fresque au plafond décore une pièce du premier étage. Elle fut certainement réalisée à l'occasion des noces d'Alvise et de Giustiniana Pisani en 1775. Dans cette fresque on retrouve la Religion, la Justice et la Charité ; les deux personnages centraux représentant la Générosité et la Bravoure.

PALAZZETTO PISANI

PALAZZETTO PISANI

The grandiose palace that the Pisanis of Santo Stefano built in the course of about a hundred years, making it one of the most impressive buildings in the city, had one drawback – it did not face onto the Grand Canal.

It was only in 1751 that Andrea Pisani was able to purchase from Marquis Giovanni Poleni (for the sum of eight thousand ducats) the little palace which backed onto Palazzo Pisani and faced onto the Grand Canal and could therefore easily be connected to the great building behind. In this way the Pisanis finally acquired their façade, albeit of modest size, onto the prestigious waterway which wound through the city.

The Palazzetto, whose façade originated in the late 16th or early 17th century, was connected to the building in Santo Stefano by various inner passageways which can still be seen today, though the two buildings have since been separated.

The family did not enjoy ownership of the elegant little building for long, as in 1816 it was once again sold, following the destiny of most of the fortune of the Pisanis of Santo Stefano.

Its previous owner, Giovanni Poleni, had been a man of great standing in the cultural and scientific life of Venice in the 18th century. He was already Professor of Astronomy at the University of Padua at a very early age and had subsequently held the Chairs of Mathematics and Physics. The Venetian Republic had appointed him Superintendent of the Waterways.

The Palazzetto bears no trace of his stay within its walls, however. The Pisani family must have considerably altered its interior when they became its owners. In their memory, there remains the splendid wooden lacunar ceiling of the dining room, enclosing repeated examples of the rampant lion from the family's coat of arms.

By a twist of fate, after passing through the hands of a number of owners, including the Duke of Genoa (who chose it as his private residence during his stays in Venice), the Palazzetto was repurchased by the Pisanis in 1945 (not the Santo Stefano branch, but indirect descendants of the Pisanis of San Polo).

Der imposante Palast, den die Pisani di Santo Stefano im Laufe eines Jahrhunderts erbaut hatten, hatte trotz allen Prunks einen entscheidenden Nachteil: ihm fehlte die Aussicht auf den Canal Grande.

Erst im Jahre 1751 gelang es Andrea Pisani, Marchese Giovanni Poleni für 8000 Dukaten den kleinen, an den Palazzo Pisani angrenzenden und am Canal Grande gelegenen Palast abzukaufen, der ohne Schwierigkeiten mit dem Hauptbau verbunden werden konnte. So erhielten die Pisani nun endlich an der zentralen »Prachtstraße« ihre Fassade, wenn auch in nur bescheidenen Ausmaßen.

Der Palazzetto, dessen Fassade aus dem späten Cinquecento oder aus dem frühen Seicento stammt, wurde mit dem Gebäude bei Santo Stefano durch interne Durchgänge verbunden. Diese Verbindungsgänge sind heute noch erkennbar, obwohl die beiden Bauten später wieder getrennt wurden.

Im Jahre 1816 wurde das elegante kleine Gebäude schon wieder verkauft. Es teilte somit das Schicksal vieler anderer Besitztümer der Pisani di Santo Stefano.

Der frühere Besitzer des Palazzetto, Giovanni Poleni, war eine bekannte Persönlichkeit im kulturellen und wissenschaftlichen Venedig des 18. Jahrhunderts. Schon in jungen Jahren wurde er Professor der Astronomie an der Universität Padua. Später hatte er auch die Lehrstühle für Mathematik und Physik inne und wurde vom Senat zum Oberaufseher der Wasserwege ernannt.

Offensichtlich veränderten die Pisani die Innenräume so radikal, daß der Palazzetto keine Spuren mehr aus der Zeit Polenis trägt. Sie ließen die herrliche Holzdecke des Speisesaals einziehen, in deren Kassetten mehrmals der sich aufbäumende Löwe aus dem Familienwappen dargestellt ist.

Häufig wechselten die Besitzer; einer von ihnen, der Herzog von Genua, wählte den Palazzetto als Privatresidenz während seiner Aufenthalte in Venedig. Durch eine Schicksalsfügung gelangte der kleine Palast 1945 wieder in den Besitz der Pisani. Diese Pisani gehörten nicht zum Santo-Stefano-Zweig, sondern waren indirekte Nachkommen der Pisani di San Polo.

Le palais grandiose, que les Pisani avaient construit au cours d'un siècle environ, pour en faire l'un des édifices les plus imposants de la ville, ne donnait pas sur le Grand Canal.

Ce fut seulement en 1751 qu'Andrea Pisani put acheter au marquis Giovanni Poleni, pour la somme de 8 000 ducats, le petit palais qui, adossé au Palazzo Pisani et donnant sur le Grand Canal, put facilement être relié au grand édifice situé derrière. Ainsi, les Pisani eurent leur façade, quand bien même de dimensions modestes, sur le cours d'eau prestigieux qui traverse la ville.

Le petit palais, dont la façade date de la fin du XVIème ou du début du XVIIème siècle, fut relié à l'édifice de Santo Stefano par des passages intérieurs que l'on peut encore repérer, bien que les deux constructions soient maintenant séparées.

Les Pisani n'en jouirent cependant pas longtemps puisqu'en 1816 l'élégant petit édifice était déjà vendu, ayant subi le sort de nombreux autres biens des Pisani de Santo Stefano.

Giovanni Poleni, qui avait possédé la demeure avant les Pisani, avait été un personnage de premier plan dans la vie culturelle et scientifique du XVIIIème siècle en Vénétie : devenu très jeune professeur d'astronomie à l'Université de Padoue, il avait par la suite occupé les chaires de mathématiques et de physique, et il avait été nommé Surintendant des eaux par le Sénat de la Sérénissime.

Le petit palais ne conserve entre ses murs aucune trace de l'époque de Poleni. Les Pisani, une fois entrés en possession de l'édifice, en modifièrent manifestement les intérieurs de manière radicale ; ils firent supprimer le splendide plafond en bois de la salle à manger, dans les caissons duquel apparaît itérativement le lion rampant de l'écusson de la maison.

Par un hasard étrange, après avoir été possédé par différents propriétaires, parmi lesquels le duc de Gênes qui le choisit comme résidence privée pendant sa permanence à Venise, le petit palais fut racheté vers 1945 par les Pisani, non pas de la branche de Santo Stefano cette fois-ci, mais descendant indirectement de celle de San Polo.

Palazzetto Pisani

179 Staircase with vaulted lacunar ceiling and stucco rosettes.

180/181 Detail of the gilt wooden lacunar ceiling, with floral decorations, mythological figures, and the Pisani family's coat of arms. It dates from the 17th and 18th centuries.

183 The little *portego* with a lacunar wooden ceiling where the motive of the vault over the staircase is repeated. The floor is made of typical Venetian *terrazzo* from the 18th century and is framed by a decorative band featuring the ducal horn. The branching Murano glass chandeliers with floral decorations date from the end of the 18th century.

184 The drawing-room facing onto the Grand Canal, equipped with 18th-century furniture and decorated with a handsome fireplace lined with Delft tiles.

185 The bedroom. The 18th-century bed is particularly worthy of note, with its carved wooden headboard lacquered in green and yellow. It is decorated with an oval landscape and three round mirrors with floral decorations.

187 Detail of the carved lacunar ceiling in the bedroom, with cupids in the centre panel.

179 Aufgang mit Kassettengewölbe und Stuckrosetten.

180/181 Detail der vergoldeten Kassettenholzdecke mit floralen Verzierungen, mythologischen Motiven und dem Wappen der Familie Pisani. Die Decke entstand zwischen dem 17. und 18. Jahrhundert.

183 Kleiner *portego* mit Kassettenholzdecke, auf der das Motiv des Treppengewölbes wiederholt wird. Der Bodenbelag aus venezianischem Terrazzo stammt aus dem 18. Jahrhundert und wird von einem dekorativen Band mit dem Motiv des Dogen-Horns eingefaßt. Die Murano-Kronleuchter mit floralem Zierat entstanden Ende des 18. Jahrhunderts.

184 Der Salon mit Blick auf den Canal Grande ist mit Möbeln aus dem 18. Jahrhundert und einem Kamin mit Delfter Kacheln eingerichtet.

185 Schlafzimmer. Besonders wertvoll ist das Bett aus dem 18. Jahrhundert. Das geschnitzte und grüngelb lackierte Kopfteil zieren eine ovalförmige Vedute und drei Spiegel mit eingeritzten Blumenmotiven.

187 Detail der geschnitzten Kassettendecke des Schlafzimmers mit Amoretten in der Mitte.

179 Escalier d'accès avec plafond à voûte à compartiments avec rosettes en stuc.

180/181 Détail du plafond en bois doré, à compartiments, avec décoration florale, sujets mythologiques et blason de la famille Pisani. XVII–XVIIIème siècle.

183 Petit *portego* avec plafond en bois à compartiments où est reproduit le motif de la voûte de l'escalier. Le sol en terrasse caractéristique du XVIIIème siècle est entouré d'une bande décorative avec le motif du bonnet ducal. Lustres de Murano à branches ornées de fleurs datant de la fin du XVIIIème siècle.

184 Salon donnant sur le Grand Canal. Décoré avec des meubles du XVIIIème siècle, il est orné d'une belle cheminée recouverte de carreaux de Delft.

185 Chambre à coucher. Le lit XVIIIème est de grande valeur ; la tête de lit en bois est en laque de couleur vert-jaune et décorée par un ovale et trois miroirs avec des motifs de fleurs gravés.

187 Détail du plafond à caissons de la chambre à coucher avec amours dans le cadre central.

PALAZZO SANDI, PORTO, CIPOLLATO

SANDI, PORTO, CIPOLLATO

PALAZZO SANDI, PORTO, CIPOLLATO

With its plain, almost severe façade, the palace faces onto a quiet Venetian square, the Corte dell'Albero, in the parish of Sant'Angelo not far from the Grand Canal (though it has no direct view), which was famous in the 18th century for the Sant'Angelo theatre.

The construction was entrusted to the architect Domenico Rossi by Tommaso Sandi about the year 1721. The Sandis were originally from Feltre and had been accepted into the Venetian nobility only very late (in 1685), thanks to a donation to the State of a hundred thousand ducats by a member of the family named Vettor. They were traditionally linked with the legal profession. One Tommaso, born in 1647, was *avogador;* half a century later, another Tommaso held the position of Podestà in Chioggia, Bergamo and Brescia.

The palace has a plain front, animated only by the balcony and the loggia on the first and second floors, but it has a remarkable majesty inside, in the vast *portego* on the ground floor and the ample, flowing staircase which is unusual for palaces of the period.

The layout of the first floor features a "T" shape (according to a scheme already obsolete by the 18th century) comprising a *portego* closed by a much larger oblong hall facing onto a narrow canal.

As was the habit in Venetian palaces, the other rooms led off from either side of the *portego,* responding in this case to the new demands for comfort which were most keenly felt by those who had most recently acquired a noble title. Being of bourgeois origin, they were not obliged to stage any official functions or to decorate their homes accordingly.

This period therefore saw the banishment of all those decorations of late-Baroque taste intended to visually extend spaces that were already vast. Following the new trend, the architect probably also helped to plan the decoration of the interior, especially the great frescoes which cover the ceiling of the drawing-room. These reveal the exceptional artistic talent of Giambattista Tiepolo, who also produced three other paintings for the

Der Palast mit der schlichten und geradezu strengen Fassade steht an einem kleinen, stillen Platz Venedigs, dem Corte dell'Albero. Dieser liegt in dem nur wenige Schritte vom Canal Grande entfernten Stadtteil Sant'Angelo, der im 18. Jahrhundert für sein angesehenes gleichnamiges Theater berühmt war.

Um 1721 gab Tommaso Sandi den Bau des Palastes bei dem Architekten Domenico Rossi in Auftrag. Die aus Feltre stammende Familie Sandi erhielt erst sehr spät ihren Adelstitel. Im Jahre 1685 veranlaßte Vettor Sandi eine Schenkung von 100 000 Dukaten an die Republik Venedig und wurde daraufhin in das Patriziat aufgenommen. Die Sandi waren seit jeher im Justizwesen tätig. Der 1647 geborene Tommaso war *avogador* (venezianischer Richtertitel), und ein anderer Tommaso sollte 50 Jahre später das Bürgermeisteramt in Chioggia, Bergamo und Brescia übernehmen.

Der Palast mit der glatten Fassade, die lediglich durch einen Balkon und eine Loggia an den beiden Obergeschossen rhythmisiert wird, weist im Inneren einen großartigen, weitläufigen *portego* im Erdgeschoß auf und besitzt einen großzügigen Treppenaufgang, dessen dynamischer Verlauf für jene Zeit recht ungewöhnlich ist.

Im ersten Obergeschoß befindet sich ein vergleichsweise viel kleinerer *portego* mit dem veralteten T-förmigen Abschluß, den ein großer, eher länglicher als breiter Saal mit Blick auf einen schmalen Kanal bildet.

Vom *portego* gelangt man, wie in den venezianischen Palästen allgemein üblich, in die übrigen Räume des Stockwerkes. Sie entsprechen den neuen Vorstellungen von Bequemlichkeit, auf die hauptsächlich der Neuadel bürgerlicher Abstammung Wert legte, denn die Emporkömmlinge waren an keine besonderen Repräsentationsverpflichtungen gebunden.

Sämtliche Dekorationen im Stil des Spätbarock wurden nach und nach entfernt, um die an sich schon weiten Räume noch größer wirken zu lassen. Der Architekt, der jenen Tendenzen Folge leistete, plante wahrscheinlich auch die Innenausstattung und vor allem die großen Deckenfresken im

Le palais donne, avec sa façade sobre et presque sévère, sur une petite place vénitienne tranquille, la Cour de l'Arbre, dans la paroisse de Sant'Angelo, peu éloignée du Grand Canal, dans un endroit de la ville célèbre au XVIIIème siècle pour son célèbre théâtre Sant'Angelo.

La construction fut commandée à l'architecte Domenico Rossi par Tommaso Sandi vers 1721. Les Sandi, originaires de Feltre, avaient eu accès à la noblesse très tard, seulement en 1685, en vertu d'une donation de 100 000 ducats à l'Etat de la part d'un membre de la famille, Vettor. Ils étaient liés par tradition à la carrière juridique : l'un d'entre eux, Tommaso, né en 1647, fut *avogador* (un des trois magistrats défendant les intérêts de la République de Venise) et un autre Tommaso, environ un demi-siècle plus tard, aurait occupé la charge de podestat à Chioggia, à Bergame et à Brescia.

Le palais avec sa façade nue, égayée seulement par les balcons à balustrades des deux étages nobles, révèle une majesté unique en son genre à l'intérieur, dans le vaste *portego* au rez-de-chaussée et dans l'escalier spacieux dont le développement mouvementé est inhabituel pour l'époque.

Au premier étage se trouve un *portego* aux dimensions plus réduites en comparaison, fermé en « T », selon un plan désormais désuet au XVIIIème siècle, par un grand salon plus long que large, qui donne sur un canal étroit.

Le long du *portego,* comme il est de coutume dans les palais vénitiens, s'ouvrent les autres pièces de la maison qui répondent aux nouvelles exigences de confort, ressenties surtout dans la noblesse la plus récente d'extraction bourgeoise, dont la vie, moins tapageuse, n'est pas liée à de particuliers devoirs de représentation.

A cette époque, on commence à bannir toutes les décorations de goût typiquement fin baroque afin d'agrandir optiquement des espaces en eux-mêmes déjà vastes. L'architecte suivant ces nouvelles tendances intervint aussi probablement dans la disposition des ornements intérieurs et surtout de la grande fresque qui couvre le plafond du

same palace (unfortunately no longer in place).

The palace contains one of Tiepolo's first ceiling frescoes. This is one of the artist's most brilliant and successful works, though it is not among the most famous. It is usually described as the *Allegory of the Power of Eloquence.* This unusual theme probably refers to the owners' profession, that of lawyers, and therefore to the triumph of the word, and hence also of music (inasmuch as it is sound) over brute force.

The centre of the composition is dominated by episodes involving Minerva and Mercury, the divinities presiding over wisdom and eloquence. Four heroic episodes are depicted along the sides in compositions with a triangular arrangement resting on the margins of the fresco, thus leaving an ample central space for depicting the two deities, which are painted smaller than the others.

Represented on the longer sides of the fresco are Amphion, who with the power of his music built the walls of Thebes, and Orpheus, who with his music succeeded in conducting Euridice out of Hades. On the shorter sides, the frescoes illustrate Hercules Gallicus enchanting the people with his words and Bellerophon riding the winged charger Pegasus and slaying the Chimera.

The painted musical episodes are obviously closely linked with the function of the room, which was intended for concerts, receptions, and dances.

The fresco is characterized by its brilliant colours and carefully thought-out compositions which are almost geometrically structured by means of light, in which the images are animated by an uncontainable vitality, so that mythology and allegory merge into one and are transformed into dramatic reality, almost as if it were a theatre stage. The room's relatively plain decor contrasts with the brilliant fresco. The walls have slightly projecting pilasters, and the single ornament is a stucco female figure over the entrance.

The frieze of animals, centaurs, and male figures providing a frame for the fresco at the top of the walls was created by another hand and is probably attributable to a painter who used less modern methods, very likely Nicolò Bambini.

Tiepolo's great work is not the only decoration in the palace, whose rooms underwent extensive renovation towards the end of the 18th century, probably for the marriage between Vettor Sandi and Laura Minelli in 1795.

Salon. In ihnen manifestiert sich die außerordentliche Begabung des jungen Giambattista Tiepolo. Der Maler schuf für den Palast noch drei weitere Gemälde, die heute bedauerlicherweise nicht mehr vorhanden sind.

In diesem Palast befindet sich aber noch heute eine der ersten Deckenmalereien Tiepolos. Es ist eine der brillantesten und gelungensten Darstellungen, wenn sie auch nicht zu den bekanntesten Werken des Malers gehört. Gewöhnlich wird sie als die *Allegorie über die Macht der Beredsamkeit* bezeichnet. Das ungewöhnliche Thema bezieht sich offensichtlich auf den Juristenberuf der Auftraggeber und folglich auf den Triumph des Wortes und der Musik über die rohe Gewalt.

Das Zentrum der Komposition beherrschen Episoden, die von Minerva und Merkur erzählen, Gottheiten, denen Weisheit und Beredsamkeit zugeordnet wird. Vier heroische Begebenheiten sind an den Freskenrändern in dreieckigen Rahmen dargestellt.

An den Längsseiten des Deckenfreskos sind Amphion, der durch sein Leierspiel Thebens Stadtmauern errichtete, und Orpheus dargestellt, dem es gelingt, Eurydike durch den Zauber seines unwiderstehlichen Gesangs aus dem Hades zu führen. An den Querseiten sieht man, wie Herkules Gallicus die Menschen mit seinen Worten fesselt und wie Bellerophon auf Pegasus die Chimäre tötet.

Die dargestellten Episoden stehen offensichtlich in unmittelbarer Verbindung zur Funktion des Saals. Hier sollten nämlich Konzerte, Empfänge und Bälle stattfinden.

Das Fresko prägen leuchtende Farben und eine durchdachte, fast geometrisch angelegte Komposition. Mythologie und Allegorie scheinen miteinander zu verschmelzen und sich dadurch in dramatische Realität zu verwandeln, geradezu als handele es sich um eine Theaterbühne. Im Kontrast zu dem brillanten Fresko steht die relativ schlichte Raumausstattung. An den Wänden befinden sich kaum merklich vorgelagerte Pilaster, und über dem Eingang erhebt sich als einziges Ornament eine weibliche Stuckfigur.

Ein Fries mit Tieren, Kentauren und männlichen Figuren rahmt das Fresko. Ihn schuf eine andere Hand. Aufgrund der vorherrschenden konventionellen Malweise ist der Fries eher einem Künstler wie Nicolò Bambini zuzuschreiben.

Das großartige Werk Tiepolos bildet aber nicht die einzige Dekoration im Palast,

salon dans lequel se révèle l'exceptionnelle trempe artistique de Giambattista Tiepolo jeune, qui peignit trois autres toiles malheureusement disparues aujourd'hui.

La fresque qui orne le plafond est l'une des premières créations de Tiepolo, et l'une des œuvres les plus brillantes et les mieux réussies du peintre, même si elle ne fait pas partie des plus connues.

Désignée habituellement comme *Allégorie du Pouvoir de l'éloquence,* avec son thème insolite, elle se réfère probablement à la profession des commanditaires, donc au triomphe de la parole – et par conséquent aussi de la musique, en tant que son – sur la force brute.

Au centre de la composition dominent les épisodes traitant de Minerve et Mercure, en tant que divinités de la Sagesse et de l'Eloquence. Quatre événements héroïques se répartissent sur les côtés en des compositions à schéma triangulaire, sur les bords de la fresque, laissant donc un large fond central pour les représentations des divinités aux dimensions plus limitées par rapport aux autres dieux.

Sur les longs côtés de la fresque, on peut admirer Amphion qui, en jouant de la lyre, fait s'élever les murs de Thèbes et Orphée qui, en vertu de sa musique, réussit à conduire Eurydice hors de l'Hadès. Sur les côtés courts : Hercule Gallicus qui enchaîne les gens avec sa parole et Bellérophon qui tue la Chimère, monté sur Pégase, le cheval ailé.

L'importance attribuée aux épisodes musicaux doit évidemment aussi être mise en étroite relation avec la fonction de la salle qui devait accueillir concerts, réceptions et bals.

La fresque présente de lumineuses couleurs et une composition réfléchie, presque géométriquement agencée par la lumière, dans laquelle les images sont animées d'une irrésistible vitalité, à tel point que mythologie et allégorie fusionnent, se transformant en réalité dramatique, comme s'il s'agissait de la scène d'un théâtre. Elle contraste avec un milieu sobrement décoré : aux murs, des piliers à peine saillants, et pour unique ornement, un personnage féminin en stuc au-dessus de l'entrée.

La frise avec animaux, centaures, personnages masculins qui sert de cadre à la fresque, dans la partie supérieure des murs de la salle, est l'œuvre d'une autre main, et on l'attribue plutôt à un peintre aux méthodes moins modernes, probablement Nicolò Bambini.

Mais l'œuvre magnifique de Tiepolo n'est pas le seul ornement de la maison qui,

In an overall redistribution of space to suit family intimacy rather than a showy lifestyle, the now smaller rooms were decorated with frescoes on the ceiling and delicate stucco work of neo-classical style.

It is at this point in the history of the palace that Costantino Cedini (1741–1811) set to work, creating a series of frescoes on the theme of marital happiness. According to the dictates of the new trends in taste, instead of expanding the space illusionalistically, the artist confined his elegant compositions in regular compartments, paying particular attention to antique forms taken from manuals of archaeology. At the same time, the stucco work, mainly floral in tones of pink and pale blue, became lighter.

Cedini's frescoes all refer to mythological episodes, for example *Venus and Mars Caught by Surprise in Vulcan's Net,* a monochromatic work framed by stucco garlands and rosettes. This scene also contains putti and the images of four deities: Juno, Cybele, Pluto and Mercury. Cedini also painted the *Triumph of the Arts,* with Apollo and the Muses; *Venus and Adonis,* with putti, and the *Triumph of Eros* in a fine frame decorated with delicate branches.

From the point of view of colour, the harmony between the stucco work and the frescoes now shows a taste for soft and delicate pastels. Among other objects from the end of the last century, the house still preserves a fireplace decorated with Delft china tiles painted with landscapes. In contrast to the decorative richness of the fireplaces of the first half of the 18th century, the simplicity of this example is functional, in accordance with the new criteria of comfort and cosiness.

The palace had a series of owners after the Sandis and is now the seat of the Association of Building Contractors.

dessen Räume gegen Ende des 18. Jahrhunderts, vermutlich anläßlich der Hochzeit von Vettor Sandi und Laura Minelli im Jahre 1795, grundlegend umstrukturiert wurden.

Bei der Änderung der Raumfolge, die weniger repräsentativen Ansprüchen als familiärer Intimität genügen sollte, wurden die nunmehr kleineren Säle mit Deckenmalereien und zarten Stukkaturen in klassizistischer Manier dekoriert.

Zu jener Zeit begann Costantino Cedini (1741–1811) für die Sandi zu arbeiten. Er schuf eine Reihe von Fresken, die das Eheglück thematisieren. Unter dem Diktat des neuen Geschmacks zwängte der Künstler seine eleganten Kompositionen in regelmäßige Felder, anstatt den Raum optisch zu erweitern. Dabei richtete er seine spezielle Aufmerksamkeit auf die Darstellung antiker Formen, die Archäologiehandbüchern entnommen waren. Zugleich wirkten die hauptsächlich floralen Stuckmotive, die in rosa und blaßblauen Farbtönen gehalten waren, leichter.

Alle Fresken Cedinis erzählen mythologische Episoden, beispielsweise *Venus und Mars werden im Netz Vulcanus' überrascht.* In den Ecken des Stuckrahmens, der diese Szene einfaßt, sind auch Juno, Kybele, Pluto und Merkur sowie Putten dargestellt. Die monochrome Malerei rahmen zwei Stuckgirlanden und ein Stuckrosettenband. Außerdem schuf Cedini *Der Triumph der Künste* mit Apoll und den Musen, *Venus und Adonis* mit Putten und den *Triumph des Eros* in feinem, mit Ranken verziertem Rahmen.

In der Farbgebung von Stuck und Fresken dominieren nun zarte Pastelltöne. Neben seinen übrigen Objekten aus der zweiten Hälfte des 19. Jahrhunderts bewahrt das Haus einen Kachelofen. Die Delfter Kacheln sind mit Landschaftsdarstellungen bemalt. Im Gegensatz zu den aufwendig dekorierten Kaminen der ersten Hälfte des 18. Jahrhunderts wirkt diese schlichte Feuerstelle eher funktional. Sie steht damit im Zeichen der neuen Kriterien von Bequemlichkeit und Wohnlichkeit.

Nach den Sandi hat der Palast noch mehrmals den Besitzer gewechselt. Heute ist er Sitz eines Bauunternehmerverbandes.

vers la fin du XVIIIème siècle, subit de profondes restructurations à l'intérieur, peut-être à l'occasion des noces de Vettor Sandi et de Laura Minelli, célébrées en 1795.

Dans une révision générale de la distribution des espaces répondant aux exigences d'une vie orientée davantage sur la famille, les pièces, plus réduites désormais, furent décorées, en plus des fresques du plafond, de stucs délicats d'une harmonie toute néoclassique.

C'est à ce moment que commence l'activité de Costantino Cedini (1741–1811), qui exécuta une partie des fresques liées au thème du bonheur conjugal, dans lesquelles, en accord avec les nouvelles tendances de goût, plutôt que de développer l'espace, l'artiste étend les compositions avec une élégance nette dans des subdivisions régulières, en accordant une attention particulière aux formes antiques tirées des manuels d'archéologie. En même temps, on voit s'alléger les cadres en stuc surtout ornés d'éléments floraux dans des tons de rose et de bleu pâle.

Toutes les fresques de Cedini représentent des épisodes mythologiques, par exemple *Vénus et Mars surpris dans le filet de Vulcain,* en camaïeu, scène encadrée de deux guirlandes en stuc et d'un ruban en stuc à petites roses dans lesquelles s'insèrent deux reliefs avec jeux de putti et les images de quatre divinités : Junon, Cybèle, Pluton et Mercure ; *Le Triomphe des Arts* avec Apollon et les Muses ; *Vénus et Adonis* avec putti et le *Triomphe d'Eros* dans le cadre à sarments délicats.

Sur le plan de la couleur, l'harmonie entre stucs et fresques met en évidence une prédilection désormais affirmée pour les tons pâles et délicats. La maison conserve, parmi d'autres témoignages de la fin du siècle, une cheminée dont les parois intérieures sont décorées de carreaux de Delft ornés de paysages ; bien loin de la richesse décorative des cheminées de la première moitié du XVIIIème siècle, elle manifeste dans sa simplicité des caractères fonctionnels liés aux critères de confort et d'habitabilité de la demeure.

Le palais qui eut d'autres propriétaires après les Sandi, est aujourd'hui le siège de l'Association des Constructeurs du Bâtiment.

194 · PALAZZO SANDI, PORTO, CIPOLLATO

Palazzo Sandi, Porto, Cipollato

192 The *portego,* or central reception hall, on the first floor, with stucco decorations and large looking-glasses dating from the end of the 18th century.

193 Giambattista Tiepolo, *Allegory of the Power of Eloquence.* The detail shows the episode of Bellerophon who rides the winged horse Pegasus and slays the Chimera. The fresco was made between 1721 and 1726, when Tiepolo left Venice for Udine to paint the frescoes for the archbishop's palace.

194 Detail of the frieze with animals, centaurs, and male figures surrounding Tiepolo's fresco. The frieze was created by another artist, probably Nicolò Bambini.

195 Giambattista Tiepolo, *Allegory of the Power of Eloquence.* The detail shows the episode of Hercules Gallicus enchanting the people with his words. This part of the fresco was reworked by the artist some years after it had been made (possibly due to damage caused by damp); in fact, there is a visible change in style by comparison with the other compositions on the ceiling.

196 Costantino Cedini, *Venus and Adonis.* The artist's activity at Palazzo Sandi probably began with the renovation and redecoration of the home for the marriage of Vettor Sandi to Laura Minelli in 1795.

197 Costantino Cedini, *Triumph of the Arts,* with Apollo and the Muses. The fresco decorates a ceiling and is surrounded by a stucco frame with restrained floral motives which reflect the new artistic taste at the turn of the century.

198 Costantino Cedini: details with images of *Pluto* and *Juno* which, together with those of Cybele and Mercury, decorate the corners of the stucco frame surrounding the fresco of *Venus and Mars Caught by Surprise in Vulcan's Net.* There is a noteworthy simplicity and elegance in these compositions, which are of classical inspiration.

199 Costantino Cedini, *Venus and Mars Caught by Surprise in Vulcan's Net.* This fresco, decorating the ceiling of one of the rooms in the palace possibly created in 1795, is marked by soft colours and framed by a floral stucco decoration containing monochromatic panels with groups of putti and deities.

192 Der *portego* oder zentrale Saal des ersten Obergeschosses mit Stuckdekorationen und großen Spiegeln aus dem späten 18. Jahrhundert.

193 Giambattista Tiepolo, *Allegorie über die Macht der Beredsamkeit.* Der Ausschnitt zeigt die Geschichte von Bellerophon, der auf dem geflügelten Pferd Pegasus die Chimäre tötet. Das Fresko entstand zwischen 1721 und 1726, als Tiepolo Venedig verließ, um sich in Udine der Ausmalung des erzbischöflichen Palastes zu widmen.

194 Detail des Frieses mit Tieren, Kentauren und männlichen Figuren, der Tiepolos Fresko umgibt. Diesen Fries schuf ein anderer Künstler, vermutlich Nicolò Bambini.

195 Giambattista Tiepolo, *Allegorie über die Macht der Beredsamkeit.* Der Auschnitt zeigt Herkules Gallicus, der die Menschen mit seinen Worten fesselt. Diesen Freskenteil überarbeitete der Künstler einige Jahre später, weil er wohl aufgrund der Feuchtigkeit Schaden erlitten hatte. Im Vergleich zu den übrigen Darstellungen an der Decke ist hier ein Stilwandel festzustellen.

196 Costantino Cedini, *Venus und Adonis.* Mit der Renovierung und neuen Ausschmückung des Gebäudes anläßlich der Hochzeit von Vettor Sandi und Laura Minelli im Jahre 1795 begann Cedinis Wirken im Palazzo Sandi.

197 Costantino Cedini, *Der Triumph der Künste* mit Apoll und den Musen. Das Deckenfresko umgibt ein maßvoll mit floralen Motiven dekorierter Stuckrahmen, der den neuen Geschmack der Jahrhundertwende widerspiegelt.

198 Costantino Cedini, *Pluto und Juno.* Zusammen mit Darstellungen von Kybele und Merkur schmücken sie die Ecken des Stuckrahmens, der das Fresko *Venus und Mars werden im Netz Vulcanus' überrascht* umgibt. Bemerkenswert sind Schlichtheit und Eleganz der klassisch inspirierten Kompositionen.

199 Costantino Cedini, *Venus und Mars werden im Netz Vulcanus' überrascht.* Das Fresko in weicher Farbgebung ziert die Decke eines Palastraumes, der vermutlich 1795 im Zuge der Umstrukturierung entstand. Die Deckenmalerei umgibt ein floral gestalteter Stuckrahmen, in den wiederum monochrom gehaltene rechteckige Bilder mit Putten und Gottheiten eingelassen sind.

192 Le *portego* ou salon central du premier étage avec décors en stuc et grands miroirs datant de la fin du XVIIIème siècle.

193 Giambattista Tiepolo, *Allégorie du Pouvoir de l'éloquence.* Le détail présente l'épisode de Bellérophon qui, monté sur Pégase, tue la Chimère. La fresque fut exécutée entre 1721 et 1726, quand Tiepolo quitta Venise pour Udine où il travailla aux fresques du palais archiépiscopal.

194 Détail d'une frise avec animaux, centaures et personnages masculins qui délimite la fresque de Tiepolo. La frise révèle l'intervention d'un autre artiste, probablement Nicolò Bambini.

195 Giambattista Tiepolo, *Allégorie du Pouvoir de l'éloquence.* Le détail présente Hercule Gallicus qui enchaîne les gens en leur parlant. Cette partie de la fresque fut retouchée par l'artiste quelques années après son exécution, sans doute en raison des dommages provoqués par l'humidité ; on note en effet un changement stylistique par rapport aux autres compositions du plafond.

196 Costantino Cedini, *Vénus et Adonis.* L'activité de l'artiste pour le Palazzo Sandi est probablement liée à la restructuration et la nouvelle décoration de la demeure à l'occasion des noces de Vittor Sandi et de Laura Minelli en 1795.

197 Costantino Cedini, *Le Triomphe des Arts,* avec Apollon et les Muses. La fresque qui décore un plafond est entourée d'un cadre en stuc au sobre dessin ornemental végétal qui répond bien aux nouvelles tendances du goût de la fin du siècle.

198 Costantino Cedini, détails avec *Pluton* et *Junon* dont les images, avec celles de Mercure et de Cybèle, décorent les sommets du cadre en stuc qui entoure la fresque représentant *Vénus et Mars surpris dans le filet de Vulcain.* A noter, la netteté et l'élégance des compositions d'inspiration classique.

199 Costantino Cedini, *Vénus et Mars surpris dans le filet de Vulcain.* La fresque qui décore le plafond d'une pièce du palais restructurée sans doute en 1795, est caractérisée par des couleurs pâles et est encadrée d'un décor en stuc de petites roses et de motifs ornementaux de type floral, à l'intérieur duquel s'intègrent des peintures en camaïeu avec angelots et divinités.

PALAZZO MANIN

PALAZZO MANIN   PALAIS MANIN

Venise Joseph Kier Editeur Place St Marc. N°117

Palazzo Dolfin Manin

As its name suggests, the palace's history is linked with two of the most prestigious Venetian families, who unfortunately did not live there for long.

In 1536, construction was begun on a building on the Grand Canal, near Rialto, based on a plan by Jacopo Sansovino commissioned by the Procurator of St. Mark, Giovanni Dolfin, on a site where he owned a few modest houses.

The façade over the Canal was completed in 1540. After a brief interval, the works began again in 1545, and Vasari notes that, by the time it was completed, the building had come to cost thirty thousand ducats.

The Dolfins were a family of very ancient origins which had provided Venice with a doge, Giovanni (1356–1361) and a Dogaressa, Chiara Corner née Dolfin (1530–1590), as well as a number of officials and dignitaries.

The origins of the family are lost in legend, according to which the Dolfins were descended from the *Gens Memmia.* At some unspecified time, a Memmio apparently fell from the last step of a staircase and was left with a limp; in memory of this event, he was nicknamed Gradinicus, which changed into Gradenigo in Venice, becoming his family's surname. Later on, a certain Zuanne Gradenigo, nicknamed "dolphin" because of his handsome physical appearance, finally abandoned his previous surname in favour of the name of Dolfin.

The palace built by Giovanni Dolfin was praised unreservedly by Francesco, the son of Jacopo Sansovino, in *Venetia città nobilissima,* where it was described as "one of the principal palaces on the Grand Canal for architecture, for artifice of live stone, for majesty, for magnitude of body and expense".

Sansovino had created a building which was unusual for Venice, where palaces usually had a broad façade and at the centre a courtyard surrounded by loggias in the Roman style. This building was made "with a well-designed façade on the outside and very long and comfortable rooms on the inside", as the architect's son explained in his writing.

Wie sein Name bereits besagt, verbindet dieser Palast seine Geschichte mit zwei der angesehensten venezianischen Familien, die ihn allerdings nicht lange bewohnten.

Das Gebäude am Canal Grande in der Nähe der Rialto-Brücke wurde im Jahre 1536 nach einem Plan Jacopo Sansovinos und im Auftrag des Prokuratoren von San Marco, Giovanni Dolfin, begonnen. Im Jahre 1540 wurde die Fassade am Canal Grande fertiggestellt. Nach einer kurzen Bauunterbrechung nahm man die Arbeiten 1545 wieder auf. Vasari zufolge soll die Errichtung des Palastes 30 000 Dukaten gekostet haben.

Die Dolfin waren eine alteingesessene venezianische Familie. Sie stellten der Republik Venedig einen Dogen, Giovanni (1356–1361), und eine Dogaressa, Chiara Dolfin verheiratete Corner (1530–1590), sowie zahlreiche andere Amtspersonen und Würdenträger.

Einer Legende zufolge sollen die Dolfin Nachkommen der *Gens Memmia* gewesen sein. In grauer Vorzeit, so die Überlieferung, ist ein Memmio von der letzten Stufe einer Treppe gestürzt und hat wegen seines Hinkens den Spitznamen Gradinicus erhalten, der sich dann in Venedig in Gradenigo verwandelte und zum Familiennamen wurde. Ein gewisser Zuanne Gradenigo, der wegen seiner hübschen Erscheinung Dolfin (Dialektform für Delphin) genannt wurde, gab schließlich seinen alten Familiennamen zugunsten des Nachnamens Dolfin auf.

Den von Giovanni Dolfin errichteten Palast lobt der Sohn Jacopo Sansovinos, Francesco, in seinem Werk *Venetia città nobilissima* vorbehaltlos. Er bezeichnet ihn »auf Grund der Architektur, Erlesenheit der Materialien, Erhabenheit, Größe und Kostenaufwendung als einen der bedeutendsten Palazzi des Canal Grande«.

Sansovino hatte ein für Venedig ungewöhnliches Gebäude geschaffen, denn in der Regel wiesen die breit angelegten Paläste einen zentralen Hof mit römischen Loggien auf. Diesen Palazzo zeichnen eine »wohlproportionierte Fassade und innen lange und bequeme Räume« aus, wie der Sohn des Baumeisters erklärt.

Comme le nom du palais l'indique, son histoire est liée à deux des plus prestigieuses familles vénitiennes qui, n'eurent ni l'une ni l'autre la chance de l'habiter longtemps.

La construction de l'édifice sur le Grand Canal, à proximité du Rialto, débuta en 1536, sur un projet de Jacopo Sansovino et par la volonté du Procurateur de San Marco, Giovanni Dolfin, à l'endroit où il possédait de modestes maisons. En 1540, la façade donnant sur le Canal Grande était terminée ; après une brève interruption, les travaux reprirent en 1545 et, si l'on en croit Vasari, la construction achevée aurait coûté 30 000 ducats.

Les Dolfin étaient une famille très ancienne qui avait donné un doge à Venise, Giovanni (1356–1361), et une dogaresse, Chiara Corner née Dolfin (1530–1590), en plus des nombreux autres fonctionnaires et dignitaires.

Les origines de la maison se perdent dans la légende selon laquelle les Dolfin seraient des descendants de la *Gens Memmia ;* un Memmio, à une époque non précisée, tombant de la dernière marche d'un escalier, se serait retrouvé boiteux et, en souvenir de l'événement, on lui aurait attribué le nom de Gradinicus, transformé ensuite à Venise en Gradenigo et devenu patronyme. Par la suite, un certain Zuanne Gradenigo, surnommé dolfin, forme dialectale de dauphin, à cause de son physique avenant aurait définitivement adopté pour la famille le nom de Dolfin, abandonnant le précédent.

Le palais érigé par Giovanni Dolfin est loué sans réserve par le fils de Jacopo Sansovino, Francesco, dans *Venetia città nobilissima* où il le décrit comme l'un des palais majeurs du Grand Canal pour « l'architecture, l'artifice de pierres vives, la maîtrise, la grandeur du corps et de la dépense ».

Sansovino avait créé un projet inhabituel pour Venise où les palais se déployaient en longueur, avec au centre une cour entourée de loges selon l'usage romain, alors que l'édifice se présentait « à l'extérieur avec une façade bien proportionnée et à l'intérieur avec de très longues et confortables pièces » comme le spécifie dans son ouvrage le fils de l'architecte.

Today, after restoration of the interior by the architect Giannantonio Selva in the last years of the 18th century, there is virtually no trace of the palace's original layout. The palace was once notable for its great refinement and opulence with "the rooms going straight from one side of the building to the other[;] all the bedrooms had a fireplace…" and "…the floors were made not of bricks but of a particular material called *terrazzo*".

The palace had ceilings with exposed beams decorated with coloured or gilt decorations, some of which only came to light as a result of restoration work in 1968. Francesco Sansovino also claimed that it was virtually impossible to describe the pomp and richness of the furnishings and ornaments in the house, which seemed to him of uncommon opulence.

The Dolfins only lived in the palace for a few years however, as it appears to have been rented out to the Bonvisi family in 1603. After the death of Lorenzo Dolfin in 1664, the building passed into the hands of various heirs, who rented it in 1700 to the nobleman Ludovico Manin.

The fame of the Manin family is sadly linked mainly with the Venetian Republic's last doge, Ludovico (who saw Venice fall into the hands of the French), but the family was of very ancient tradition and extremely rich.

The Manins had taken refuge in Friuli in the 14th century and, after various travels, had so actively supported the Venetian Republic in its battle against the Patriarchate of Aquileia that, in 1385, Nicolò Manin received Venetian citizenship by unanimous vote of the Great Council. In the 15th century, another Manin was responsible for the restitution of Udine after the city had fallen into the hands of Sigmund of Hungary, and the conquest of the Carnia, Cadore, and Istria regions for the Republic of Venice.

In the 16th century, various members of the family came to Venice's aid in times of danger, providing money for mercenaries. The Senate and the Great Council included Ludovico I Manin among the Venetian nobility in 1651 for having conspicuously aided the Republic in the war of Crete by providing the sum of sixty thousand ducats.

Ludovico was also famous as a patron of the arts. At his own expense, he ordered the building of the Venetian church of the Scalzis, the royal Villa of Passariano and the choir in Udine Cathedral. It was also he who established in his will that all the first-born

Heute, nach der von Giannantonio Selva in den letzten Jahren des 18. Jahrhunderts durchgeführten Neustrukturierung der Innenräume, ist fast nichts von der ursprünglichen Raumfolge und -ausstattung erhalten. Der Palast war einst für seine raffinierten und üppigen Dekorationen bekannt, mit »den Sälen… gerade von einer zur anderen Fassade des Wohnsitzes reichend… alle Schlafzimmer mit Kaminen…« und »die Böden nicht aus Ziegeln, sondern aus einem *terrazzo* genannten Material«.

Das offen liegende Gebälk der Palastdecken war mit mehrfarbigen oder vergoldeten Verzierungen dekoriert. 1968 wurde ein Teil des Gebälks bei der Restaurierung freigelegt. Francesco Sansovino schreibt außerdem, daß der Prunk und der Reichtum der Einrichtung und Ausstattung des Wohnsitzes kaum zu beschreiben und in seinen Augen außergewöhnlich üppig war.

Die Dolfin lebten jedoch nur wenige Jahre im Palast. 1603 wurde das Gebäude an die Bonvisi verpachtet. Nach dem Tod Lorenzo Dolfins im Jahre 1664 fiel der Besitz mehreren Erben zu, die ihn schließlich 1700 dem Adeligen Ludovico Manin vermieteten.

Der Ruhm der alteingesessenen und wohlhabenden Familie Manin ist vor allem mit dem letzten Dogen der Serenissima, Ludovico, verbunden, der miterleben mußte, wie die Republik in die Hände der Franzosen fiel.

Nach verschiedenen Irrfahrten fanden die Manin im 14. Jahrhundert in Friaul Zuflucht. Sie unterstützten den Kampf der Serenissima gegen das Patriarchat von Aquileia so entschieden, daß Nicolò Manin im Jahre 1385 mit Zustimmung des Großen Rates die venezianische Staatsangehörigkeit erhielt. Im 15. Jahrhundert erreichte ein weiterer Manin die Rückgabe von Udine, das in die Hände Sigismunds von Ungarn gefallen war, und konnte Carnia, Cadore und Istrien Venedig unterwerfen.

Im 16. Jahrhundert halfen verschiedene Mitglieder der Familie Manin Venedig in Zeiten der Gefahr, indem sie Heerestruppen anwarben. 1651 schließlich nahmen der Senat und der Große Rat Ludovico I. Manin in die venezianische Aristokratie auf, da er der Serenissima im Kreta-Krieg mit der Schenkung von 60 000 Dukaten hervorragende Dienste geleistet hatte.

Ludovico trat auch durch sein Mäzenatentum rühmlich hervor. So ließ er die venezianische Kirche der Scalzi, die königliche Villa von Passariano und den Chor des Domes von Udine errichten. In seinem Te-

Aujourd'hui, après la restructuration des intérieurs réalisée par l'architecte Giannantonio Selva durant les dernières années du XVIIIème siècle, il ne reste presque plus de traces du plan d'origine du palais, qui devait toutefois être caractérisé par un grand raffinement et une opulence certaine avec les « salles… de l'une à l'autre façade de l'habitation… toutes les chambres avec cheminées… » et « …les sols ou carrelages non pas en briques, mais faits dans une matière appelée terrasse ».

Outre les terrasses à la vénitienne, le palais avait des plafonds aux poutrages décorés de frises polychromes ou dorées, dont certaines, suite à la restauration de 1968, ont été revalorisées. Francesco Sansovino déclare également qu'il est impossible de décrire le faste et la richesse de l'ameublement et des bibelots de la demeure qui apparaît à ses yeux d'une opulence hors du commun.

Les Dolfin ne vécurent toutefois que peu d'années dans le palais puisqu'en 1603 il apparaît loué par la famille Bonvisi ; à la mort de Lorenzo Dolfin, en 1664, l'édifice devint la propriété de divers héritiers qui, en 1700, le louèrent à N. H. Ludovico Manin.

La notoriété des Manin est surtout tristement liée au dernier doge de la Sérénissime, Ludovico, qui vit tomber la République entre des mains françaises, mais la famille était ancienne et très riche.

S'étant réfugiés en Frioul au XVIème siècle, après diverses pérégrinations, les Manin avaient activement appuyé la Sérénissime dans sa lutte contre le Patriarcat d'Aquilée, à tel point qu'en 1385 Nicolò reçut la nationalité vénitienne après vote unanime du Grand Conseil ; au XVème siècle, on doit à un autre Manin la restitution d'Udine, après que la ville eut risqué de tomber dans les mains de Sigismond de Hongrie, et la soumission de la Carnie, du Cadore et de l'Istrie à la République de Venise.

Au XVIème siècle, divers membres de la famille vinrent en aide à Venise dans les moments dangereux, recrutant des soldats, jusqu'à ce qu'en 1651 le Sénat et le Grand Conseil admissent au patriciat Ludovico Ier Manin pour avoir considérablement aidé la Sérénissime, engagée dans la guerre de Candie, par le versement de 60 000 ducats.

On doit également à Ludovico de nombreuses initiatives dans le domaine artistique : il fit dresser, à ses frais, l'église vénitienne des Scalzi, la ville royale de Passariano et le chœur du dôme d'Udine. Il établit, par testament, que tous les premiers

males in the family should be called Ludovico.

In 1787, the palace already rented by the Manins was granted in perpetual concession to Piero and to Ludovico, who was to become the last doge of Venice. After his election, Ludovico ultimately purchased the palace with a view to transforming it into a home suited to his new rank.

Shortly after the year 1700, the palace had already undergone restoration work because it had been somewhat neglected during the period of joint ownership by the Dolfin heirs. In 1708, for the marriage of Daniele Bragadin and Taddea Manin, the apartments had been sumptuously furnished and restored to their original splendour.

The chronicles of the period provide a description of the magnificent ceremony and the opulence of the stately home's furnishings, emphasising the astonishing costs involved and the wealth of art works it contained.

After acting as Podestà in Vicenza, Verona, and Brescia and holding the most important positions in the Venetian magistrature, Ludovico IV Manin (who became doge in 1789) purchased the palace following long negotiations and the expenditure of considerable sums of money, and decided to have the building renovated in order to preserve Sansovino's work. He called in the architect Giannantonio Selva, who presented a report on the subject in 1793, following up with plans for the renovation of both façades, at the rear of the palace and onto the Grand Canal.

The architect was obliged to give up this scheme because of the protest and debate aroused in Venice by his intention to demolish a façade created by Sansovino on the Grand Canal. Selva's intervention was therefore limited to the restoration of the interior. It was meant to increase the number of rooms and make them more comfortable, according to the doge's wishes.

Work was begun in 1794 and finished in 1801, but many innovations were not put into effect because of the political unrest and the fall of the Republic; this was also the fate of the majestic façade that should have added dignity to the rear of the palace. On the arrival of the French troops in Venice, Doge Ludovico Manin had already abandoned the city, where he returned in 1802 to die as a private citizen a year later.

As he had no heirs, the property passed to his brother Giovanni, who left it to his son, whose descendants sold it in 1867 to the

stament bestimmte er, daß alle Erstgeborenen der Familie auf den Namen Ludovico getauft werden sollten.

Der von den Manin gemietete Palast ging 1787 in Erbpacht an Piero und Ludovico, den letzten Dogen. Nachdem Ludovico das höchste Staatsamt erreicht hatte, erwarb er den Palazzo, um ihn in einen seiner Würde angemessenen Wohnsitz zu verwandeln.

Schon vorher, wenige Jahre nach 1700, waren am Palast Restaurierungsarbeiten vorgenommen worden, da während des gemeinsamen Besitzes der Dolfin-Erben die Instandhaltung des Gebäudes vernachlässigt worden war. Im Jahre 1708, anläßlich der Hochzeit von Daniele Bragadin und Taddea Manin, war der ursprüngliche Glanz der prunkvoll eingerichteten Wohnräume wieder hergestellt.

Die glanzvolle Zeremonie und die opulente Ausstattung des Wohnsitzes mit zahlreichen Kunstwerken beschreiben die zeitgenössischen Chronisten. Auch die gewaltigen Kosten werden erwähnt.

Ludovico IV. Manin, der bereits Bürgermeister von Vicenza, Verona und Brescia gewesen war und die wichtigsten Ämter in der Magistratur Venedigs bekleidet hatte, wurde 1789 Doge. Nachdem er den Palast nach zahlreichen Verhandlungen und Zahlung ungeheurer Summen erworben hatte, ließ er das Gebäude restaurieren, um das Werk Sansovinos zu erhalten. Zu diesem Zweck beauftragte er den Architekten Giannantonio Selva, der 1793 einen Baubericht abfaßte und unter anderem Pläne für die Neugestaltung beider Fassaden vorlegte.

Doch allein der Gedanke an einen Abriß der Sansovino-Fassade am Canal Grande rief allgemeine Proteste hervor und ließ das Vorhaben des Architekten scheitern. Selvas Umbaumaßnahmen beschränkten sich daher nur auf die Neustrukturierung der Innenräume. Auf Wunsch des Dogen sollte der Palast mehr Säle erhalten und der allgemeine Komfort erhöht werden.

Der Umbau begann 1794 und endete 1801. Auf Grund der politischen Unruhen und des Untergangs der Republik konnten jedoch zahlreiche Erneuerungen, darunter die majestätische Fassade, die der Rückseite des Palastes neue Würde verleihen sollte, nicht ausgeführt werden. Der Doge Ludovico Manin hatte beim Einmarsch der französischen Truppen Venedig verlassen. Er kehrte erst 1802 als privater Bürger in die Lagunenstadt zurück, wo er ein Jahr später starb.

Da Ludovico keine Erben hinterließ, fiel der Besitz an seinen Bruder Giovanni,

nés masculins de la famille devraient s'appeler Ludovico.

En 1787, le palais déjà loué par les Manin fut donné en concession emphytéotique perpétuelle à Piero et Ludovico, le futur dernier doge de Venise, qui l'aurait finalement acheté, après être arrivé à la plus haute charge de l'Etat, avec l'intention de le transformer en une demeure appropriée à sa dignité.

Quelques années après 1700, le palais avait toutefois été soumis à des interventions de restauration, vu que, durant la période de copropriété des héritiers de Dolfin, l'entretien de l'édifice avait été négligé ; en effet en 1708, à l'occasion des noces de Daniele Bragadin et Taddea Manin, les appartements somptueusement meublés apparaissaient de nouveau dans toute leur splendeur du passé.

Les chroniques de l'époque évoquent la cérémonie fastueuse et la magnificence de l'ameublement de la demeure, en soulignant les coûts extraordinaires et la richesse des œuvres d'art qu'elle contenait.

Ludovico IV Manin, devenu doge en 1789, après avoir été podestat à Vicence, Vérone et Brescia, avoir couvert les plus hautes charges dans la magistrature de Venise, et avoir acheté le palais suite à « l'intervention de nombreuses négociations et à la dépense de sommes considérables parce que, se vantant d'être une œuvre de Sansovino, il était considéré d'une valeur élevée », décida de procéder à la restauration de l'immeuble, en consultant l'architecte Giannantonio Selva. Celui-ci présenta en 1793 un rapport auquel fit suite un projet de construction d'une nouvelle façade aussi bien derrière le palais que sur la partie donnant sur le Grand Canal.

Les protestations et les polémiques que suscitèrent à Venise le projet de démolition de la façade de Sansovino sur le Grand Canal firent renoncer l'architecte à cette idée. Les interventions de Selva se limitèrent par conséquent à la restructuration des intérieurs, avec l'objectif d'augmenter le nombre des pièces et leur confort, selon les vœux du doge.

Les travaux débutèrent en 1794 et s'achevèrent en 1801, mais à cause de la chute de la République, de nombreuses innovations, parmi lesquelles la façade majestueuse qui aurait dû donner une nouvelle dignité à la partie arrière du palais, ne furent pas réalisées. Au moment de l'entrée des troupes françaises à Venise, le doge Ludovico Manin avait abandonné le palais où il serait revenu, en tant que citoyen privé, en 1802 pour y mourir l'année suivante.

Banca Nazionale del Regno, which subsequently became the Banca d'Italia in 1893. The building was sold with the walls laid bare and there is no trace of any of the furnishings, which were shared among the Manin heirs. Fortunately, there are still the pictorial decorations and stucco works with which Selva had decided to embellish the interior, relying on the most famous artists of the time: the painters Pierantonio Novelli, Jacopo Guarana, Costantino Cedini, Pietro Moro, and Giuseppe Bison; the ornamentalists Antonio Zanetti and Davide Rossi; and the stucco worker Giambattista Castelli.

At the end of the 17th century, the palace interior was re-furnished in the classical style, following the new trend already making itself felt in Venice.

The rooms became a virtual art gallery of the best Veneto painting of the period.

Restoration work begun in 1968 has returned a number of rooms to their original appearance, equipped with antique furniture; at the same time, the Sansovinian *portego* has also been restored, bringing to light the old pediments.

der ihn wiederum seinem Sohn vermachte. Die Nachkommen des Neffen veräußerten das Gebäude 1867 an die Banca Nazionale del Regno, die 1893 die Banca d'Italia wurde. Der Palast wurde unmöbliert verkauft, denn die unter den Manin-Erben aufgeteilte Einrichtung war inzwischen in alle Winde verstreut. Geblieben sind nur die Ausmalungen und die Stuckarbeiten, mit denen Selva die Innenräume verschönern wollte und für die er sich der Mitarbeit der berühmtesten Künstler der Epoche versicherte. Die Werke der Maler Pierantonio Novelli, Jacopo Guarana, Costantino Cedini, Pietro Moro und Giuseppe Bison, der Ornamentisten Antonio Zanetti und Davide Rossi sowie des Stukkateurs Giambattista Castelli sind glücklicherweise erhalten geblieben.

Die Ausstattung der Räume erfolgte im ausklingenden 18. Jahrhundert im klassizistischen Stil, der dem bereits seit einiger Zeit in Venedig herrschenden Geschmack entsprach. Darüber hinaus hingen im Palazzo Dolfin Manin die Gemälde der besten zeitgenössischen Maler Venetiens.

Die Restaurierungen von 1968 beförderten die ursprüngliche Ausstattung einiger Räume wieder zu Tage. Diese Säle wurden dann mit Möbeln der Epoche eingerichtet. Im Zuge dieser Maßnahme wurde auch der *portego* Sansovinos restauriert und das alte Gebälk freigelegt.

Puisqu'il n'avait pas d'héritiers, la propriété fut transmise à son frère Giovanni, qui la laissa à son fils, dont les descendants la vendirent en 1867 à la Banque Nationale du Royaume, changée en 1893 en Banque d'Italie. L'édifice fut vendu complètement vide, et il n'est resté aucune trace du mobilier partagé entre les héritiers Manin. Il reste heureusement les décorations picturales et en stuc avec lesquelles Selva comptait embellir les intérieurs, en ayant recours aux artistes les plus renommés de l'époque, les peintres Pierantonio Novelli, Jacopo Guarana, Costantino Cedini, Pietro Moro, Giuseppe Bison, les ornemanistes Antonio Zanetti et Davide Rossi, en plus du stucateur Giambattista Castelli.

L'aménagement du palais prit, à la fin du siècle, un aspect achevé et homogène orienté vers le classicisme, selon la tendance déjà en pratique depuis quelque temps à Venise. Il abritait de surcroît une véritable galerie de la meilleure peinture vénitienne de l'époque.

Des travaux de restauration entrepris en 1968 ont reconduit à leur aspect d'origine une série de pièces qui ont été ensuite meublées avec des meubles d'époque ; à cette occasion le *portego* de Sansovino a été intégralement restauré, ce qui valorise les vieux entablements.

PALAZZO DOLFIN MANIN

205 The Sala dell'Alcova. The room is decorated on the ceiling and over the doors with stucco work by Castelli. At the four corners of the ceiling, the spindle-shaped medallions with allegories of the seasons are the work of Giuseppe Bernardino Bison, as are the eight panels with festoons on the walls, celebrating the Arts, the Sciences and the Activities of Man. On the ceiling is the fresco by Jacopo Guarana, *Sleep.*

206 The so-called Academy of Music. The corner of the room that looks onto the Grand Canal and the San Salvador canal is furnished with large looking-glasses from the end of the 18th century, three armchairs and a neoclassical divan, plus a lacquered harpsichord from the end of the 17th century. On the walls, there are gilt bronze brackets from the Louis Seize period.

207 The central hall on the second floor. This very spacious room has a lacunar ceiling divided into one hundred and ten recesses. The furniture, with the round table and four sofas decorated with lions' paws and heads, is in the Empire style. The floor is the typical Venetian *terrazzo* made of doline lime, from the end of the 18th century.

208/209 The corner room. The ceiling is decorated with stucco-work by Castelli. The oval table in the centre is probably the work of the Venetian architect Giuseppe Jappelli (1783 – 1852) who was also responsible for the furnishing of the Pedrocchi café in Padua.

210 Pierantonio Novelli, *The Centaur Chiron Teaches Music to Achilles with Thetis Looking on.* The ceiling of the room called the Academy of Music on the second floor over the Grand Canal is decorated with another two works by the same artist. The central fresco represents *Mercury Offering the Lyre He Has Made to Apollo* while the other lunette illustrates *Pan Teaching Love to Play the Bagpipes.* These are the only frescoes by this artist in the palace.

211 The reception room on the second floor. The Empire furnishings include console tables with looking-glasses, chairs, armchairs, and round tables with Carrara marble tops. The painting on the wall is by Angelica Kauffmann (1741 – 1807) and represents a bacchante.

205 Sala dell'Alcova. Diesen Saal schmücken an der Decke und den Sopraporten Stuckarbeiten Castellis. In den vier Ecken der Decke befinden sich spindelförmige Medaillons mit Allegorien der Jahreszeiten. Sie sind wie die acht Wandtafeln mit Festons, die die Künste, die Wissenschaften und die Tätigkeiten des Menschen darstellen, Werke Giuseppe Bernardino Bisons. Die Deckenmalerei *Der Schlaf* schuf Jacopo Guarana.

206 Der »Akademie der Musik« genannte Raum. Die Saalecke, die zum Canal Grande und zum Rio San Salvador weist, ist mit großen Spiegeln aus dem späten 18. Jahrhundert verkleidet und mit drei klassizistischen Sesseln, einem Diwan sowie einem lackierten Clavicembalo aus dem späten 17. Jahrhundert eingerichtet. An den Wänden befinden sich vergoldete Bronzeleuchter aus der Zeit Ludwigs XVI.

207 Zentraler Saal des zweiten Obergeschosses. Dieser weitläufige Raum hat eine Kassettendecke, die aus 110 Feldern besteht. Der runde Tisch und die vier Sofas, die Löwenköpfe und -tatzen schmücken, sind im Empire-Stil gehalten. Der Fußbodenbelag aus dem späten 18. Jahrhundert besteht aus dem typischen venezianischen *terrazzo* aus Covolo-Kalk.

208/209 Ecksaal. Die Decke schmücken Stuckarbeiten Castellis. Der ovale Tisch in der Mitte stammt wahrscheinlich von dem venezianischen Architekten Giuseppe Jappelli (1783 – 1852), der auch die Einrichtung des Cafés Pedrocchi in Padua entwarf.

210 Pierantonio Novelli, *Der Kentaur Chiron unterweist Achilles in Gegenwart von Thetis in die Musik.* Die Decke des Raums im zweiten Obergeschoß am Canal Grande, der »Akademie der Musik« genannt wird, schmücken zwei weitere Werke desselben Künstlers. Das zentrale Fresko stellt *Merkur reicht Apoll die von ihm selbst hergestellte Kithara* dar, und das andere Bogenfeld zeigt *Pan lehrt Amor, Dudelsack zu spielen.* Dies sind die einzigen Fresken, die der Künstler für den Palast ausführte.

211 Empfangssaal im zweiten Obergeschoß. Die Einrichtung im Empire-Stil umfaßt Konsoltische mit Spiegeln, Stühle, Sessel und runde Tische mit Marmorplatten aus Carrara. An der Wand hängt ein Gemälde von Angelica Kauffmann (1741 – 1807) mit der Darstellung einer Bacchantin.

205 Salle de l'alcôve. La salle est décorée de stucs de Castelli au plafond et sur les dessus-de-porte. Aux quatre coins du plafond, les médaillons fusiformes avec allégories des saisons sont l'œuvre de Giuseppe Bernardino Bison, tout comme les huit panneaux avec festons sur les murs qui célèbrent les Arts, les Sciences et les Activités de l'homme. Au plafond, la fresque de Jacopo Guarana, *Le Sommeil.*

206 Salle dite « Académie de la musique ». La salle d'angle qui donne sur le Grand Canal et sur le canal de San Salvador est meublée de quatre grandes glaces de la fin du XVIIIème siècle, de trois fauteuils et d'un divan néoclassiques et d'un clavecin laqué de la fin du XVIIème siècle. Aux murs, des appliques Louis XVI en bronze doré.

207 Salon central du deuxième étage. Le plafond subdivisé en cent-dix caissons est très vaste. Le mobilier, qui comprend une table ronde et quatre canapés ornés de pattes et têtes de lion, est de style Empire. Le sol est la typique terrasse à la vénitienne en chaux de doline de la fin du XVIIIème siècle.

208/209 Salle d'angle. Le plafond est décoré de stucs de Castelli. La table ovale, au centre, est probablement l'œuvre de l'architecte Giuseppe Jappelli (1783 – 1852) qui conçut l'ameublement du café Pedrocchi de Padoue.

210 Pierantonio Novelli, *Le Centaure Chiron enseigne la musique à Achille en présence de Thétys.* Le plafond de la pièce appelée « Académie de la musique », au deuxième étage sur le Grand Canal, est orné de deux autres œuvres du même artiste. La fresque centrale représente *Mercure donnant la cithare qu'il a fabriquée à Apollon* tandis que dans l'autre lunette apparaît *Pan apprenant à jouer de la cornemuse à Amour.* Ce sont les seules fresques que le peintre exécuta pour le palais.

211 Salle de réception au deuxième étage. Le mobilier style Empire est constitué de consoles avec miroirs, chaises, fauteuils et tables rondes avec plateaux en marbre de Carrare. Au mur, tableau d'Angelica Kauffmann (1741 – 1807) représentant une bacchante.

PALAZZO SAGREDO

a S.ᵃ Sofia

PALAZZO SAGREDO   ✳   PALAIS SAGREDO

a S.ta Sofia   à S.te Sophie

Venise, Joseph Kier, Editeur, place S. Marc. 12 27

PALAZZO SAGREDO

This palace was originally owned by the Morosini family and was purchased at the start of the 18th century by the Sagredos, a noble family who had lived in the Santa Sofia district for centuries.

The façade onto the Grand Canal is proof of the Byzantine origin of the building, which was altered several times in subsequent centuries.

The original ground floor, with the doors leading onto the water, and the first floor with its tall windows topped by raised ogival arches supported on slim pillars, were completed in the 14th century by the addition of the second floor, which has a tracery frieze around the middle mullioned windows of the *portego* or central hall.

On purchasing the palace, the Procurator of St. Mark Gherardo Sagredo had it renovated to make it suitable for the social standing of his family. He ordered the architect Andrea Tirali to design a grandiose indoor staircase to replace the long since demolished outdoor Gothic stairway. He had the walls of the new staircase decorated by Pietro Longhi in 1734 with a fresco representing *The Fall of the Giants,* inspired by Giulio Romano's *Battle of the Giants* for the Palazzo del Tè in Mantua.

At the same time, the interior was luxuriously covered by Abbondio Stazio and Carpoforo Mazzetti Tencalla with stucco work, much of which is still in place. The same artists also created the decorations in the alcove, an exceptional example of a purely rococo-style bedroom, now preserved at the Metropolitan Museum in New York.

As the father of two daughters who married into rich and noble families (the Pisanis of Santo Stefano and the Barbarigos) and being the last male heir in his lineage, on his death Gherardo left his palace to the wealthiest branch of the Sagredo family, arranging in his will for the façade to be restored according to the plan of the architect Tommaso Temanza.

But the legal battle that ensued among the various branches of the Sagredo family considerably delayed the execution of his will, to such a degree that by the time the

Der Palazzo Sagredo, der ursprünglich im Besitz der Morosini war, wurde Anfang des 18. Jahrhunderts von den Sagredo erworben, einer seit Jahrhunderten im Stadtteil Santa Sofia ansässigen Adelsfamilie.

Die Fassade zum Canal Grande erinnert noch an die byzantinischen Wurzeln des Gebäudes. In den folgenden Jahrhunderten wurde der Palazzo mehrmals umgebaut.

Über dem Erdgeschoß mit den Portalen zum Wasser und dem ersten Obergeschoß mit den gestelzten byzantinischen Fenstern auf schlanken Säulen wurde im 14. Jahrhundert das zweite Obergeschoß errichtet, das einen Maßwerkfries an den mittleren Arkaturen des zentralen Saals oder *portego* aufweist.

Nach dem Erwerb des Palastes veranlaßte der Prokurator von San Marco, Gherardo Sagredo, die Modernisierung des Gebäudes, um es der gesellschaftlichen Stellung seiner Familie anzupassen. An Stelle der ursprünglichen und seit langem schon zerstörten gotischen Außentreppe ließ Gherardo nach einem Entwurf des Architekten Andrea Tirali einen grandiosen Innenaufgang bauen. Die Wände des Treppenhauses schmückte Pietro Longhi im Jahre 1734 mit dem *Gigantensturz* aus. Dieses Motiv lehnt sich an die von Giulio Romano für den Palazzo del Tè in Mantua geschaffene *Gigantenschlacht* an.

Gleichzeitig statteten Abbondio Stazio und Carpoforo Mazzetti Tencalla die Innenräume luxuriös mit Stukkaturen aus, von denen viele noch heute erhalten sind. Dieselben Künstler schufen auch die Dekorationen des Rokoko-Schlafzimmers, das heute im Metropolitan Museum in New York ausgestellt ist.

Ohne männlichen Nachkommen – seine zwei Töchter heirateten in die adligen und wohlhabenden Familien Pisani di Santo Stefano und Barbarigo ein – hinterließ Gherardo den Palast dem reichsten Zweig der Sagredo. In seinem Testament bestimmte er, daß die Fassade nach dem Plan des Architekten Tommaso Temanza erneuert werden sollte. Doch die folgenden gerichtlichen Auseinandersetzungen zwischen den verschiedenen Zweigen der Familie Sagredo verzögerten die Ausführung seines letzten Willens.

Le palais, qui appartenait à l'origine aux Morosini, fut acheté au début du XVIIIème siècle par les Sagredo, famille noble qui habitait depuis des siècles dans le quartier Santa Sofia.

L'origine byzantine de l'édifice est manifeste dans la façade donnant sur le Grand Canal tandis que le reste de la construction fut soumise à de multiples interventions au cours des siècles.

Au rez-de-chaussée avec les portes sur l'eau et au premier étage, doté de hautes fenêtres à arc surhaussé surmonté d'une flèche et soutenu par de fines colonnes, on ajouta au XIVème siècle le second étage noble, indiqué par la présence de la fenêtre bigéminée centrale entourée d'un encadrement richement sculpté et surmontée de quatre-feuilles au niveau du portego ou salon central.

Après avoir acheté le palais, le Procurateur de Saint Marc, Gherardo Sagredo, entreprit de le moderniser pour l'adapter à la position sociale de sa famille, en y faisant construire sur projet de l'architecte Andrea Tirali, à la place de l'escalier extérieur gothique qui avait déjà été supprimé, un grandiose escalier interne dont les murs furent décorés en 1734 par Pietro Longhi avec une fresque représentant *La Chute des Géants,* s'inspirant de la *Bataille des Géants* peinte par Jules Romain pour le Palazzo del Tè à Mantoue.

A la même époque, Abbondio Stazio et Carpoforo Mazzetti Tencalla recouvrirent les murs intérieurs de stucs luxueux, dont beaucoup sont encore in situ ; les mêmes artistes décorèrent la chambre à coucher en pur style rococo, conservée aujourd'hui au Metropolitan Museum de New York.

Père de deux filles entrées par leur mariage dans les riches et nobles familles Pisani de Santo Stefano et Barbarigo, et dernier descendant mâle de sa propre lignée, Gherardo laissa à sa mort le palais à la branche la plus riche des Sagredo, avec comme disposition testamentaire de refaire la façade suivant le projet réalisé par l'architecte Tommaso Temanza.

Mais le litige qui s'ensuivit entre les différentes branches Sagredo retarda l'exécution des volontés du défunt, au point que quand

Santa Ternita branch of the family gained possession of the inheritance, the fall of the Republic was already drawing near. Because of the consequent impoverishment of the great noble families, the palace remained as it was.

The surname Sagredo is a corrupted form of the word "secret", as the family was said to be secret advisors to the emperor. They boasted remote Roman origins having been governors of Dalmatia who apparently arrived in Venice in the ninth century. There they joined the Great Council in 1100 as a result of their restoring the city of Sibenik to obedience to the Republic.

The Santa Sofia branch of the family included one Giovanni, chancellor and treasurer of the Republic, who acted as ambassador to the court of Louis XIV, where he managed to obtain support for Venice's war in Crete and the personal privilege of adding the French lilies to his family's coat of arms. Later, during another diplomatic mission to England, he was received with all honours by Oliver Cromwell and was so successful that, on the renewal of the treaty of friendship between Venice and England in 1655, he was elected Procurator.

A number of the Sagredos were great lovers of the arts and sciences. Gianfrancesco was a remarkable scholar and a friend of Galileo's, who dedicated his *Dialogo dei massimi sistemi* to him. Zaccaria had one of the most renowned art galleries in Europe. Gherardo himself, who had purchased the palace, was the owner of four frescoes and a painting by Giambattista Tiepolo which disappeared in the 19th century.

The imposing staircase constructed by Tirali and frescoed by Longhi leads up to the *portego* with its huge paintings carried out between 1770 and 1780 by Andrea Urbani; these were great landscapes contained in sumptuous stucco frames with ovals representing allegorical figures over the doors.

A number of rooms lead off from the *portego,* many of which are decorated with very refined and elegant stucco work by Abbondio Stazio and Carpoforo Mazzetti Tencalla, who were also responsible for decorating the palace's mezzanine floor.

The ballroom is particularly interesting: as in other examples of the period, it extends to a height of two floors and is decorated with a series of illusionistic architectural frescoes containing two chiaroscuro figures representing *Minerva* and *Venus,* the work of the Belluno artist Gaspare Diziani.

Als schließlich die Sagredo di Santa Ternita das Erbe antraten, stand bereits der Untergang der Republik, der die Verarmung der adligen Familien zur Folge hatte, kurz bevor, und der Palast blieb letztendlich unverändert.

Wie der Familienname besagt, der eine abgewandelte Form für *segreto* (geheim) ist, waren die Sagredo kaiserliche Geheimräte. Sie hatten römische Wurzeln und waren vermutlich als Statthalter von Dalmatien im 9. Jahrhundert nach Venedig gelangt. Dort wurden sie im Jahre 1100 in den Großen Rat aufgenommen, weil sie die Stadt Sebeniko wieder der Obhut der Republik zugeführt hatten.

Zu den Sagredo di Santa Sofia gehörte Giovanni, Kanzler und Schatzmeister der Republik. Dieser konnte als Botschafter am Hofe Ludwigs XIV. die Unterstützung Frankreichs im Kreta-Krieg erringen. Bei einer anderen Mission in England wurde Giovanni von Oliver Cromwell mit allen Ehren empfangen. Zum Dank für seine erfolgreichen Bemühungen 1655 um die Erneuerung der Freundschaft zwischen Venedig und England wurde er zum Prokurator ernannt.

Unter den zahlreichen Mitgliedern der Familie Sagredo waren Liebhaber der Kunst und der Wissenschaft. Gianfrancesco Sagredo war ein hochgebildeter Gelehrter und Freund Galileo Galileis, der ihm den *Dialog über die beiden großen Weltsysteme* widmete. Zaccaria Sagredo besaß eine der berühmtesten Kunstgalerien Europas. Gherardo Sagredo, der den Palast erwarb, war unter anderem Besitzer von vier Fresken und einem Gemälde Giambattista Tiepolos, die im 19. Jahrhundert allerdings verlorengingen.

Über die imposante von Tirali erbaute und von Longhi mit Fresken ausgemalte Treppe erreicht man den *portego,* den Andrea Urbani zwischen 1770 und 1780 mit großformatigen Landschaftsdarstellungen und allegorischen Figuren ausschmückte.

Vom *portego* gelangt man in weitere Säle, die mit äußerst raffinierten und eleganten Stukkaturen von Abbondio Stazio und Carpoforo Mazzetti Tencalla ausgestattet sind. Diese beiden Künstler dekorierten auch das Mezzanin des Palastes.

Die Raumhöhe des Ballsaals, wie zu jener Zeit allgemein üblich, nimmt zwei Stockwerke ein. Unter den Fresken mit Scheinarchitekturen befinden sich zwei Figuren in Helldunkelmalerei, die *Minerva* und *Venus* darstellen und von Gaspare Diziani stammen.

la lignée de Santa Ternita entra en possession de l'héritage, la chute de la République entraînant l'appauvrissement des grandes familles était proche et la palais resta comme il était.

Les Sagredo, si l'on en croit la tradition et comme l'indique leur nom qui serait une déformation de *segreto* (secret) à cause de leur rôle de conseillers secrets impériaux, avaient de lointaines origines romaines ; gouverneurs de la Dalmatie, ils seraient arrivés à Venise au IXème siècle et auraient été acceptés dans le Grand Conseil en 1100 pour avoir ramené la ville de Sebenico sous la domination de la Sérénissime.

C'est à la branche de Santa Sofia qu'appartenait Giovanni, Chancelier et Trésorier de la République qui, en qualité d'ambassadeur à la cour de Louis XIV, réussit à obtenir des aides en faveur de Venise pour la guerre de Candie et le privilège personnel de pouvoir ajouter au blason de sa famille les lys de France. Plus tard, dans une autre mission diplomatique en Angleterre, il fut accueilli avec tous les honneurs par Oliver Cromwell et après le succès de cette mission qui renouvela en 1655 les liens d'amitié entre Venise et l'Angleterre, il fut élu procurateur.

La famille des Sagredo compta de nombreux amateurs d'art et savants. Gianfrancesco fut un grand chercheur et ami de Galilée qui lui avait dédié le *Dialogue sur les deux grands systèmes du monde,* tandis que Zaccaria possédait l'une des collections d'art les plus célèbres d'Europe ; Gherardo, celui même qui avait acheté le palais, était propriétaire entre autres de quatre fresques et d'une toile de Giambattista Tiepolo, œuvres disparues au XIXème siècle.

Par le large escalier construit par Tirali et orné de fresques par Longhi, on accède au *portego* qui abrite les grandes décorations exécutées entre 1770 et 1780 par Andrea Urbani, avec de grands paysages entourés de faux cadres et des dessus-de-porte ovales ornés de figures allégoriques.

A partir du *portego,* on accède à plusieurs salles, souvent décorées de stucs très élégants qui sont probablement de la main d'Abbondio Stazio et de Carpoforo Mazzetti Tencalla, auteurs également de la décoration de la mezzanine.

La salle de bal présente un intérêt particulier : comme d'autres de la même époque, elle se développe sur la hauteur de deux étages et est ornée de fresques de style architectural parmi lesquelles deux figures en grisaille représentant *Minerve* et *Vénus,* œuvres de Gaspare Diziani, originaire de Belluno.

215 Detail of the ballroom with illusionistic architectural frescoes containing two chiaroscuro works by Gaspare Diziani representing *Minerva* and *Venus.* True to 18th-century convention, the ballroom extends twice the height of the other rooms.

216 A row of rooms lying parallel to the longer side of the *portego.* They preserve valuable stucco decorations by Abbondio Stazio and Carpoforo Mazzetti Tencalla, who also decorated the palace's mezzanine floor.

217 Detail of one of the 18th-century doors in the main hall, or *portego,* contained by sham pilasters and topped by a sham stucco medallion.

218 The palace's *portego* with the mullioned window facing onto the Grand Canal; the walls are lined with vast landscapes contained in illusionist frames, the work of Andrea Urbani between 1770 and 1780.

215 Teilansicht des Ballsaals. Unter den Fresken mit Scheinarchitekturen befinden sich zwei Figuren in Helldunkelmalerei von Gaspare Diziani, *Minerva* und *Venus.* Wie im 18. Jahrhundert üblich, nimmt die Raumhöhe des Ballsaals zwei Stockwerke ein.

216 Eine Saalflucht erstreckt sich parallel zur Längsseite des *portego.* Diese Räume sind mit wertvollen Stukkaturen von Abbondio Stazio und Carpoforo Mazzetti Tencalla ausgestattet, die auch das Mezzanin des Palastes ausschmückten.

217 Eine der Türen aus dem 18. Jahrhundert des zentralen Saals oder *portego.* Scheinpilaster und ein gemaltes Stuckmedaillon rahmen bzw. bekrönen die Tür.

218 *Portego* des Palastes mit dem Fensterband zum Canal Grande. An den Wänden befinden sich die weiten Landschaftsdarstellungen mit gemalten Rahmen, die zwischen 1770 und 1780 Andrea Urbani ausführte.

215 Détail de la salle de bal : fresques de style architectural avec les deux grisailles de Gaspare Diziani représentant *Minerve* et *Vénus.* La salle de bal, suivant une typologie courante au XVIIIème siècle présentait une hauteur de deux étages.

216 Enfilade de salles qui se succèdent parallèlement au côté long du *portego.* Elles conservent de riches décors en stuc probablement réalisés par Abbondio Stazio et Carpoforo Mazzetti Tencalla qui décorèrent également l'entresol du palais.

217 Détail d'une porte XVIIIème du salon central ou *portego,* entourée de fausses parastates et surmontée d'un médaillon en stuc.

218 *Portego* avec la baie donnant sur le Grand Canal ; les murs sont ornés de grands paysages entourés de faux cadres exécutés par Andrea Urbani de 1770 à 1780.

PALAZZO FALIER

D. Moretti

PALAZZO FALIER

Palazzo Falier is a Gothic construction, probably dating from the first half of the 15th century, which has since undergone a number of alterations at various times. The palace features two covered projecting loggias, called *liagò,* on either side of the central mullioned windows, which rise flush with the Grand Canal, resting on the façade which thus recedes slightly from the canal bank.

For a time it was assumed that these elements were a 19th-century addition; but in fact, they are all that remains of the 15th-century *liagò,* as represented for example in paintings by Vettore Carpaccio.

The palace belonged for many centuries to the Faliers, a family of ancient nobility residing in the San Vidal district, where the building existed already in the 9th century. It was apparently due to the will of Vitale Falier, the first doge in the family (1084–1096), that the first church dedicated to San Vitale was built; it was renovated in the 18th century.

An episode in the 14th-century St. Mark's mosaics reminds us that it was this same Vitale who apparently rediscovered the lost remains of Saint Mark which had been buried in the Palatine chapel. It was also Vitale who consecrated the third construction of the Basilica of St. Mark's in 1094.

Among numerous other famous personalities, the Falier family also gave the Republic two further doges: Ordelaffo, who was a valiant military man and an ally of Baldwin, King of Jerusalem, conquered Accra. This conquest brought Venice considerable commercial privileges, which were renewed in subsequent years by the Byzantine emperors, and which also laid the foundations for the future Venetian Empire in the east. After a series of victories, Ordelaffo died in 1118 in a battle beneath the walls of Zara.

Another branch of the Falier family included Marino, who was doge from 1354 to 1355. His name is remembered for the conspiracy he hatched to gain absolute power. His plan was discovered before it could be put into effect and finished tragically in 1355 with the doge beheaded and his accomplices also sentenced to death.

Der gotische Palazzo Falier stammt vermutlich aus der ersten Hälfte des 15. Jahrhunderts. Im Laufe der Zeit erfuhr das Gebäude zahlreiche Umbaumaßnahmen.

Besonders charakteristisch für diesen Palast sind die beiden vorspringenden überdachten Loggen oder *liagò* zu Seiten der zentralen Arkadenbögen. Sie liegen auf der zurückgesetzten Fassade des Gebäudes auf. Eine Zeitlang ging man davon aus, daß diese Terrassen im 19. Jahrhundert hinzugefügt worden waren. Tatsächlich aber sind sie die einzigen erhaltenen *liagò* aus dem 15. Jahrhundert, so wie sie beispielsweise Vettore Carpaccio in seinen Gemälden darstellte.

Viele Jahrhunderte lang war der Palast im Besitz der Falier, einer alteingesessenen Patrizierfamilie aus dem Stadtviertel San Vidal, wo sich auch das Gebäude seit dem 9. Jahrhundert befindet. Auf Wunsch Vitale Faliers, des ersten Dogen der Familie (1084–1096), erfolgte wohl der Bau der ersten Kirche San Vitale, die im 18. Jahrhundert neu errichtet wurde. Vitale weihte auch im Jahre 1094 den dritten Bau der Basilika von San Marco ein.

Neben zahlreichen anderen berühmten Persönlichkeiten stellten die Falier der Republik zwei Dogen. Ordelaffo war ein ruhmreicher Krieger und Verbündeter Balduins, König von Jerusalem, der Akkra einnahm. Diese Eroberung ging einher mit enormen Handelsprivilegien für Venedig, die die byzantinischen Herrscher in den folgenden Jahren erneuerten und die den Grundstein für das zukünftige venezianische Reich im Osten bildeten. Nach zahlreichen siegreichen Schlachten starb Ordelaffo im Jahre 1118 im Kampf in der Nähe Zaras.

Aus einem anderen Zweig der Falier entstammte Marino, der zwischen 1354 und 1355 Doge war. Marino stiftete eine Verschwörung an, um die absolute Macht zu erringen. Das Komplott wurde aber rechtzeitig aufgedeckt und der Doge im Jahre 1355 geköpft. Seine Verbündeten wurden ebenfalls hingerichtet.

Bis zum 17. Jahrhundert wurde zwar eine Statue mit abgeschlagenem Kopf erwähnt, die an das tragische Ereignis erin-

Le Palais Falier, une construction gothique datant probablement de la première moitié du XVème siècle, a subi de nombreuses modifications à différentes époques ; il possède deux loggias très caractéristiques, couvertes et en saillie. Ces éléments ou *liagò,* flanquent la grande baie centrale ; ils surplombent le Grand Canal et s'appuient sur la façade proprement dite qui apparaît ainsi en recul.

On a pensé que ces éléments avaient été ajoutés au XIXème siècle, mais en réalité ce sont les uniques témoignages de *liagò* du XVème siècle tels qu'on peut en voir par exemple dans les peintures de Vettore Carpaccio.

Le palais a appartenu pendant plusieurs siècles aux Falier, vieille famille de la noblesse vénitienne dont la présence est attestée dans le quartier de San Vidal où s'élève justement le palais dès le IXème siècle.

C'est à la volonté de Vitale Falier, premier doge de la famille (1084–1096) que l'on doit la construction de la première église, refaite ensuite au XVIIIème siècle et consacrée au saint du même nom.

Comme le rappelle un épisode des mosaïques de Saint-Marc datant du XIVème siècle, ce même Vitale aurait redécouvert la dépouille de saint Marc, inhumé dans la chapelle palatine et dont on avait perdu les traces. Par ailleurs, c'est lui qui consacra en 1094 la troisième construction de la basilique Saint-Marc.

En plus de nombreux autres personnages célèbres, les Falier donnèrent à la République deux autres doges : Ordelaffo qui fut un vaillant guerrier, allié de Baudouin, roi de Jérusalem, il conquit Acre et obtint de grands privilèges commerciaux en faveur de Venise, renouvelés ensuite par les empereurs byzantins et jetant ainsi les bases du futur empire vénitien à l'Est. Après une série de batailles victorieuses, il mourut en 1118 en combattant sous les remparts de Zara.

Marino, de la famille des Falier mais d'une autre branche, fut doge en 1354 et 1355 : son nom est lié au complot qu'il ourdit pour s'emparer du pouvoir absolu mais qui, démasqué avant d'être mis en acte, se conclut tragiquement en 1355 avec la décapitation du

Although popular tradition has it that up until the 17th century there was a statue of his headless figure to commemorate the dismal affair at the top of a staircase in Palazzo Falier, he was not even a member of the San Vidal branch of the family and his own palace, which is still standing today, is in the Santi Apostoli district.

Marino was a descendant of Anzolo, a Procurator of St. Mark, son of the Doge Vitale and brother of another Ordelaffo, who was the founder of the San Vidal branch of the family.

The same San Vidal lineage also included Francesco, who was exiled in 1492 because, as head of the Great Council – one of the highest judicial appointments in the state – he had proposed a law whereby every nobleman in need should be granted a hundred gold ducats. Such a move would have caused the Republic's financial collapse, considering the enormous number of impoverished noblemen.

In addition to their roles in the administration and defence of the state, the Faliers were also patrons of the arts. Francesco's father, Giovanni, who died after the fall of the Republic having held some of the highest appointments in the Venetian navy, was a great patron of Antonio Canova, whose talent he had foreseen even in the artist's youth.

Despite much renovation work over the centuries which has altered its structure, the palace still retains most of its original features intact, for example the long and narrow *portego* with its row of rich mullioned windows facing onto the Grand Canal, flanked by two projecting *liagò* structures. These have now been transformed into two elegant drawing-rooms, from which one can observe the bustling life on the busiest of the city's waterways.

The last owners of the palace, who died in this century, have donated to the city's collections many precious objects and art works recalling the history and the life of the Falier family.

Today the state apartments at Palazzo Falier are used to house the Veneto Sviluppo company which, with all due respect for the nature of the interior, has furnished the rooms with modern and functional good taste, proving yet again how the Venetian home can adapt to the needs of the times.

nern sollte und oberhalb einer heute zerstörten Treppe des Palazzo Falier als Mahnmal stand, doch Marino gehörte nicht zu den Falier di San Vidal. Sein Palast, der heute noch besichtigt werden kann, liegt im Stadtviertel Santi Apostoli. Marino stammte von Anzolo ab, Prokurator von San Marco, Sohn des Dogen Vitale und Bruder eines anderen Ordelaffo, Stammvater der Falier di San Vidal.

Demselben Zweig von San Vidal gehörte auch Francesco an. In seiner Eigenschaft als Vorsitzender des Großen Rates hatte er eine der höchsten richterlichen Machtbefugnisse des Staates inne. Als er ein Gesetz vorschlug, auf Grund dessen jedem notleidenden Patrizier 100 Golddukaten ausgezahlt werden sollten, wurde er im Jahre 1492 kurzerhand verbannt. Dieses Gesetz hätte nämlich der Republik den finanziellen Ruin beschert, denn die Zahl der mittellosen Patrizier war überaus groß.

Die Falier wirkten nicht nur in Staatsämtern von Verwaltung und Verteidigung. Sie machten sich auch einen Namen als Kunstmäzene. So war der Vater Francescos, Giovanni, der nach dem Untergang der Serenissima starb und höchste Ämter in der venezianischen Marine bekleidet hatte, ein großer Gönner Antonio Canovas, dessen Talent er frühzeitig erkannte.

Trotz der zahlreichen Umbauten, die die Anlage des Palastes im Laufe der Jahrhunderte verändert haben, sind seine ursprünglichen Merkmale zu einem guten Teil erhalten geblieben: beispielsweise der lange, enge *portego*, dessen reich gestaltetes Fensterband zum Canal Grande weist und der von den beiden Vorbauten der *liagò* eingerahmt wird. Sie sind heute in zwei elegante Salons verwandelt worden, von denen aus das Leben und Treiben auf der belebtesten Wasserstraße der Stadt beobachtet werden kann.

Die letzten Besitzer des Palastes verstarben in diesem Jahrhundert. Sie haben den städtischen Sammlungen Kostbarkeiten und Kunstwerke hinterlassen, die an die Geschichte und das Leben der Familie Falier erinnern.

Heute ist das Obergeschoß des Palazzo Falier Sitz der Gesellschaft Veneto Sviluppo. Sie hat den Palast unter Berücksichtigung der originalen Ausstattung mit modernem und funktionalem Geschmack eingerichtet und so den Beweis für die Anpassungsfähigkeit der venezianischen Häuser an die heutigen Anforderungen erbracht.

doge et la condamnation à mort de ses complices.

Bien que la tradition cite la présence jusqu'au XVIIème siècle d'une statue le représentant décapité, pour rappeler ce sombre événement, et placée dans le palais Falier, au sommet d'un escalier aujourd'hui disparu, Marino n'appartenait pas à la branche de San Vidal et son palais, qui existe encore aujourd'hui, s'élevait dans le quartier des Santi Apostoli.

Il descendait en effet d'Anzolo, Procurateur de Saint Marc, fils du doge Vitale et frère d'un autre Ordelaffo, chef de la branche de San Vidal.

A la branche de San Vidal appartenait également Francesco qui fut condamné à l'exil en 1492 parce que du temps où il était haut magistrat de la République, à savoir Chef des Quarante, il avait proposé une loi sur la base de laquelle il aurait fallu attribuer à chaque noble indigent la somme de cent ducats d'or, ce qui aurait provoqué une véritable faillite pour le Trésor de Venise vu le grand nombre de nobles sans le sou.

A côté de leurs hautes fonctions dans l'administration et dans la défense de l'Etat, les Falier furent aussi de grands mécènes : Giovanni, par exemple – il mourut après la chute de la Sérénissime –, le père de Francesco, commandant de la flotte vénitienne, fut le protecteur d'Antonio Canova dont il avait deviné le talent dès son plus jeune âge.

Malgré les nombreuses interventions qui ont modifié la structure du palais au cours des siècles, celui-ci conserve en bonne partie ses caractéristiques d'origine dans le long et étroit salon central qui donne à travers la baie sur le Grand Canal, flanqué par les deux avant-corps des *liagò*, transformés aujourd'hui en deux élégants salons desquels on peut admirer l'animation de la voie d'eau la plus fréquentée de Venise.

Les derniers propriétaires du palais, disparus au cours du XXème siècle, ont laissé aux collections de la ville des reliques et des œuvres d'art rappelant l'histoire et la vie de la famille Falier.

Aujourd'hui le premier étage du Palais Falier est le siège de la Société Veneto Sviluppo qui, tout en respectant les espaces internes, l'a aménagé dans un goût moderne et fonctionnel prouvant, une fois de plus, que la maison vénitienne peut s'adapter aux exigences du temps.

223 The end section of the *portego,* facing onto the Grand Canal, has been transformed into a meeting room and furnished with a table designed by Tobia Scarpa.

224 The long and narrow *portego* in the palace's state apartments, where the beams in the ceiling have been restored to view, receives light through the mullioned windows at the end.

225 The *liagò* or covered loggia, which extends flush with the Grand Canal, has been transformed into a modern drawing-room.

226 The left-hand *liagò* has also been transformed into a drawing-room with its interior space delineated by a pair of Corinthian columns.

223 Der hintere Teil des *portego* zum Canal Grande wurde zu einem Versammlungssaal. Er ist mit einem von Tobia Scarpa entworfenen Tisch eingerichtet.

224 Der lange, enge *portego* des Obergeschosses, in dem das Deckengebälk freigelegt wurde, erhält durch das dreibogige Fenster Licht.

225 Die *liagò* oder überdachte Loggia zum Canal Grande wurde in einen modernen Salon verwandelt.

226 Die linke, ebenfalls als Salon dienende *liagò* wird von zwei korinthischen Säulen begrenzt.

223 L'extrémité du *portego,* vers le Grand Canal, transformée en salle de réunion et meublée d'une table dessinée par Tobia Scarpa.

224 Le *portego* du palais, long et étroit, où l'on a dégagé les poutres du plafond, avec fenêtre tripartite.

225 *Liagò* ou loggia couverte qui surplombe le Grand Canal, transformé en salon moderne.

226 *Liagò* de gauche, transformé en salon, délimité vers l'intérieur par deux colonnes corinthiennes.

PALAZZO BOLDÙ

D. Moretti

PALAZZO BOLDÙ

The palace stands in the San Felice parish in one of the city's most densely populated districts, facing onto the Grand Canal alongside the Palazzo Contarini Pisani.

In its current form, the building presents a 17th-century facade marked by an ashlar-worked stone covering on the ground floor, topped by the first mezzanine floor, two floors of state apartments, and a second mezzanine floor.

The façade has a characteristically asymmetrical layout with the axis of the main door and the mullioned window of the main hall shifted considerably to the right. The windows are still linked with 16th-century tradition, with a balcony and a round arch, enclosed in a frame at the top and sides.

The interior reflects the outside structure of the building: the long but relatively narrow main hall, or *portego,* with its mullioned window, only leads off to rooms on the left-hand side of the home, clearly identifiable from the outside, whereas the right-hand wing seems nonexistent.

The present 17th-century palace stands in the place of an earlier building which once belonged to the Ghisi family and was passed on to the Boldù family as a result of the marriage of Adriana Ghisi and Cristoforo Boldù in 1657, which is probably when the palace was restored.

The Ghisi family were originally from Aquileia and belonged to the group of families which moved to the lagoon city between the 8th and 9th centuries and thus to the most ancient of Venetian nobility. A number of the family's members had been on the Great Council or held important appointments in the city's government. At the time of the Second Crusade, they had also conquered certain Aegean islands, and these they governed for many years.

The Boldùs also had a long-standing aristocratic background: they had come to Venice from Conegliano at the start of the 9th century and had been among those who had been responsible for the construction (around the year 1000 according to the chronicles of the time) of the church of San Samuele. They took an active part in public

Der Palazzo Boldù steht in der Pfarrei San Felice, einem der dichtbevölkertsten Viertel der Stadt, und blickt neben dem Palazzo Contarini Pisani auf den Canal Grande.

In seiner heutigen Gestalt weist das Gebäude eine Fassade aus dem Seicento auf, die sich durch eine Rustika-Erdgeschoßzone auszeichnet, über der sich das erste Mezzanin, die beiden Obergeschosse und das zweite Mezzanin erheben.

Charakteristisch ist die asymmetrische Gestaltung der Fassade: Die Achsen von Portal und vom Dreibogenfenster des Salons sind ganz nach rechts verschoben. Noch in der Tradition des 16. Jahrhunderts stehen die Rundbogenfenster mit Balkon, die seitlich und oben eingerahmt sind.

Die äußere Struktur des Bauwerkes spiegelt das Innere wider. So führen nur die Säle des linken Flügels, die von außen leicht erkennbar sind, zu dem langen und nicht sehr breiten Hauptsaal oder *portego* mit Drillingsfenster, während der rechte Flügel wie nicht vorhanden erscheint.

Der heutige Palazzo aus dem 17. Jahrhundert erhebt sich auf einem älteren Bau, der zunächst der Familie Ghisi gehörte und dann durch die Heirat von Adriana Ghisi und Cristoforo Boldù im Jahre 1657 in den Besitz der Boldù gelangte. Aus diesem Anlaß wurde vermutlich auch die Restaurierung des Palastes durchgeführt.

Die ursprünglich aus Aquileia stammenden Ghisi gehörten zu jenen Familien, die sich bereits zwischen dem 8. und 9. Jahrhundert in der Lagunenstadt niederließen und somit zur ältesten venezianischen Aristokratie zählten. Zahlreiche Mitglieder der Familie gehörten dem Großen Rat an oder bekleideten Ämter in der Stadtverwaltung. Zur Zeit des zweiten Kreuzzugs hatten sie einige Inseln der Ägäis erobert, auf denen sie viele Jahre ihre Herrschaft ausübten.

Die Geschichte der Familie Boldù läßt sich ebenfalls weit zurückverfolgen: Zu Beginn des 9. Jahrhunderts waren die Boldù von Conegliano nach Venedig gekommen. Sie zählten zu jener Gruppe, die alten Chroniken zufolge um 1000 die Kirche von San Samuele errichten ließ. Aktiv am öffentli-

Le palais s'élève dans la paroisse de San Felice, l'un des quartiers les plus habités de la ville, et donne sur le Grand Canal à côté du Palais Contarini Pisani.

Dans sa forme actuelle, le palais présente une façade du XVIIème siècle avec un revêtement en bossage au rez-de-chaussée sur lequel s'élève la première mezzanine, les deux étages nobles et la seconde mezzanine.

La façade est caractérisée par le dessin asymétrique constitué par l'axe du portail et celui de la fenêtre triple du salon complètement déplacés à droite, tandis que les fenêtres avec balcon et arc en plein cintre, entourées sur les côtés et au-dessus par une moulure, manifestent encore l'influence du style du XVIème siècle.

L'intérieur reflète la structure externe de l'édifice et, en effet, au niveau de la triple fenêtre seules les salles de l'aile gauche du palais donnent sur le salon central, long et pas très large ; elles sont clairement identifiables de l'extérieur alors que le salon apparaît mutilé de son aile droite.

Le palais actuel datant du XVIIème siècle s'élève sur une construction antérieure ayant appartenu à la famille Ghisi et passée aux Boldù à la suite du mariage entre Adriana Ghisi et Cristoforo Boldù, en 1657, et c'est peut-être à cette occasion qu'on procéda à la restauration du palais.

Les Ghisi, originaires d'Aquilée, appartenaient au groupe de familles qui s'étaient installées dans la ville lagunaire vers le VIIIème – IXème siècle et donc à la noblesse vénitienne la plus ancienne ; de nombreux membres de la famille avaient appartenu au Grand Conseil ou occupé des charges importantes dans le cadre du gouvernement de la ville ; à l'époque de la deuxième croisade, ils avaient en outre conquis quelques îles de la mer Egée sur lesquelles ils avaient exercé leur domination de longues années durant.

Les Boldù étaient eux aussi de très ancienne noblesse : originaires de Conegliano, ils étaient arrivés à Venise au début du IXème siècle et étaient au nombre de ceux qui, suivant les chroniques, avaient fait édifier aux environs de l'an 1000 l'église de San Samuele ; en participant activement à la vie

life in the Republic and held important civilian and military positions. In the 15th century, one Leonardo was among the most capable of Venetian diplomats in negotiations with the Turks; in 1456, given his profound understanding of the situation in the Balkans, he was appointed governor of Shkoder, to which he returned in 1473 as quartermaster-general of all of Albania. In 1489 a Boldù named Antonio was sent to the Habsburg court of Friedrich III to bring Venice's good offices to bear in the imperial conflict with Hungary, while another Venetian nobleman, Domenico Bollani, was sent on a similar mission to Matthias Corvinus.

When the peace was signed, Antonio Boldù was appointed to important posts at home. In 1492 he became a magistrate, together with the same Bollani, whom he accused two years later of corruption, thus bringing about his exile. Antonio died in Genoa on a diplomatic mission to negotiate a peace between Ferdinand of Aragon and Charles VIII of France. He was a highly educated man and his friends included the anatomist Alessandro Benedetti and Pietro Bembo, who dedicated one of his *Epistole familiari* to him.

Jacopo Boldù was a famous orator and clever politician, who wrote a funeral speech on the death of the Patriarch of Venice Tommaso Donato in 1504. One Filippo Boldù showed great courage in defending his position in Crete against the Turks in 1646, until he received the order from his superiors to abandon the effort.

The San Felice branch of the Boldù family came to an end in 1837 with Giuseppe. He was a man of great learning, an art lover, and also the first Podestà of Venice, an appointment he held for a number of years with considerable ability and dedication.

The palace, which was built in the 17th century, probably was renovated for the marriage of Zuane Boldù to Benizia Rubbi in 1745, when the interior was also remodelled. The long *portego*, which faces onto the Grand Canal from the state apartments, and one of the adjacent rooms still preserve their stucco decorations, frescoes, and paintings and can rightly be considered among the most beautiful examples of the period.

The Boldùs commissioned Francesco Fontebasso to do the frescoes and Jacopo Guarana to do the paintings. No one knows who was responsible for the stucco work, which provides an admirable, purely rococo framework with lively tones of various colours and a very rich repertoire of elegant

chen Leben der Serenissima teilnehmend, bekleideten sie wichtige zivile und militärische Ämter. Ein gewisser Leonardo war während der Verhandlungen mit den Türken im Quattrocento einer der geschicktesten venezianischen Diplomaten und wurde im Jahre 1456 aufgrund seiner genauen Kenntnis des Balkans zum Statthalter von Skutari ernannt, wohin er 1473 als Aufsichtsbeamter für ganz Albanien zurückkehrte. Antonio Boldù wurde 1489 an den Hof Friedrichs III. von Habsburg gesandt, um beim kaiserlichen Konflikt mit Ungarn zu vermitteln, während ein anderer Patrizier der Serenissima, Domenico Bollani, eine ähnliche Mission bei Matthias Corvinus erfüllte.

Nach dem Friedensschluß bekleidete Antonio Boldù in Venedig wichtige Ämter. Im Jahre 1492 wurde er zusammen mit Bollani Friedensrichter. Zwei Jahre später klagte er Bollani der Korruption an und veranlaßte dessen Verbannung ins Exil. Antonio Boldù starb während einer diplomatischen Mission in Genua, wo er sich wegen der Friedensverhandlungen zwischen Ferdinand von Aragón und Karl VIII. von Frankreich befand.

Antonio Boldù war ein hochgebildeter Mann. Zu seinen Freunden zählten der Anatom Alessandro Benedetti und Pietro Bembo, der ihm eine seiner *Epistole familiari* widmete.

Der berühmte Redner und kluge Politiker Jacopo Boldù schrieb im Jahre 1504 eine Grabrede zum Tode des Patriarchen von Venedig, Tommaso Donato. Ein gewisser Filippo Boldù verteidigte im Jahre 1646 Kreta mit großer Tapferkeit gegen die Türken, bis er abberufen wurde.

Die Linie der Boldù di San Felice starb 1837 mit Giuseppe aus. Der hochgebildete Bewunderer der schönen Künste war auch der erste Podestà von Venedig. Dieses Amt übte er viele Jahre lang kompetent und hingebungsvoll aus.

Der im 17. Jahrhundert restaurierte Palast wurde wahrscheinlich anläßlich der Vermählung von Zuane Boldù und Benizia Rubbi im Jahre 1745 umgebaut. Auch die Innenausstattung wurde erneuert. So finden sich in dem langgestreckten *portego* des Obergeschosses, der zum Canal Grande weist, und in einem anliegenden Saal noch Stukkaturen, Fresken und Gemälde, die zu den schönsten bis heute erhaltenen Beispielen jener Epoche gezählt werden dürfen.

Während die Boldù die Fresken bei Francesco Fontebasso und die Gemälde bei Jacopo Guarana in Auftrag gaben, bleibt die Herkunft der Stukkaturen unklar. Die

publique de la Sérénissime, ils avaient rempli de nombreuses fonctions de caractère civil et militaire : Leonardo au XVème siècle fut l'un des plus habiles diplomates vénitiens dans les négociations avec les Turcs ; en 1456, vu sa profonde connaissance des affaires balkaniques, il fut nommé recteur de Scutari où il retourna en 1473 en qualité de gouverneur de toute l'Albanie ; Antonio, en 1489, fut envoyé à la cour de Frédéric II de Habsbourg pour proposer les bons offices de Venise dans le conflit qui opposait l'Empire à la Hongrie tandis qu'un autre noble de la Sérénissime, Domenico Bollani, remplissait une mission analogue auprès de Mathias I Corvin.

Une fois la paix conclue, Boldù occupa des charges très importantes à Venise ; en 1492 il fut Avogador de Comun (haut magistrat) avec Bollani qu'il accusa deux ans plus tard de corruption en demandant sa condamnation a l'exil. Il mourut à Gênes tandis qu'en mission diplomatique il s'apprêtait à négocier la paix entre Ferdinand d'Aragon et Charles VIII de France.

Il fut également un homme de grande culture : citons parmi ses amis l'anatomiste Alessandro Benedetti et Pietro Bembo qui lui adressa l'une de ses *Epîtres confidentielles.*

Jacopo Boldù fut, quant à lui, un célèbre orateur de même qu'un homme politique avisé ; il écrivit en 1504 une oraison funèbre pour la mort du patriarche de Venise Tommaso Donato. Filippo défendit en 1646 avec grand courage l'emplacement des citernes à Candie contre les Turcs jusqu'à ce qu'il fût obligé d'abandonner cette entreprise sur l'injonction de ses supérieurs.

La branche des Boldù de San Felice s'éteignit en 1837 avec Giuseppe qui, en plus de sa profonde culture et de son amour des Beaux-Arts, fut également le premier podestat de Venise et remplit cette fonction pendant plusieurs années en manifestant une grande compétence et un dévouement sans borne.

Le palais, restauré au XVIIème siècle, peut-être à l'occasion du mariage entre Zuane Boldù et Benizia Rubbi, fut remis à neuf également à l'intérieur en 1745 : en effet le long *portego* du premier étage, qui donne sur le Grand Canal, et une salle adjacente conservent encore la décoration de stucs, fresques et tableaux qui peut être jugée à juste titre comme l'une des plus belles de cette époque à être parvenues jusqu'à nous.

Tandis que les Boldù s'adressèrent pour les fresques à Francesco Fontebasso et pour les tableaux à Jacopo Guarana, les stucs sont restés anonymes. Ils constituent un magnifi-

floral motives and other decorative elements. These link the work directly to the tradition created in Venice by the Ticino-born Abbondio Stazio and his pupil Carpoforo Mazzetti Tencalla.

In the *portego,* the walls are decorated with paintings by Guarana in stucco frames depicting mythological subjects: *Hercules and Omphale, Bacchus and Ariadne,* and *Zephyr.* Three great frescoes by Fontebasso are unfurled on the ceiling, representing *Diana and Endymion, The Judgement of Paris,* and *Andromeda Rescued from the Sea Monster.* Fontebasso was also responsible for the ceiling in the room facing onto the Grand Canal with *The Rape of Europe* contained by four chiaroscuro mythological subjects in the corners and accompanied by two compositions over the doors.

As a whole, the decoration of these rooms shows a great unity, not only in chronological terms but also in terms of theme. Fontebasso's elegant frescoes can be dated between 1744 and 1745. They are finely finished and use bright and luminous colours which wrap the compositions in a transparent atmosphere. These frescoes bear witness to the artist's Arcadian-narrative vein and can be considered among his best works. Although the influence of Tiepolo and Ricci is apparent, his interpretation is absolutely novel and personal.

aufwendigen Stuckarbeiten bilden wunderschöne polychrome Rokoko-Rahmen, die ein reiches Repertoir an eleganten floralen Motiven und anderem Zierat aufweisen. Diese Dekorationen knüpfen direkt an die von dem Tessiner Abbondio Stazio und seinem Schüler Carpoforo Mazzetti Tencalla eingeführte Tradition an.

Die Wände des *portego* schmücken die stuckgerahmten Gemälde Guaranas mit Szenen aus der Mythologie: *Herkules und Omphale, Bacchus und Ariadne* sowie *Zephir.* Die drei großen Deckenfresken Fontebassos zeigen *Diana und Endymion, Das Urteil des Paris* und *Die befreite Andromeda.* Ebenfalls von Fontebasso stammt die Deckenmalerei des zum Canal Grande weisenden Saals. Dort ist *Der Raub der Europa* dargestellt, den vier mythologische Szenen in Helldunkelmalerei an den Ecken rahmen. Außerdem dekorierte Fontebasso in diesem Saal zwei Sopraporten.

Da diese Räume zur selben Zeit ausgestattet wurden, weisen sie sowohl stilistische wie auch thematische Einheitlichkeit auf. Die eleganten Fresken Fontebassos können auf 1744 bis 1745 datiert werden. Sie wurden überaus sorgfältig unter Verwendung heller, leuchtender Farben ausgeführt, die die Kompositionen in eine transparente Atmosphäre tauchen. Diese Fresken bezeugen das erzählerische Talent des Künstlers und können zu den besten Werken Fontebassos gezählt werden. Zwar sind der Einfluß Tiepolos und Riccis spürbar, die sehr persönliche Interpretation ist jedoch unverkennbar.

que encadrement en pur style rococo, jouant sur une polychromie de tons vifs avec un riche répertoire d'images très variées et d'élégantes vrilles qui sont en relation directe avec la tradition inaugurée à Venise par Abbondio Stazio, artiste originaire du Tessin, et son élève Carpoforo Mazzetti Tencalla.

Dans le *portego,* les tableaux de Guarana sont encadrés de stucs et présentent des sujets mythologiques : *Hercule et Omphale, Bacchus et Ariane* et *Zéphyr,* tandis qu'au plafond on peut admirer les trois grandes fresques de Fontebasso représentant *Diane et Endymion, Le Jugement de Pâris* et *Andromède libérée du monstre.*

Fontebasso est également l'auteur du plafond de la salle donnant sur le grand Canal et qui représente *L'Enlèvement d'Europe* entouré aux quatre coins de quatre grisailles à sujets mythologiques auxquels font pendant deux dessus-de-porte.

Dans son ensemble, la décoration de ces pièces manifeste une grande unité, non seulement du point de vue chronologique mais aussi sur le plan thématique ; les fresques de Fontebasso, qui peuvent être datées vers 1744 – 1745 présentent une facture très raffinée avec un soin élégant des détails et l'emploi de couleurs claires et lumineuses qui baignent les compositions dans une atmosphère transparente. Ces fresques qui témoignent de la veine arcadienne et narrative de l'artiste peuvent être considérées comme faisant partie de ses plus belles réalisations où, sans oublier les leçons de Tiepolo et de Ricci, son interprétation est absolument personnelle et innovatrice.

231 The *portego* in the state apartments is decorated with three frescoes by Francesco Fontebasso on the ceiling and three paintings by Jacopo Guarana on the walls, enframed by one of the richest and most elegant stucco decorations of the century.

232 The *portego* in the state apartments. Detail of the mirror in an exuberant frame of stucco foliage with a double chandelier.

233 The *portego* in the state apartments. Detail of the wall with a huge painting by Jacopo Guarana representing *Bacchus and Ariadne,* enclosed in a sumptuous frame of coloured stucco work.

234 Francesco Fontebasso, *The Rape of Europe.* This fresco decorates the ceiling of a room leading off from the *portego* and facing onto the Grand Canal. In addition to the fresco, the room contains what is probably the most beautiful coloured stucco decoration in the palace.

234 Francesco Fontebasso, *The Judgement of Paris.* This is one of the frescoes decorating the ceiling in the *portego,* carried out between 1744 and 1745.

231 Den *portego* des ersten Obergeschosses schmük-ken an der Decke drei Fresken Francesco Fonte-bassos und an den Wänden drei Gemälde Jacopo Guaranas, die in eine der reichsten und elegante-sten Stuckdekorationen des Jahrhunderts einge-fügt sind.

232 *Portego* des ersten Obergeschosses. Ansicht eines Spiegels in atemberaubendem Stuckrahmen mit Rankenwerk und zweiflammigem Leuchter.

233 *Portego* des ersten Obergeschosses. Teilansicht der Wand mit dem großen Gemälde *Bacchus und Ariadne* Jacopo Guaranas in einem prächtigen polychromen Stuckrahmen.

234 Francesco Fontebasso, *Der Raub der Europa.* Die-ses Fresko schmückt die Decke eines dem *portego* benachbarten Saals zum Canal Grande. Neben dem Fresko weist dieser Raum die vielleicht schönste polychrome Stuckarbeit des Wohnsitzes auf.

234 Franceso Fontebasso, *Das Urteil des Paris.* Eines der Deckenfresken des *portego,* die zwischen 1744 und 1745 entstanden.

231 *Portego* du premier étage. Il est décoré de trois fresques de Francesco Fontebasso sur le plafond et de trois tableaux de Jacopo Guarana sur les murs, encadrés par l'une des décorations en stuc les plus riches et élégantes du siècle.

232 *Portego* du premier étage. Détail du miroir dans un exubérant cadre en stuc de style végétal avec double torchère.

233 *Portego* du premier étage. Détail du mur avec le grand tableau de Jacopo Guarana représentant *Bacchus et Ariane,* entouré d'un cadre opulent en stucs polychromes.

234 Francesco Fontebasso, *L'Enlèvement d'Europe.* La fresque décore le plafond de la salle contiguë au salon et donnant sur le Grand Canal. En dehors de la fresque, la salle est décorée de stucs poly-chromes qui figurent parmi les plus beaux de tout le palais.

234 Francesco Fontebasso, *Le Jugement de Pâris.* Une des fresques décorant le plafond du *portego,* exécutées entre 1744 et 1745.

PALAZZO GAMBARA

D. Moretti

Palazzo Mocenigo Gambara

The current palace building dates back to the second half of the 17th century, as demonstrated by the façade comprising a high mezzanine floor topped by two floors of state apartments. The second is lower than the first and features a mullioned window with a central arch and side lintels, with a triangular pediment off-center to the right and a series of single windows with gables to the left.

The *campiello* (or small square) and the *calle* (or narrow street) adjacent to the building both take the name Gambara from the family, who owned the palace after the marriage of Eleonora Gambara to Francesco, of the Carità branch of the Mocenigo family, in 1678.

It seems that in 1634 this palace was the birthplace of Lazzaro Mocenigo, one of the most famous and valiant of Venetian admirals. His enterprises included a part in the war of Crete, where he defeated the Turks on various occasions, causing them considerable losses of men and arms. He became Procurator of St. Mark and later admiral General and died in battle in 1665 during the Dardanelles blockade.

With its various branches, the Mocenigo family was one of the oldest and most powerful in Venice, providing the Republic with six doges.

The Gambara family joined the Venetian nobility late, in 1653. It did not have to buy its title of nobility, as other families did by, for example, financing the war against the Turks. Francesco Gambara received the title of nobility for himself and his family on account of the merit of his ancestor Nicolò Gambara, who had recruited soldiers for Venice in the war against the Turks in 1571.

Nonetheless, the family boasted titles of a very ancient order in Germany, from where they had moved to Brescia. It was held in great esteem by the Venetian Republic, partly because of its solid links with the court of Rome.

The Gambara family could count four cardinals among its members and also a poetess, Veronica, who married Gilberto X,

Der heutige Palazzo Mocenigo Gambara stammt aus der zweiten Hälfte des 17. Jahrhunderts, wie das hohe Zwischengeschoß verdeutlicht, über dem sich die beiden Hauptstockwerke erheben. Das zweite Obergeschoß hat eine geringere Höhe als das erste und wird von einem zentralen Giebel mit dreigeteiltem Fenster bekrönt.

Der kleine Platz und die Gasse beim Palazzo erhielten den Namen Gambara von der Familie, die den Palast nach der Hochzeit von Eleonora Gambara und Francesco Mocenigo aus der Linie der Carità im Jahre 1678 besaß.

Vermutlich wurde in einem früheren Bau 1634 Lazzaro Mocenigo geboren. Er war einer der berühmtesten venezianischen Admirale. Neben seinen vielen anderen Unternehmungen nahm er auch am Kreta-Krieg teil, wo er die Türken in mehreren Schlachten besiegte und ihnen große Verluste zufügte. Nachdem er Prokurator von San Marco und dann Generaladmiral geworden war, fiel er im Jahre 1665 während der Blockade der Dardanellen im Kampf.

Die in verschiedene Zweige aufgeteilten Mocenigo waren eine der ältesten und mächtigsten Familien der Stadt, die der Serenissima sechs Dogen stellte.

Die Gambara wurden erst spät, im Jahre 1653, in den venezianischen Adelsstand erhoben. Sie mußten sich aber nicht wie andere Familien, die etwa den Krieg gegen die Türken finanzierten, die Aufnahme in die Aristokratie erkaufen. Francesco Gambara erhielt den Titel für sich und seine Familie für die Verdienste seines Vorfahren Nicolò Gambara, der 1571 Soldaten im Dienste der Serenissima gegen die Türken anwarb.

Die Gambara waren jedoch schon seit alters von deutschem Adel. Von Deutschland aus waren sie nach Brescia übergesiedelt. In der Republik Venedig wurden sie wegen ihrer soliden Verbindungen mit dem römischen Hof hoch geachtet.

Zur Familie Gambara zählten vier Kardinäle und eine Dichterin. Veronica Gambara heiratete Gilberto X., Signore di Correggio, und regierte nach dessen Tod den kleinen Staat mit Weisheit und Geschick. Die

L'architecture actuelle du palais remonte à la deuxième moitié du XVIIème siècle, comme l'atteste la façade constituée d'un haut entresol surmonté des deux étages nobles ; le deuxième a une hauteur légèrement plus réduite que le premier et est caractérisé par une fenêtre tripartite avec fronton triangulaire, complètement déplacée sur la droite, tandis qu'à gauche on trouve une série de fenêtres simples surmontées elles aussi d'un tympan.

La petite place et la ruelle adjacentes tirent leur nom, Gambara, de la famille qui posséda le palais à la suite du mariage entre Eleonora Gambara et Francesco Mocenigo, de la branche Della Carità, qui eut lieu en 1678.

Il semble que ce palais ait vu naître en 1634 Lazzaro Mocenigo, l'un des plus célèbres et courageux capitaines de marine vénitiens qui participa, entre autres, à la guerre de Candie ; il battit à plusieurs reprises les Turcs auxquels il infligea des pertes considérables en hommes et en armement. Devenu Procurateur de Saint Marc puis Capitaine Général, il mourut au combat en 1665, durant le blocus des Dardanelles.

Les Mocenigo, divisés en différentes branches, étaient l'une des familles les plus anciennes et puissantes de la ville et lui donnèrent pas moins de six doges.

La noblesse des Gambara est, quant à elle, beaucoup plus récente : 1653. Contrairement à de nombreuses autres familles vénitiennes, elle ne fut pas achetée en ces temps critiques où la République avait besoin d'argent pour financer la guerre contre les Turcs, mais parce que Nicolò Gambara en 1571, avait fait preuve d'un grand mérite en maintenant des soldats en faveur de la Sérénissime contre les Turcs. C'est pourquoi l'un de ses descendants, Francesco, obtint le titre de noblesse pour lui-même et sa famille.

Quoi qu'il en soit, les Gambara possédaient de longue date des titres de noblesse en Allemagne, d'où ils s'étaient installés à Brescia, et ils étaient en outre fort estimés par la République de Venise pour les liens solides qui les unissaient à la cour de Rome.

Les Gambara comptaient dans leurs rangs quatre cardinaux et une femme poète,

Lord of Correggio, and governed that little state with great wisdom and ability after her husband's death.

She enjoyed great fame as a poetess in her time and associated with important personalities of the literary world such as Bembo, Tasso, Ariosto, and Aretino. She wrote refined and elegant rhymes in the style of Petrarch and letters revealing a deep-felt humanity and a lively and subtle spirit.

As for the palace, the records show that its façade onto the inner court was frescoed on historical and allegorical themes by Pordenone, obviously before it was restored in the 17th century.

In addition to the visual arts, the Mocenigos must have also been sensitive to literature, as Sanudo recalls that in 1514, on the last day of Carnival, they presented a play by Plautus at their home in the Carità district.

Especially in the state apartments, the palace has preserved its original layout as well as its stucco and fresco decorations. True to Venetian style, the rooms all face onto a central *portego* or main hall. The frescoes decorating the central hall and four side rooms are the work of Giambattista Canal, who painted mythological themes and six portraits of illustrious members of the Gambara family. The artist worked in the palace during the very last years of the 18th century, as demonstrated by a letter he wrote in 1798 requesting payment of the balance owing for five decorations over doors in the main hall, two portraits, and the frieze in the dining-room. Canal was well-known as a "historical figure painter" and was much in demand. He was also a member of the Venice painters' guild between 1768 and 1780.

He was constantly active: he decorated churches and palaces in Venice, Treviso, Udine, and Rovigo, with occasional trips to other Veneto cities. Above all, he painted numerous frescoes for ceilings in churches in the Veneto hinterland. He was among the artists most in demand in his lifetime, in particular filling the gap created by the departure of Giambattista Tiepolo. Among other things, he frescoed a ceiling in the Mocenigo home at San Stae in 1790 with the *Glorification of Aeneas.*

In the last decade of the century, his original rococo vein was influenced by the neoclassic style. This was the time when he was collaborating with the architectural illusionist painter Giuseppe Borsato, who remained a faithful friend during his final years.

bereits zu Lebzeiten berühmte Poetin pflegte den Umgang mit bedeutenden Dichtern wie Bembo, Tasso, Ariost und Aretino. Sie verfaßte elegante und raffinierte Reime im Stil Petrarcas und schrieb Briefe, die eine tiefempfundene Humanität und einen lebendigen und scharfsinnigen Geist bezeugen.

Die Palastfassade zum Hof schmückten vor der Neustrukturierung im 17. Jahrhundert – laut überlieferter Quellen – historisch-allegorische Außenfresken Pordenones.

Neben der Kunst liebten die Mocenigo offensichtlich auch die Literatur. So berichtet Sanudo, daß sie am letzten Karnevalstag des Jahres 1514 in ihrem Wohnsitz im Carità-Viertel eine Komödie Plautus' aufführten.

Vor allem im Obergeschoß des Palastes sind die ursprüngliche Raumfolge und die Stukkaturen und Fresken erhalten geblieben. Die Räume dieses Stockwerkes gruppieren sich, wie in venezianischen Palästen üblich, um den zentralen *portego*. Die Fresken des *portego* und weiterer vier Säle schuf Giambattista Canal. Er malte mythologische Szenen und sechs Bildnisse illustrer Mitglieder der Familie Gambara. Wie aus einem seiner Briefe aus dem Jahre 1798 hervorgeht, arbeitete der Maler in diesem Palast während der letzten Jahre des 18. Jahrhunderts. Schriftlich forderte er das Honorar für fünf Sopraporten des Hauptsaals, zwei Porträts und den Fries im Speisezimmer ein. Canal war zu jener Zeit allgemein als »historischer Figurenmaler« bekannt und daher sehr gefragt. Von 1768 bis 1780 war er Mitglied der Malerzunft von Venedig.

Unermüdlich und ohne Unterlaß schmückte Canal Kirchen und Paläste in Venedig, Treviso, Udine und Rovigo aus. Er wirkte auch in anderen Städten Venetiens. Vor allem schuf er zahlreiche Deckenfresken für Kirchen im Hinterland Venetiens und war, besonders nach der Abreise von Giambattista Tiepolo, einer der gefragtesten Künstler seiner Zeit. Unter anderem schuf er 1790 auch eine Deckenmalerei im Wohnsitz der Mocenigo in San Stae mit der Darstellung der *Verherrlichung Äneas'.*

Während der letzten Jahre des ausgehenden Jahrhunderts veränderte sich sein ursprünglicher Rokokostil durch klassizistische Einflüsse. In jener Zeit begann er, mit Giuseppe Borsato zusammenzuarbeiten. Der Maler von Scheinarchitekturen war ihm auch während seiner letzten Jahre ein treuer Freund.

Die Fresken Canals im Palazzo Mocenigo Gambara zeigen die Verschmelzung klassizistischer Elemente, zu denen auch Motive

Veronica qui, mariée à Gilberto X, Seigneur de Correggio, avait gouverné avec beaucoup de sagacité et d'habileté le petit Etat après la mort de son époux.

Ses poésies la rendirent très célèbre à son époque, et elle fréquenta les plus grandes personnalités du monde littéraire comme Pietro Bembo, le Tasse, l'Arioste et l'Arétin. Elle écrivit des vers élégants et raffinés dans le style de Pétrarque, ainsi que des lettres témoignant d'une profonde humanité et d'un esprit vif et subtil.

En ce qui concerne le palais, les sources rappellent que la façade interne donnant sur la cour avait été décorée de fresques historiques et allégoriques par Pordenone, évidemment avant la restauration au XVIIème ; en dehors de l'art, les Mocenigo semblent avoir été sensibles à la littérature, si l'on en croit Sanudo qui rappelle qu'en 1514, le dernier jour du Carnaval, ils avaient présenté une comédie de Plaute dans leur demeure du quartier de La Charité.

Le palais a conservé, surtout au premier étage, la planimétrie originale avec les décors de stucs et de fresques. Il se développe suivant la coutume vénitienne autour du *portego* central sur lequel donnent toutes les autres pièces. Les fresques ornant le salon central et quatre autres salles sont de Giambattista Canal qui y peignit des scènes de caractère mythologique et six portraits de membres célèbres de la famille Gambara. Le peintre travailla dans le palais durant les dernières années du XVIIIème siècle comme l'atteste une de ses lettres de 1798 où il réclame le solde de son dû pour cinq dessus-de-porte de la salle, deux portraits et la frise de la salle à manger. Canal était très connu à l'époque comme peintre d'histoire et donc très recherché ; il fut membre de la corporation des artistes-peintres de Venise de 1768 à 1780.

Ne connaissant pas de pauses créatives, il décora des églises et des palais à Venise, Trévise, Udine et Rovigo et réalisa également quelques œuvres dans d'autres villes de la Vénétie ; mais il exécuta surtout de nombreuses fresques pour les églises de l'arrière-pays vénitien et fut parmi les artistes les plus demandés de son époque, surtout après le vide créé par le départ de Giambattista Tiepolo. Entre autres, il orna de fresques un plafond du palais des Mocenigo à San Stae en 1790, représentant la *Glorification d'Enée.*

Dans la dernière décennie du siècle, sa veine rococo originale connut quelques influences néoclassiques : c'est de cette époque que date sa collaboration avec Giuseppe

Canal's frescoes at Palazzo Mocenigo Gambara show the merging of neoclassic elements, including Pompeian motives, with Rococo forms and Arcadian elements. The result is a refined style which forms a bridge between Rococo and Romanticism.

The elegant stucco work framing his painting is clearly of the same period, though it is from an unknown hand.

der pompejanischen Wandmalerei gehören, mit Rokokoformen und arkadischen Elementen. So entstand ein raffinierter Stil, der das Rokoko mit der Romantik verbindet.

Zur selben Zeit wurden die eleganten Stukkaturen, die seine Malerei rahmen, von einem unbekannten Künstler ausgeführt.

Borsato, en qualité de peintre de perspectives, avec lequel il entretint une amitié fidèle jusqu'à sa mort.

Les fresques de Canal au Palais Mocenigo Gambara témoignent de sa tentative d'adopter les éléments néoclassiques avec l'introduction dans la composition de motifs pompéiens qui se fondent avec son éducation rococo et avec une veine arcadienne, donnant lieu à une stylisation raffinée qui constitue un pont entre le style rococo et le romantisme.

Contemporains des fresques, les stucs de la main d'un artiste resté anonyme créent un cadre élégant à ses créations picturales.

241 Giambattista Canal, *Apollo and Diana.* This fresco is one of the four semicircles arranged around the sides of the central composition, in which the artist represented Jupiter, Juno and Mercury.

242 The Council Chamber. Detail of the huge red marble fireplace with a mirror inserted between coloured stucco decorations with mythological figures and a great central medallion representing Vulcan's workshop and topped by cherubs.

243 The Council Chamber. Green marble console table against a wall decorated with coloured stucco work in which garlands of flowers frame an altar with a central medallion that depicts a girl dancing with a tambourine.

244 Detail of the main hall with a great mirror between sham stucco decorations with trompe-l'œil architectural effects that include Corinthian pillars.

245 The Council Chamber. This is decorated entirely with coloured stucco work dating from the late 18th and early 19th centuries. In the detail, a landscape is surrounded by stylized floral elements.

246 Giambattista Canal, *Aeneas on Olympus.* This fresco decorates the ceiling of the main hall in the palace's state apartments and is enclosed by a rich frame of flowers and foliage. The painter worked on numerous frescoes in the palace during 1796.

247 The main hall with the fresco representing *Aeneas on Olympus.* The illusionist perspectives on the walls with trompe-l'œil effects and Corinthian pillars are also the work of Canal, who was responsible for the ovals over the doors with portraits of famous members of the Gambara family.

241 Giambattista Canal, *Apoll und Diana.* Dieses Fresko gehört zu den vier seitlichen, halbkreisförmigen Darstellungen, die um die zentrale Komposition mit Jupiter, Juno und Merkur angeordnet sind.

242 Ratssaal. Ansicht des großen Kamins aus rotem Marmor mit Spiegel, den polychrome Stuckdekorationen mit mythologischen Figuren und einem großen Mittelmedaillon mit Putten rahmen. Auf dem Stuckmedaillon ist die Werkstatt Vulcanus' dargestellt.

243 Ratssaal. Ein Konsoltisch aus grünem Marmor lehnt an einer mit polychromen Stukkaturen geschmückten Wand. Die Stuckdekorationen zeigen Blumengirlanden um ein zentrales Medaillon, auf dem eine Tänzerin mit Tamburin dargestellt ist.

244 Detail des zentralen Salons mit einem großen Spiegel zwischen gemalten Stuckdekorationen und Scheinarchitekturen mit korinthischen Säulen.

245 Der Ratssaal ist vollständig mit polychromen Stuckarbeiten aus dem späten 18. bzw. frühen 19. Jahrhundert ausgestattet. Das Detail zeigt eine Landschaft zwischen stilisierten floralen Elementen.

246 Giambattista Canal, *Äneas im Olymp.* Dieses Fresko schmückt die Decke des zentralen Saals im Obergeschoß. Es wird von einem reichen Blüten- und Blätterband gerahmt. Im Jahre 1796 schuf Canal zahlreiche Fresken in diesem Palast.

247 Zentraler Saal mit der Deckenmalerei *Äneas im Olymp.* Die gemalten Architekturelemente an den Wänden schuf ebenfalls Canal, der auch die ovalen Porträts berühmter Mitglieder der Familie Gambara über den Türen malte.

241 Giambattista Canal, *Apollon et Diane.* La fresque est l'un des quatre demi-cercles latéraux disposés autour de la composition centrale où l'artiste a représenté Jupiter, Junon et Mercure.

242 Salle du Conseil. Détail de la grande cheminée en marbre rouge au miroir encadré de stucs polychromes avec figures mythologiques et un grand médaillon central surmonté d'amours dans lequel est représentée la forge de Vulcain.

243 Salle du Conseil. Console en marbre vert appuyée contre un mur décoré de stucs polychromes avec guirlandes de fleurs encadrant un autel au centre duquel est représentée, dans un médaillon, une danseuse au tambourin.

244 Détail du salon central orné d'un grand miroir encadré de décorations en stuc avec fausses architectures et colonnes corinthiennes.

245 Salle du Conseil. Elle est entièrement décorée de stucs polychromes datant de la fin du XVIIIème et du début du XIXème siècle. Détail : un paysage encadré de grands candélabres végétaux.

246 Giambattista Canal, *Enée dans l'Olympe.* La fresque décore le plafond du salon central du premier étage et est entourée d'un riche cadre de fleurs et de feuilles. Le peintre exécuta de nombreuses fresques dans le palais en 1796.

247 Salon central avec la fresque représentant *Enée dans l'Olympe.* L'encadrement des murs avec de fausses architectures et des colonnes corinthiennes est également l'œuvre de Canal qui réalisa aussi les tableaux ovales avec les portraits des personnages célèbres de la famille Gambara, placés au-dessus des portes.

Palazzo Barozzi

Sul Rio di S. Mose'

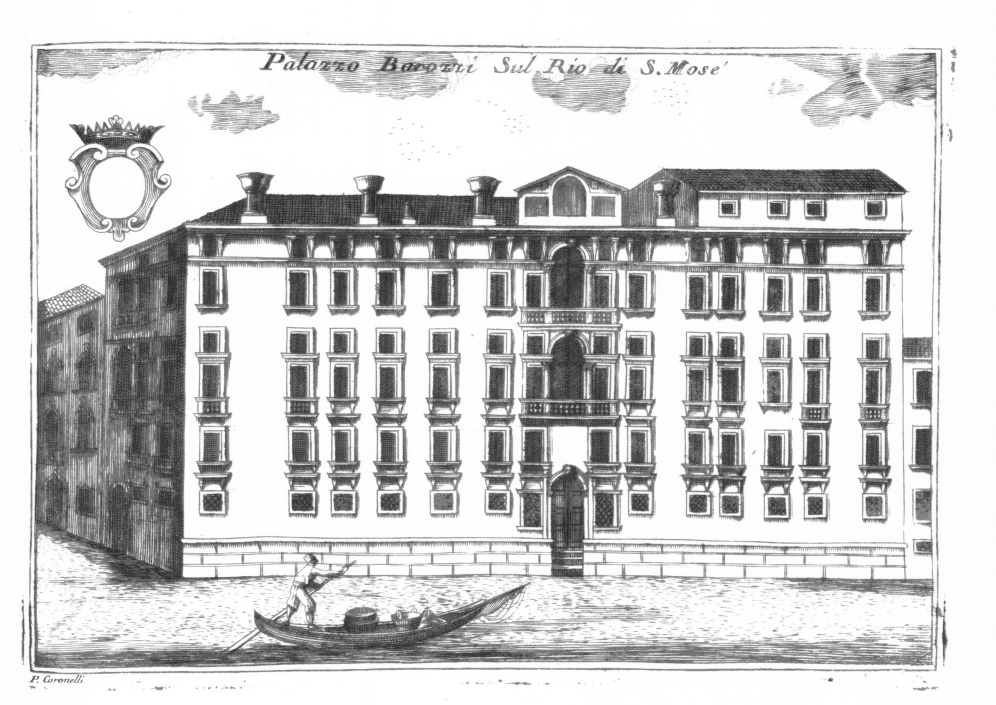

Palazzo Barozzi Sul Rio di S. Mosé

P. Coronelli

Palazzo Barozzi, Emo, Treves de'Bonfili

This palace stands on a corner where the Rio di San Moisè joins the Grand Canal. De'Barbari's plan of Venice, drawn up in the year 1500, already indicated a palace with several floors and two square towers on this site.

The palace belonged to the Barozzi family, who had been resident in the San Moisè parish ever since 1164, when one Domenico Barozzi had purchased the piece of land where the palace was later to be built. The palace stood opposite a building owned by another branch of the family which was subsequently razed to the ground as punishment because some of that family's members had taken part in the Baiamonte Tiepolo conspiracy of 1310.

The fact that the family's name is borne by various roads, courts, porticoed passageways and bridges near the palace shows that the Barozzis had lived for a long time in this part of the city.

Unlike their relations who had fallen into disgrace on amount of their treasonable behaviour, this branch of the family, called the Barozzi della Ca' Grande, was highly respected in Venice.

In 1204 (after the fall of the Byzantine Empire), one Jacopo Barozzi from the district of San Moisè conquered the islands of Santorini and Thirasia, where he became a feudal lord. His dominion over these two Aegean islands passed on to his son Andrea, who added to his possessions two feudal estates on the island of Crete, granted to him by the Venetian Republic.

While he was Venice's ambassador at Negroponte in 1258–59, Andrea Barozzi commanded some victorious military campaigns and, in a battle near Halkidiki, he succeeded in conquering William II of Achaia, whose feudal subjects had rebelled against him with the support of Venice.

Towards the end of the 13th century, Andrea lost his domains on Santorini and Thirasia (which were re-occupied by the Byzantines) but his right to the islands was passed on to his son Jacopo, who rose to important positions in the government of the Venetian colonies in the Aegean during the last few years of the 13th century and the

Dieser Palast liegt an der Mündung des Rio di San Moisè in den Canal Grande. Bereits auf dem Venedig-Plan de'Barbaris aus dem Jahre 1500 ist dieses Areal mit einem mehrstöckigen Palast mit zwei quadratischen Türmen bebaut.

Der Palazzo gehörte der Familie Barozzi, die nachweislich seit 1164 in der Pfarrei San Moisè ansässig war. In jenem Jahr erwarb ein gewisser Domenico Barozzi das Grundstück, auf dem der Palast später errichtet werden sollte. Auf der gegenüberliegenden Seite befand sich ein Gebäude, das einem anderen Zweig der Barozzi gehörte. Diese sollten wegen ihrer Beteiligung an der Verschwörung Baiamonte Tiepolos im Jahre 1310 hingerichtet werden.

Da die Straßen, Höfe und Brücken in der Nähe des Palastes den Namen der Familie tragen, ist dies ein weiteres Indiz dafür, daß die Barozzi schon seit langer Zeit in diesem Stadtteil lebten. Sie wurden Barozzi della Ca' Grande genannt und waren in Venedig im Gegensatz zum anderen, eher subversiven Familienzweig sehr angesehen.

Im Jahre 1204 eroberte ein gewisser Jacopo Barozzi aus dem Stadtviertel San Moisè die Inseln Santorin und Thirassia. Die Herrschaft über die beiden Inseln in der Ägäis ging auf seinen Sohn Andrea über, der seine Besitztümer unter Billigung der Republik Venedig um zwei Lehen auf der Insel Kreta vergrößerte. Während Andrea Barozzi zwischen 1258 und 1259 Botschafter in Negroponte war, führte er einige erfolgreiche Feldzüge. Außerdem gelang es ihm, in einer Schlacht bei Chalkis Wilhelm II. von Achaia zu schlagen, dessen Lehnsherren – unterstützt von Venedig – rebellierten.

Gegen Ende des 13. Jahrhunderts verlor Andrea die Herrschaft über Santorin und Thirassia, die von den Byzantinern zurückerobert wurden. Die Ansprüche auf die Inseln gingen aber auf seinen Sohn Jacopo über, der in den letzten Jahren des 13. und den ersten Jahren des 14. Jahrhunderts wichtige Ämter in der Regierung der venezianischen Kolonien in der Ägäis bekleidete. So war er zwischen 1301 und 1303 Prokurator von Candia, Botschafter von Negroponte und Herzog von Kreta. Er nutzte

Le Palais se dresse au confluent du canal San Moisè et du Grand Canal, en un lieu qui possédait déjà sur le plan de Venise de'Barbari en 1500 un palais crénelé à plusieurs étages et garni de deux tours carrées.

Il appartenait à la famille Barozzi, présente dans la paroisse de San Moisè depuis 1164. Cette année-là un certain Domenico acheta le terrain, sur lequel s'éleva plus tard le palais situé en face d'un autre édifice, appartenant à une autre branche des Barozzi. Celui-ci fut rasé pour infamie, à la suite de la participation de certains membres de la famille au complot de Baiamonte Tiepolo, en 1310.

Le fait que des rues, des cours et des ponts des environs portent le nom de la famille, prouve que l'établissement des Barozzi dans cette partie de la ville remonte à une époque très éloignée.

Cette branche de la famille, appelée de la Ca' Grande, contrairement à l'autre, marquée par la trahison, fut récompensée par la cité et jouit d'une grande considération.

De fait, en 1204, immédiatement après la chute de l'empire byzantin, un certain Jacopo Barozzi, de San Moisè conquit les îles de Santorin et de Thyrasie dont il devint le seigneur. La domination sur les deux îles de la mer Egée passa ensuite à son fils Andrea qui augmenta ses possessions avec la concession de la part de la cité de deux fiefs dans l'île de Crète.

Andrea Barozzi, alors consul de Venise à Negroponte entre 1258 et 1259, dirigea des campagnes militaires victorieuses ; lors d'une bataille près de Calcide, il réussit à infliger une défaite à Guillaume II d'Achaia dont les serfs appuyés par Venise, s'étaient révoltés.

Vers la fin du XIIIème siècle, il perdit son pouvoir sur Santorin et Thyrasie qui furent à nouveau occupées par les Byzantins, mais les droits sur les îles passèrent à Jacopo, son fils, qui endossa d'importantes responsabilités dans le gouvernement des colonies vénitiennes de la mer Egée au cours des dernières années du XIIIème siècle et au début du XIVème. Il fut recteur de la Canée, de Negroponte et duc de Candie en 1301 – 1303. Il profita alors de sa position pour recon-

early 14th century. In fact he became the Procurator of Canea, the ambassador at Negroponte, and the Duke of Crete between 1301 and 1303. He profited from his position to regain the possessions his father had lost, succeeding in becoming the "dominator insularum Sancte Eritni et Thyrasie".

Among the members of the family, there were also a Patriarch of Grado, a Patriarch of Venice, various bishops, and several eminent politicians. Thus during the 15th and 16th centuries the palace at San Moisè was host to many illustrious personalities on good terms with the Barozzis, such as the Turkish ambassador (in 1497) and the Lord of Correggio (in 1499), who was also Benedetto Barozzi's brother-in-law.

At the start of the 17th century, the Barozzis decided to alter the appearance of their castle-home, but they did not complete their restoration work – probably owing to economic difficulties, but possibly because the Emo family which inherited the palace in 1632 decided not to make any further changes.

The renovation was reportedly carried out by, among others, the architect Bartolomeo Manopola, who is mentioned in the records of the years 1597 to 1623 as overseer and designer of various engineering works in the Palazzo Ducale.

Manopola was responsible for making the palace's main façade the one onto the rio. The other façade onto the Grand Canal was left asymmetrical because the rooms inside were extended beyond the renovated part of the palace into a building with ogival-arched windows that was clearly what remained of the original palace.

The façade onto the rio included interesting solutions, such as the first-floor triple-mullioned window with side lintels and a central arch (once topped by another similar window that was subsequently walled up).

In 1827 the palace was purchased by the bankers Isacco and Jacopo Treves, whose father had been made a baron in 1811 by Napoleon Bonaparte. The new owners made only modest changes to the outside, renovating the annex on the Grand Canal which Manopola had left unfinished. This was transformed into an architecturally insignificant extension, which was used to house the Treves' rich collection of art works.

Without interfering a great deal with the layout of the palace, the Treves had all the rooms redecorated and refurnished so that now it is probably the best example of Venetian taste of the early 19th century, after the fall of the Republic.

seine Stellung aus, um die vom Vater verlorenen Besitzungen zurückzuerobern – ein erfolgreiches Unternehmen, denn er wurde »dominator insularum Sancte Eritni et Thyrasie«.

Zur Familie Barozzi gehörten auch ein Patriarch von Grado und einer von Venedig, mehrere Bischöfe und eminente politische Persönlichkeiten. Im Palast von San Moisè wurden im 15. und 16. Jahrhundert berühmte Gäste empfangen, die mit den Barozzi gute Beziehungen pflegten, wie beispielsweise der türkische Botschafter im Jahr 1497 und zwei Jahre später der Signore von Correggio, der außerdem Benedetto Barozzis Schwager war.

Zu Beginn des 17. Jahrhunderts beschlossen die Barozzi, ihren Wohnsitz zu verändern. Der Umbau blieb aber vermutlich wegen finanzieller Schwierigkeiten unvollendet; es ist aber auch möglich, daß die Emo, die den Palast 1632 erbten, es als nicht erforderlich erachteten, die Umstrukturierung zu vollenden. Bei der Renovierung des Gebäudes soll der Architekt Bartolomeo Manopola, dessen Wirken als Baumeister und Ingenieur am Dogenpalast von 1597 bis 1623 belegt ist, beteiligt gewesen sein.

Unter Mitwirkung von Manopola wurde die zum Rio gelegene Palastseite zur Hauptfassade umgestaltet. Die andere Fassade zum Canal Grande blieb asymmetrisch, weil sich die Wohnräume über den renovierten Teil hinaus auf einen Bau mit Spitzbogenfenstern ausdehnten, der offensichtlich zum ursprünglichen Palast gehörte. Die Fassade mit Blick auf den Rio zeigt interessante Lösungen, wie beispielsweise das dreiteilige Fenster des ersten Obergeschosses, über dem sich ein zweites ähnliches Fenster öffnete, das heute zugemauert ist.

Im Jahre 1827 erwarben die Bankiers Isacco und Jacopo Treves den Palast. Ihr Vater war 1811 von Napoleon Bonaparte zum Baron ernannt worden. Die neuen Eigentümer veränderten das Äußere des Palazzo nur geringfügig: Sie ließen den unvollendet gebliebenen Anbau von Manopola zum Canal Grande renovieren. Es entstand ein allerdings nur unbedeutender architektonischer Zusatz, der die reiche Kunstsammlung der Treves beherbergte.

Die Treves ließen die Säle, ohne die Raumfolge des Hauses merklich zu verändern, vollständig neu ausschmücken und einrichten. So spiegelt der Palazzo heute sehr eindrucksvoll den venezianischen Geschmack der ersten Jahre des 19. Jahrhunderts nach dem Untergang der Republik wider.

Jacopo Treves war nicht nur tapferer Verfechter der Revolution von Manin im

quérir les possessions perdues par son père, une entreprise qui lui réussit, et il devint « dominator insularum Sancte Eritni et Thyrasie ».

La famille comptait aussi un patriarche de Grado et un de Venise, divers évêques et d'éminents hommes politiques, et au cours des XVème et XVIème siècles, le Palais de San Moisè reçut des personnages illustres qui entretenaient de bonnes relations avec les Barozzi, notamment l'Ambassadeur de Turquie en 1497, et en 1499 le Seigneur de Correggio qui était aussi le beau-frère de Benedetto Barozzi.

Au début du XVIIème siècle, les Barozzi décidèrent de modifier l'aspect de leur demeure, mais ils n'en terminèrent pas la restructuration, probablement pour des raisons financières. Peut-être aussi que les Emo, auxquels le Palais fut donné en héritage en 1632, jugèrent inutile d'apporter d'autres changements.

La restructuration semble avoir été dirigée par l'architecte Bartolomeo Manopola, sur lequel on a des informations de 1597 à 1623, prote du Palais ducal, et maître d'œuvre d'un grand nombre de travaux d'ingénierie.

Avec l'intervention de Manopola, la façade orientée sur le canal devint la principale, mais l'autre resta asymétrique, sur le Grand Canal, puisque les pièces d'habitation se prolongeaient au-delà de la partie restructurée dans une construction aux fenêtres à arcs brisés qui de toute évidence étaient ce qui restait du Palais initial.

La façade sur le canal bénéficia de solutions intéressantes, comme la fenêtre trilobée de l'étage noble au-dessus de laquelle il y en avait une autre, aujourd'hui murée.

En 1827, le Palais fut acheté par les banquiers Isacco et Jacopo Treves, dont le père avait été fait baron en 1811 par Napoléon. Ils intervinrent de manière très limitée sur l'extérieur de l'édifice, se contentant de restructurer l'annexe sur le Grand Canal restée inachevée depuis l'intervention de Manopola et qui devint une annexe du XIXème siècle, assez inintéressante sur le plan architectural, où se trouvait la riche collection d'œuvres d'art de la famille Treves.

Les barons Treves, sans en changer fondamentalement la disposition, firent redécorer et remeubler complètement l'intérieur de la demeure, aussi est-elle aujourd'hui plutôt l'exemple du goût vénitien des premières années du XIXème siècle, après la chute de la cité.

Jacopo Treves ne fut pas seulement un partisan fervent de la révolution de Manin

As well as being an avid supporter of Manin's revolution in 1848, Jacopo Treves in particular had been backing and encouraging young Venetian artists ever since the twenties, offering grants and ordering works that were suitably well paid. The palace contained sculptures by Angelo Pizzi and frescoes by Giuseppe Borsato and Sebastiano Santi. It was furnished in the neoclassic style by the best artisans in the city, who had inherited a centuries-old tradition.

There was also a collection of paintings including some of the most representative examples of neoclassic and early Romantic Venetian pictorial art: Hayez, Camuccini, Grigoletti, Orsi, Besa, Lipparini, to mention just a few.

In Rome, in 1827, the family purchased two sculptures by Canova representing Ajax and Hector, created in 1811–12 and in 1816 respectively. For the arrangement of the sculptures in the palace, the Treves called in Giuseppe Borsato, the most-renowned Venetian decorator and interior designer of the time. Borsato had already done a whole range of works in some of the most prestigious public and private places in the city and was very up-to-date on French decorative and architectural models. Borsato made use of a room facing onto the Grand Canal, with a view of the Dogana and the church of the Salute. He placed the statues in an apse inundated with light, which seems to expand in relation to the delicately-coloured lacunar entablature supported by two Ionic columns – a splendid setting for Canova's masterpieces.

It was also Borsato who immortalized in a painting (now kept in the palace) the visit paid in 1838 by the Emperor Ferdinand and his wife, with the Archduke Ranieri, Prince Metternich, and a host of followers to this room in Palazzo Treves dedicated to Canova's genius.

Jahre 1848, er unterstützte und förderte auch seit den zwanziger Jahren junge venezianische Künstler durch Stipendien und angemessen bezahlte Aufträge. Sein Haus schmückten Skulpturen Angelo Pizzis sowie Fresken Giuseppe Borsatos und Sebastiano Santis. Außerdem ließ er es mit klassizistischem Mobiliar einrichten, das die besten Handwerker der Stadt fertigten – Erben einer jahrhundertealten Tradition.

Zur Bildergalerie des Palastes zählten die repräsentativsten Werke venezianischer Maler des Klassizismus und der Frühromantik. Vertreten waren unter anderem Hayez, Camuccini, Grigoletti, Orsi, Besa und Lipparini.

Im Jahre 1827 erwarb die Familie in Rom zwei Skulpturen von Antonio Canova. Sie stellen Ajax und Hektor dar und wurden in den Jahren 1811/12 und 1816 ausgeführt. Für die Aufstellung der Skulpturen im Palast wurde Giuseppe Borsato, der damals angesehenste Dekorateur und Innenarchitekt Venedigs, zu Rate gezogen. Borsato hatte schon in vielen öffentlichen und privaten Gebäuden sein Können bewiesen und war über die neuesten französischen Dekorations- und Architekturentwürfe unterrichtet. Er wählte für die Unterbringung der Statuen einen Saal zum Canal Grande, von dem man auf die Dogana (ehem. Zollstation) und die Kirche Santa Maria della Salute blickt. Die beiden Skulpturen stellte er in eine lichterfüllte Apsis. Diese scheint sich im Verhältnis zum Kassettengebälk mit erlesenem Dekor, das von zwei ionischen Säulen getragen wird, auszuweiten – ein großartiges Ambiente für die Meisterwerke Canovas.

Ein Gemälde Borsatos, das heute im Palazzo Treves aufbewahrt wird, zeigt Kaiser Ferdinand mit Gemahlin, den Erzherzog Ranieri, den Fürsten von Metternich und eine große Gefolgschaft, wie sie im Jahre 1838 diesen Saal besuchen, der dem Genius Canovas gewidmet ist.

en 1848 ; depuis 1820 il soutenait et favorisait aussi les jeunes artistes vénitiens en instituant des bourses d'études et en les rémunérant.

La demeure renfermait des sculptures d'Angelo Pizzi, des fresques de Giuseppe Borsato et de Sebastiano Santi. Elle fut meublée en faisant appel aux meilleurs artisans de la ville, héritiers d'une tradition séculaire, avec des meubles de style néoclassique.

On pouvait aussi y admirer une galerie d'art représentative de la peinture vénitienne néoclassique et du début du XIXème siècle, avec des œuvres de Hayez, Camuccini, Grigoletti, Orsi, Besa, Lipparini pour n'en citer que quelques-uns.

En 1827, la famille acquit à Rome les deux sculptures de Canova représentant Ajax et Hector, exécutées respectivement en 1811 – 12 et 1816 mais restées inachevées dans l'atelier de l'artiste. Pour leur installation dans la demeure, on fit appel à Giuseppe Borsato, le décorateur et assemblier le plus coté alors à Venise. Il avait à son actif toute une série de travaux dans les endroits publics et privés les plus prestigieux de la ville, et il suivait de très près les modèles de décoration et d'architecture français. Pour recevoir les statues, celui-ci prépara une salle qui faisait face au Grand Canal avec une vue intéressante sur la Dogana et sur l'église Santa Maria de la Salute. Il plaça les œuvres dans une baie en abside inondée de lumière qui grâce à l'entablement à caissons aux décorations raffinées, soutenu par deux colonnes ioniques, était mise en évidence, servant d'antichambre monumentale aux chefs-d'œuvre de Canova.

C'est également Borsato qui immortalisa dans un tableau, conservé aujourd'hui dans la demeure, la visite de l'empereur Ferdinand avec l'archiduc Ranieri, le prince de Metternich et une suite nombreuse en 1838, dans la salle du Palais Treves, dédiée au génie de Canova.

252 Antonio Canova, detail of *Hector.*

253 Antonio Canova, *Hector.* Marble statue sculpted after *Ajax,* although the plaster casting had been completed in 1808. It was purchased by Count Jacopo Treves de'Bonfili in Rome in 1827, together with the statue of *Ajax,* for the sum of 55 000 lire.

254/255 Antonio Canova, *Hector* and *Ajax.* The two marble statues were placed in a room facing onto the Grand Canal, arranged and decorated according to plans drawn up by Giuseppe Borsato. An especially successful solution was his idea of isolating the space around the statues, an effect underlined by the stucco lacunar entablature supported on two Ionic columns.

256 Antonio Canova, *Ajax.* Marble statue for which the artist had completed the model in 1811.

252 Antonio Canova, *Hektor* (Detail).

253 Antonio Canova, *Hektor.* Diese Marmorstatue wurde nach dem *Ajax* ausgeführt, auch wenn das Gipsmodell bereits 1808 vollendet war. Baron Jacopo Treves de'Bonfili erwarb diese Statue zusammen mit dem *Ajax* für 55 000 Lire im Jahre 1827 in Rom.

254/255 Antonio Canova, *Hektor* und *Ajax.* Die beiden Marmorstatuen wurden in einem Saal zum Canal Grande aufgestellt, der nach Entwürfen von Giuseppe Borsato eingerichtet und dekoriert worden war. Besonders gelungen wirkt die von Borsato ersonnene Lösung, die Apsis, die die Statuen aufnimmt, vom restlichen Raum zu separieren. Diesen Effekt unterstützt das weite Kassettengebälk aus Stuck, das von zwei ionischen Säulen gestützt wird.

256 Antonio Canova, *Ajax.* Das Modell für diese Marmorstatue entstand 1811.

252 Antonio Canova, Détail de la statue d'*Hector.*

253 Antonio Canova, *Hector.* Statue de marbre sculptée après l'*Ajax* dont le modèle en plâtre avait été achevé en 1808. Elle fut achetée par le baron Jacopo Treves de'Bonfili à Rome en 1827 avec l'*Ajax* pour la somme de 55 000 lires.

254/255 Antonio Canova, *Hector* et *Ajax.* Les deux statues de marbre furent installées dans une salle qui donne sur le Grand Canal, meublée et décorée par Giuseppe Borsato. Il eut une idée particulièrement heureuse en isolant l'abside qui reçoit les deux statues, mettant en évidence cet espace par une architecture en stuc soutenue par deux colonnes ioniques.

256 Antonio Canova, *Ajax.* Statue de marbre dont l'artiste acheva le modèle en 1811.

BIBLIOGRAPHY · BIBLIOGRAPHIE

1581
F. Sansovino, *Venetia città nobilissima…,* Venice

1865
G. Fontana, *Cento palazzi fra i più celebri di Venezia sul Canal Grande e nelle vie interne dei sestieri,* Venice

1910
Filocolo, *Il palazzo Albrizzi in Venezia,* in: "Emporium", pp. 467–472

1935
L. Caggiola Pittoni, *Luigi Dorigny e i suoi freschi veneziani,* in: "Rivista della città di Venezia", pp. 2–38

1942
E. Tolomei, *Patrizi veneti in Val d'Adige. Zenobio e Albrizzi,* in: "Archivio per l'Alto Adige", pp. 219–287

1945
R. Gallo, *Una famiglia patrizia. I Pisani ed i palazzi di S. Stefano e di Stra,* Venice

1954
P. Zampetti, *Il palazzo Mocenigo a San Stae donato alla città di Venezia,* in: "Arte Veneta", pp. 330–333

1961
G. Mariacher, *L'arte dello stucco a Venezia nel 1700. Palazzo Zenobio ai Carmini,* in: "Giornale Economico", July, pp. 766–775

1962
E. Bassi, *Architettura del Sei e Settecento a Venezia,* Naples
G. Damerini, *La Ca' Grande dei Cappello e dei Mocenigo a S. Samuele ora Barnabò,* Venice

1963
C. Boselli, *Un documento sul pittore G. Battista Canal,* in: "Arte Veneta", XVII, p. 160

1964
G. Mariacher, "Stuccatori ticinesi a Venezia tra la fine del '600 e la metà del '700", in: *Arte e Artisti dei laghi lombardi,* II, Como, pp. 79–91

1965
G. Mariacher, *Il palazzo Vendramin Calergi a Venezia,* Venice

1967
G. Fontana, *Venezia Monumentale. I Palazzi,* Venice

1968
E. Martini, *Due ignoti cicli pittorici di Francesco Fontebasso e altri affreschi del Diziani,* in: "Arte Illustrata", nos. 5/6, pp. 20–31

1969–1970
L. Padoan Urban, *Catalogo delle opere di Giambattista Canal (1745–1825),* in: "Atti dell'Istituto Veneto di Scienze, Lettere ed Arti", vol. CXXVIII, pp. 41–134

1970
D. R. Paolillo and C. Dalla Santa, *Il palazzo Dolfin Manin a Rialto. Storia di un'antica dimora,* Venice
G. Tassini, *Curiosità veneziane ovvero origine delle denominazioni stradali di Venezia,* Venice

1971
A. P. Zugni Tauro, *Gaspare Diziani,* Venice

1972
G. Pavanello, *Costantino Cedini (1741–1811),* in: "Bollettino del Museo Civico di Padova", pp. 179–278

1974
I. Chiappini di Sorio, *Affreschi settecenteschi veneziani: Palazzo Mocenigo,* in: "Notizie da Palazzo Albani", nos. 2/3, pp. 66–78

1976
E. Bassi, *Palazzi di Venezia,* Venice
L. Moretti, "I Pisani di Santo Stefano e le opere d'arte del loro palazzo", in: *Il Conservatorio di musica Benedetto Marcello,* Venice, pp. 135–181

G. Pavanello, *Dipinti settecenteschi in due palazzi veneziani,* in: "Antichità Viva", no. 6, pp. 39–44

1977
B. Aikema, *Giovanni Antonio Pellegrini: the early years,* in: "Notizie da Palazzo Albani", no. 2, pp. 70–80
E. Martini, *Opere di G. Diziani, J. Guarana, G. Angeli e L. Ferrari in Palazzo Pisani-Moretta,* in: "Notizie da Palazzo Albani", no. I, pp. 1–9
E. Martini, *Pittura veneta dal Ricci ai Guardi,* Venice
L. Olivato Puppi and L. Puppi, *Mauro Codussi,* Turin

1978
P. Lauritzen and A. Zielcke, *Palaces of Venice,* Florence
G. Mariacher, *Epigoni di Alessandro Vittoria negli stucchi di Palazzo Vendramin Calergi,* in: "Arte Veneta", pp. 288–292
G. Pavanello, *Giovanni Scajaro pittore tiepolesco,* in: "Arte Veneta", pp. 423–431

1979
B. Aikema, *Patronage in late baroque Venice: The Zenobio,* in: "Overdruk uit de Madedelingen van het Nederlands Instituut te Rome", no. 6, pp. 209–218

1981
I. Chiappini di Sorio, *Notizie e precisazioni sul palazzo Mocenigo di San Stae a Venezia,* in: "Notizie da Palazzo Albani", no. 2, pp. 74–82
G. Mazzariol, *I palazzi del Canal Grande,* Novara

1982
I. Chiappini di Sorio, *Gli Stuccatori delle decorazioni a Palazzo Pisani Moretta a S. Polo,* in: "Notizie da Palazzo Albani", nos. I/2, pp. 99–105
E. Martini, *La pittura del Settecento a Venezia,* Udine

1983
I. Chiappini di Sorio, *Palazzo Pisani Moret-*

ta: restauri e decorazioni (Angeli, Piazzetta, Tiepolo, Guarana), in: "Notizie da Palazzo Albani", nos. 1/2, pp. 264–273
I. Chiappini di Sorio, *Palazzo Pisani Moretta, Economica, Arte, Vita sociale di una famiglia veneziana del diciottesimo secolo,* Milan
B. Hannegan, *Antonio Zanchi and the ceiling of the Palazzo Barbaro Curtis,* in: "Arte Veneta", pp. 201–205

1985
Palazzo Loredan e l'Istituto Veneto di Scienze, Lettere ed Arti, Venice
G. Romanelli, *Affacciata sul Canal Grande una sala per il Canova,* in: "Vogue"

1986
G. Romanelli and F. Pedrocco, *Ca' Rezzonico,* Milan

1987
B. Aikema, *Le decorazioni di Palazzo Barbaro Curtis a Venezia fino alla metà del Settecento,* in: "Arte Veneta", pp. 147–153
E. Merkel, "Il mecenatismo e il collezionismo artistico dei Querini Stampali dalle origini al Settecento", in: *I Querini stampalia. Un ritratto di famiglia del Settecento veneziano,* Venice, pp. 133–153

1988
M. Magrini, *Franceso Fontebasso (1707–1769),* Vicenza

1989
Rosella Mamoli Zorzi (ed.), *H. James, Lettere da Palazzo Barbaro,* Milan

without year
S. Moronato, *Palazzo Mocenigo a San Stae,* Venice

The engravings and lithographs at the start of each chapter are reproduced by kind permission of the Museo Correr, Venice. They were taken from the following publications:

Die Stiche und Lithographien zu Beginn eines jeden Kapitels sind mit freundlicher Genehmigung des Museo Correr, Venedig, reproduziert worden. Sie wurden folgenden Publikationen entnommen:

Le Museo Correr, Venise, a aimablement donné son accord à la reproduction des gravures et des lithographies présentées en début de chapitre et extraites des publications suivantes :

Arme, Blasoni ò Insegne gentilizie delle Famiglie Patrizie esistenti nella Serenissima Repubblica di Venetia dedicata all'Ill.mo et Eccellentissimo Signore Pietro Garzoni Senatore et Bibliografo pubblico dal P. Cosmografo Coronelli, Venice 1694

V. Coronelli, *Palazzi di Venezia,* Venice 1709

Fabbriche e Vedute di Venetia disegnate, poste in prospettiva, et intagliate da Luca Carlevarijs…, Venice 1703

Venezia monumentale pittoresca o sessanta fra i palazzi più distinti ed interessanti disegnati in litografia da Marco Moro ed illustrati de Gianiacopo nob. Fontana Veneziano… per l'impressione a due tinte del litografo editore e negoziante Giuseppe Kier, Venice 1846

Il Canal Grande di Venezia descritto da Antonio Quadri… e rappresentato in LX tavole rilevate e incise da Dionisio Moretti…, Venice 1828